MW01490370

London, Europe and the Olympic Games

London hosted the Olympic Games for the third time in 2012, a mega-event where the political, economic and social expectations could hardly be compared with the previous London Games of 1908 and 1948. In addition, the Olympic Games went back to Europe in 2012 after a long period where (apart from Athens in 2004) they were held by cities in other continents. In London, the world watched the Games. Continental Europe, however, generated a particular attitude based on the special relations it had developed historically with England. At the crossing point of history, cultural studies and geopolitics, this book provides new insights on the significance of the Olympic Games. It considers that the Games are the right window to look at both the past and the current relations between England and its closest continental neighbours. The book will be ideal for students and academics working in sport sciences, cultural history, political science and European studies; amateur and professional sports historians; Olympic followers and experts in Olympic studies.

This book was previously published as a special issue of the *International Journal of the History of Sport*.

Thierry Terret is a Professor of Sports History at the University of Lyon (France) and the Rector of La Reunion Island in the Indian Ocean. His research mainly focuses on sport and gender, sport and politics, and sport and European trans-culturality.

London, Europe and the Olympic Games

Games

Historical Perspectives

Edited by
Thierry Terret

Routledge
Taylor & Francis Group

LONDON AND NEW YORK

First published 2014
by Routledge
2 Park Square, Milton Park, Abingdon, Oxon, OX14 4RN, UK

and by Routledge
711 Third Avenue, New York, NY 10017, USA

Routledge is an imprint of the Taylor & Francis Group, an informa business

© 2014 Taylor & Francis

British Library Cataloguing in Publication Data
A catalogue record for this book is available from the British Library

ISBN 13: 978-0-415-75014-1

Typeset in Times New Roman
by Taylor & Francis Books

Publisher's Note
The publisher accepts responsibility for any inconsistencies that may have arisen during the conversion of this book from journal articles to book chapters, namely the possible inclusion of journal terminology.

Disclaimer
Every effort has been made to contact copyright holders for their permission to reprint material in this book. The publishers would be grateful to hear from any copyright holder who is not here acknowledged and will undertake to rectify any errors or omissions in future editions of this book.

Contents

Series Editors' Foreword

On January 1, 2010 *Sport in the Global Society*, created by Professor J.A. Mangan in 1997, was divided into two parts: *Historical Perspectives* and *Contemporary Perspectives*. These new categories involve predominant rather than exclusive emphases. The past is part of the present and the present is part of the past. The Editors of *Historical Perspectives* are Mark Dyreson and Thierry Terret.

The reasons for the division are straightforward. *SGS* has expanded rapidly since its creation with over one hundred publications in some twelve years. Its editorial teams will now benefit from sectional specialist interests and expertise. *Historical Perspectives* draws on *International Journal of the History of Sport* monograph reviews, themed collections and conference/workshop collections. It is, of course, international in content.

Historical Perspectives continues the tradition established by the original incarnation of *Sport in the Global Society* by promoting the academic study of one of the most significant and dynamic forces in shaping the historical landscapes of human cultures. Sport spans the contemporary globe. It captivates vast audiences. It defines, alters, and reinforces identities for individuals, communities, nations, empires, and the world. Sport organises memories and perceptions, arouses passions and tensions, and reveals harmonies and cleavages. It builds and blurs social boundaries, animating discourses about class, gender, race, and ethnicity. Sport opens new vistas on the history of human cultures, intersecting with politics and economics, ideologies and theologies. It reveals aesthetic tastes and energises consumer markets.

By the end of the twentieth century a critical mass of scholars recognised the importance of sport in their analyses of human experiences and *Sport in the Global Society* emerged to provide an international outlet for the world's leading investigators of the subject. As Professor Mangan contended in the original series foreword: "The story of modern sport is the story of the modern world—in microcosm; a modern global tapestry permanently being woven. Furthermore, nationalist and imperialist, philosopher and politician, radical and conservative have all sought in sport a manifestation of national identity, status and superiority. Finally for countless millions sport is the personal pursuit of ambition, assertion, well-being and enjoyment."

Sport in the Global Society: Historical Perspectives continues the project, building on previous work in the series and excavating new terrain. It remains a consistent and coherent response to the attention the academic community demands for the serious study of sport.

Mark Dyreson
Thierry Terret

SPORT IN THE GLOBAL SOCIETY – HISTORICAL PERSPECTIVES

Series Editors: Mark Dyreson and Thierry Terret

LONDON, EUROPE AND THE OLYMPIC GAMES

Historical Perspectives

Sport in the Global Society: Historical Perspectives
Series Editors: Mark Dyreson and Thierry Terret

Titles in the Series

The Triple Asian Olympics
Asia Rising - the Pursuit of National
  Identity, International Recognition
  and Global Esteem
*Edited by J.A. Mangan, Sandra Collins
  and Gwang Ok*

**The Triple Asian Olympics - Asia
  Ascendant**
Media, Politics and Geopolitics
*Edited by J.A. Mangan, Luo Qing and
  Sandra Collins*

The Visual in Sport
*Edited by Mike Huggins and
  Mike O'Mahony*

Women, Sport, Society
Further Reflections, Reaffirming Mary
  Wollstonecraft
*Edited by Roberta Park and
  Patricia Vertinsky*

Sport in the Global Society
Past SGS publications prior to 2010

Cricket and England
A Cultural and Social History of Cricket
   in England between the Wars
Jack Williams

Cricket in Colonial India, 1780–1947
Boria Majumdar

Cricketing Cultures in Conflict
Cricketing World Cup 2003
*Edited by Boria Majumdar and
   J.A. Mangan*

Cricket, Race and the 2007 World Cup
*Edited by Boria Majumdar and
   Jon Gemmell*

Disciplining Bodies in the Gymnasium
Memory, Monument, Modernity
Sherry McKay and Patricia Vertinsky

Disreputable Pleasures
Less Virtuous Victorians at Play
*Edited by Mike Huggins and
   J.A. Mangan*

Doping in Sport
Global Ethical Issues
*Edited by Angela Schneider and
   Fan Hong*

Emigrant Players
Sport and the Irish Diaspora
Edited by Paul Darby and David Hassan

Ethnicity, Sport, Identity
Struggles for Status
*Edited by J.A. Mangan and
   Andrew Ritchie*

European Heroes
Myth, Identity, Sport
*Edited by Richard Holt, J.A. Mangan
   and Pierre Lanfranchi*

Europe, Sport, World
Shaping Global Societies
Edited by J.A. Mangan

**Flat Racing and British Society,
   1790–1914**
A Social and Economic History
Mike Huggins

**Football and Community in the
   Global Context**
Studies in Theory and Practice
*Edited by Adam Brown, Tim Crabbe and
   Gavin Mellor*

Football: From England to the World
*Edited by Dolores P. Martinez and
   Projit B. Mukharji*

Football, Europe and the Press
Liz Crolley and David Hand

Football Fans Around the World
From Supporters to Fanatics
Edited by Sean Brown

Football: The First Hundred Years
The Untold Story
Adrian Harvey

Footbinding, Feminism and Freedom
The Liberation of Women's Bodies in
   Modern China
Fan Hong

France and the 1998 World Cup
The National Impact of a World
   Sporting Event
Edited by Hugh Dauncey and Geoff Hare

Freeing the Female Body
Inspirational Icons
Edited by J.A. Mangan and Fan Hong

Sport in Australasian Society
Past and Present
Edited by J.A. Mangan and
John Nauright

Sport in Europe
Politics, Class, Gender
Edited by J.A. Mangan

Sport in Films
Edited by Emma Poulton and
Martin Roderick

Sport in Latin American Society
Past and Present
Edited by Lamartine DaCosta and
J.A. Mangan

Sport in South Asian Society
Past and Present
Edited by Boria Majumdar and
J.A. Mangan

Sport in the Cultures of the Ancient
World
New Perspectives
Edited by Zinon Papakonstantinou

Sport, Media, Culture
Global and Local Dimensions
Edited by Alina Bernstein and Neil Blain

Sport, Nationalism and Orientalism
The Asian Games
Edited by Fan Hong

Sport Tourism
Edited by Heather J. Gibson

Sporting Cultures
Hispanic Perspectives on Sport, Text
and the Body
Edited by David Wood and
P. Louise Johnson

Sporting Nationalisms
Identity, Ethnicity, Immigration and
Assimilation
Edited by Mike Cronin and
David Mayall

Superman Supreme
Fascist Body as Political Icon –
Global Fascism
Edited by J.A. Mangan

Terrace Heroes
The Life and Times of the 1930s
Professional Footballer
Graham Kelly

The Balkan Games and Balkan Politics
in the Interwar Years 1929-1939
Politicians in Pursuit of Peace
Penelope Kissoudi

The Changing Face of the Football
Business
Supporters Direct
Edited by Sean Hamil, Jonathan Michie,
Christine Oughton and Steven Warby

The Commercialisation of Sport
Edited by Trevor Slack

The Cultural Bond
Sport, Empire, Society
Edited by J.A. Mangan

The First Black Footballer
Arthur Wharton 1865–1930: An
Absence of Memory
Phil Vasili

The Football Manager
A History
Neil Carter

The Future of Football
Challenges for the Twenty-First Century
Edited by Jon Garland, Dominic Malcolm
and Mike Rowe

The Games Ethic and Imperialism
Aspects of the Diffusion of an Ideal
J.A. Mangan

The Global Politics of Sport
The Role of Global Institutions in Sport
Edited by Lincoln Allison

The Lady Footballers
Struggling to Play in Victorian Britain
James F. Lee

The Magic of Indian Cricket
Cricket and Society in India, Revised
    Edition
Mihir Bose

The Making of New Zealand Cricket
1832–1914
Greg Ryan

**The 1940 Tokyo Games: The Missing
    Olympics**
Japan, the Asian Olympics and the
    Olympic Movement
Sandra Collins

The Nordic World: Sport in Society
*Edited by Henrik Meinander and
    J.A. Mangan*

The Politics of South African Cricket
Jon Gemmell

The Race Game
Sport and Politics in South Africa
Douglas Booth

**The Rise of Stadiums in the Modern
    United States**
Cathedrals of Sport
*Edited by Mark Dyreson and
    Robert Trumpbour*

The Tour De France, 1903–2003
A Century of Sporting Structures,
    Meanings and Values
Edited by Hugh Dauncey and Geoff Hare

This Great Symbol
Pierre de Coubertin and the Origins of
    the Modern Olympic Games
John J. MacAloon

Tribal Identities
Nationalism, Europe, Sport
Edited by J.A. Mangan

**Women, Sport and Society in Modern
    China**
Holding up More than Half the Sky
Dong Jinxia

Citation Information

The chapters in this book were originally published in the *International Journal of the History of Sport*, volume 30, issue 7 (April 2013). When citing this material, please use the original page numbering for each article, as follows:

Chapter 1
In the Shadow of Myron: The Impact of the Discobolus *on Representations of Olympic Sport from Victorian Britain to Contemporary China*
Mike O'Mahony
International Journal of the History of Sport, volume 30, issue 7 (April 2013) pp. 693–718

Chapter 2
Modern Pentathlon at the London 2012 Olympics: Between Traditional Heritage and Modern Changes for Survival
Sandra Heck
International Journal of the History of Sport, volume 30, issue 7 (April 2013) pp. 719–735

Chapter 3
London is Just Around the Corner: Belgium, Britain and Sport
Pascal Delheye, Stijn Knuts and Thomas Ameye
International Journal of the History of Sport, volume 30, issue 7 (April 2013) pp. 736–756

Chapter 4
Monarchy, Socialism and Modern Capitalism: Hungary's Participation in Three London Olympic Games
Nikoletta Onyestyák
International Journal of the History of Sport, volume 30, issue 7 (April 2013) pp. 757–773

Chapter 5
From Best to Worst? Romania and Its Nostalgia for Olympic Successes
Simona Petracovschi and Thierry Terret
International Journal of the History of Sport, volume 30, issue 7 (April 2013) pp. 774–788

Chapter 6

The Olympic Games in London 2012 from a Swedish Media Perspective
Susanna Hedenborg
International Journal of the History of Sport, volume 30, issue 7
(April 2013) pp. 789–804

Chapter 7

*Close Strangers or Strange Friends? The London Olympics and
Anglo-Norwegian Sports Relations in a Historical Perspective*
Matti Goksøyr
International Journal of the History of Sport, volume 30, issue 7
(April 2013) pp. 805–824

Please direct any queries you may have about the citations to
clsuk.permissions@cengage.com

In the Shadow of Myron: The Impact of the *Discobolus* on Representations of Olympic Sport from Victorian Britain to Contemporary China

Mike O'Mahony

History of Art (Historical Studies), University of Bristol, 9 Woodland Road, Bristol BS8 1TB, UK

Without doubt, the most famous and instantly recognisable work of art associated with the Olympic Games is Myron's *Discobolus*. Originally produced in bronze in the fifth century BC, the work is now known primarily through later Roman copies in marble, discovered in Italy during the eighteenth century. Whilst much has been written about the *Discobolus* as an exemplar of antique art, less attention has been paid to the reception of the work in the modern era. Accordingly, this article shifts attention to the impact made by Myron's work in visual culture produced during the period of the modern Olympic Games; that is from the late nineteenth century to the present day. From Victorian public sculptures, to official Olympic films and posters, and even contemporary art produced for the Beijing Games of 2008, Myron's work has continued to cast an influential shadow over art practices related to the Games themselves, as it has been adopted, adapted and transformed to signify a host of new and frequently diverse meanings. The prominent display of the work at the British Museum in London during the Games of 2012 offers testimony to the work's enduring legacy and its relevance for spectators of the present day.

Introduction

Visual culture has always been a vital component in the production and historical reception of the Olympic Games. This has manifested itself in multiple forms, from the monumental and spectacular, including Olympic architecture or the theatrical opening ceremonies of recent festivals, to the ephemeral and mundane, such as cheap souvenirs or product packaging carrying images of Olympic symbols, events or personalities. Much of this material has been overlooked or marginalised in more conventional text-based research into the history of the Games. Yet, in all its diverse manifestations, visual culture constitutes a rich and vital resource for sport historians and, as a number of recent studies have shown, deserves more academic attention.[1] The important link between visual and sporting cultures at the Games is, of course, hardly a new departure. Ancient Olympia was inundated with visual representations, such as the victor monuments designed to commemorate the successes of past Olympians. Although much of this material has been lost to history, what remains has made a major contribution towards our understanding of the meaning and significance of the Games for both ancient and modern societies.

For the Games of London 2012, a plethora of Olympic-related visual material has already been produced and is clamouring for public attention. From Anish Kapoor's monumental *Orbit* sculpture, erected alongside the Olympic stadium, to lapel pins with the London 2012 logo, the sheer volume of visual and material culture associated with the Games threatens to overwhelm. Also competing for public attention, however, will be one somewhat older cultural artefact that could certainly be said to have stood the test of time. As part of the broader cultural Olympiad, the British Museum in London will be staging a special exhibition dedicated to Myron's *Discobolus*. The *Discobolus* is not only valued as a significant example of antique Greek sculpture but also remains one of the most instantly recognised and popular representations of sport in the history of art.[2] Indeed, Myron's work has come to emblematise the link between sporting and artistic culture as exemplified in both ancient and modern conceptions of Olympism. Whilst the aesthetic merits of the *Discobolus* have been widely debated, less attention has perhaps been paid to its broader reception in the modern era, not least its continuing status as a visual signifier for the Olympic Games. This essay, therefore, will focus instead on the evolution and continuing legacy of this icon of Olympic sport during the period from the Victorian era to the present day. Throughout this time the *Discobolus* has acted as a resonant, and sometimes controversial, unofficial Olympic symbol. As such it has been adopted, adapted and transformed throughout the history of the modern Games according to the needs, fashions and inclinations of different individuals and groups at specific historical moments.

The Ancient and Modern Art of Throwing the Discus

To begin this analysis, it is necessary to go back to where it all began, the inaugural Olympic Games of the modern era held in Athens in 1896. Towards the end of the first day of competition, 60,000 spectators at the newly restored Panathenaic stadium, eagerly awaited what was regarded by many as the highlight event of the first day: the discus competition. For the largely partisan crowd this event, with its rich classical heritage, was regarded not only as quintessentially Greek, but also the competition most likely to yield a victory for the home team. Amongst the competitors, however, was a young American athlete by the name of Robert Garrett Jr. The youngest son of a wealthy Baltimore banking family, Garrett was one of a small team of American athletes – primarily students and ex-students from Princeton and Harvard Universities – who had travelled to Athens to compete in the Games. Earlier that day, Garrett's compatriot, James Connolly, had become the first victor in a modern Olympic competition when he won the triple jump.[3] American, Australian and French athletes had also been victorious in the preliminary heats of the 100 m and 800 m races. Despite relatively poor performances by Greek athletes in these earlier events, a sense of hope now pervaded the crowd. As the sun began to set and a chilling breeze wafted around the stadium, the field was soon whittled down to just three competitors; two Greeks, Panagiotis Paraskevopoulos and Sotirios Versis, and Garrett. The events that unfolded next were described by A.C. Tyler, a Princetonian athlete who reported for the Associated Press:

The Greek champion, in the finals, threw first and scored 28 metres, 88 centimetres. Our champion, Garrett, followed with 28 metres, 72 centimetres. The third man was so provoked at Garrett's success that he was only able to throw 27 metres, 48 centimetres. The champion of Greece then threw the discus 28 metres, 95½ centimetres, and the other Greek hurled it 28 metres. Then came the final effort, and we all held our breath as Garrett carefully prepared for the throw. By this time he had caught the knack of hurling the discus, and had complete confidence in himself. He put all his energy into the last cast, and as the discus flew through the air the vast concourse of people were silent as if the structure were empty. When the discus struck there was a tremendous burst of applause from all sides, and we joined in with right good will ... The throw was measured, and the announcement was made that Garrett had thrown 29 metres, 15 centimetres, and had beaten the Greeks at their own game.[4]

Whilst much celebrated, Garrett's victory in the discus competition was something of a surprise, not least as he had entered the Games primarily to compete in other events.[5] The story of how he came to compete in the discus competition has subsequently attracted mythic status. According to Olympic historian Richard D. Mandell, Garrett first conceived of participating in this most classical of athletic sports on the advice of Professor William Milligan Sloane, his history teacher at Princeton and a staunch supporter of Pierre de Coubertin's plans to revive the ancient Olympic Games.[6] As discus throwing had been a component in the pentathlon at the ancient Olympics, Sloane suggested to Garrett that he conduct some library research concerning the discus in antiquity. Possibly as much out of academic, as athletic, curiosity, Garrett arranged to have an accurate reproduction of a classical discus cast in metal and subsequently practiced with this.[7] Finding the object unwieldy, he quickly gave up this plan and focused instead on his other athletic disciplines. However, on arrival at the stadium in Athens, Garrett reportedly found a discus lying on the ground and picked it up. As it was made of wood, it was much lighter than the one with which he had originally experimented, and handled much better. Thus, Garrett hesitantly decided to enter the discus competition.

Given his lack of preparation, Garrett's technique was somewhat rudimentary. As Mandell describes it, the American athlete had developed an individual technique, involving a centrifugal spin and release of the discus from a low crouching position, a technique not dissimilar, it would seem, from modern discus throwing.[8] This, however, was notably in contrast to Garrett's closest rivals, the Greeks Paraskevopoulos and Versis, whose technique was derived less from an improvised consideration of the physical movement required to achieve a long distance throw, than from a close study of classical antiquity. Indeed, both Greek athletes adopted stances that replicated the pose of Myron's *Discobolus*. This contrast between the pragmatic rationalism of the American athlete and the studied historicism of his Greek counterparts was far from lost on contemporary Greek commentators. Thus, Charalambos Anninos, writing in the *Official Report* of the Games, stated,

> By the awkward way in which some of the foreign competitors threw the discus, it was easily perceived that most of them had not been accustomed to this sort of sport; but the graceful movements, and the skill of the Greek discus throwers were admired by all beholders, strangers as well as Athenians. Mr. Versis in particular showed a harmony and a dignity in his attitudes which would not have disgraced an Ancient discus thrower. He himself is beautiful of form like an ancient statue.[9]

Anninos' claim here may well reflect a degree of sour grapes concerning Garrett's victory over the writer's own compatriots. At the same time, however, it highlights the long shadow that antiquity continued to cast not just over the Games themselves, but also over how the Games might both be understood and articulated in visual terms. Clearly, for Anninos, the harmony, dignity and classical allusion displayed by his fellow Greek athletes far outshone the raw fact of Garrett's longer throw.

Intriguingly, shortly after his victory Garrett was asked to pose for the German photographer, Albert Meyer, one of only a handful of photographers known to have documented the Athens Games (Figure 1). In the resultant image, Garrett is shown with his head in profile and torso turned towards the camera. His body squats as he leans slightly forward, one arm hovering loosely in front of his left knee whilst the other, with muscles clearly tensed, raises the discus above shoulder height. Whether the choice of pose was that of the athlete or the photographer remains unknown. What is clear, however, is that Garrett's posture consciously imitated that of Myron's famous sculptural precedent, despite the fact that he, unlike his Greek counterparts, had specifically avoided trying to replicate the classical model in competition. Further, this was far from being the only visual reference made to Myron's classical prototype in the course of the first modern Games. In September

Figure 1.   Albert Meyer, *Robert Garrett jnr, winner of the discus competitions at the inaugural Olympic Games in Athens, 1896.* © 2012 International Olympic Committee – All rights reserved.

1896, *Scribner's Magazine* published an extensive report on the Athens Games written by the classical scholar and director of the American School of Classical Studies in Athens, Rufus B. Richardson and illustrated by Corwin Knapp Linson. Although Richardson expended relatively little space on describing the discus competition, noting merely that 'Garrett beat the Greeks at what was regarded as at their own game' (and thus reiterating the widely used cliché deployed by Tyler), two of the eight illustrations representing sporting activities focused on the discus competition.[10] Unsurprisingly, perhaps, one of these, carrying the caption *The Discus, Just Before the Throw*, again deploys the *Discobolus* pose, although the unnamed athlete is represented in modern costume (Figure 2). And, as if further to canonise this visual signifier linking the ancient and modern Olympic competitions, a reproduction of Myron's *Discobolus* was embossed in silver on the cover of the *Official Report* published by the IOC shortly after the conclusion of the Games. A reproduction of the famous classical precedent and Meyer's photograph of Garrett as Myron in *tableau vivant* form, were also included in the report.[11]

All this clearly reveals that the *Discobolus* not only occupied a prominent position in the consciousness of artists and athletes alike in 1896, but also that it was readily adopted as a conventional visual signifier for the Games. Thus, from the very earliest days of the modern Olympic movement, Myron's *Discobolus* was already casting its shadow upon visual culture associated with the Games.

Rediscovering Myron

Before turning to an analysis of subsequent redeployments of the *Discobolus* form, it might be useful to offer a brief overview of the history of Myron's masterpiece and its place within the canon of classical sculpture. The original work, produced in

Figure 2.   Corwin Knapp Linson, *The Discus, Just Before the Throw*, illustration published in *Scribner's Magazine*, September 1896.

bronze in the fifth century BC by the famous sculptor Myron, does not survive, and, as a result, knowledge of its existence and importance in the ancient world has depended heavily on written descriptions in key classical sources. It is from these that it became possible to identify works later discovered in Rome, as second century marble copies of Myron's original.[12] The first of these, usually referred to as the Palombara *Discobolus*, was unearthed on the Esquiline Hill in Rome in March 1781. It was shortly thereafter identified by Carlo Fea as a copy after Myron's lost original and now resides in the Museo Nazionale in Rome (Figure 3).[13] A decade later, a second copy was discovered at Hadrian's Villa at Tivoli and acquired by the British collector of antiquities, Charles Townley. This subsequently entered the collection of the British Museum in London (Figure 4). Two years later, a third version was also found at Tivoli by the artist and antiquarian, Gavin Hamilton, and can now be found in the Vatican Museum in Rome.

From the time of their discovery, these three versions elevated Myron's *Discobolus* to canonical status. At the same time, however, they generated many confusions and controversies regarding the actual appearance of Myron's original work. The Palombara *Discobolus* was the most complete of the versions discovered at this time and, despite its damaged condition, reconstruction proved to be a fairly straightforward process. This however, could not be said for the subsequently discovered versions. Thus, the version acquired by Townley was incomplete, the most notable absence being the head. In accordance with contemporary convention, restoration work was soon undertaken by Carlo Albacini, and a replacement head of similar age was attached to the neck.[14] Yet, despite the clear evidence of the earlier discovered Palombara *Discobolus*, this

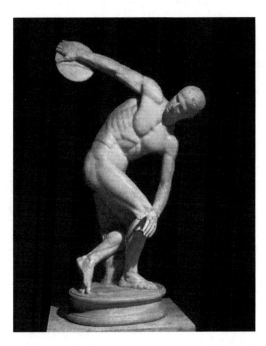

Figure 3. *The Palombara Discobolus.* Roman copy of a bronze original of the 5th century BC by Myron. Museo Nazionale, Rome. © Gianni Dagli Orti/CORBIS.

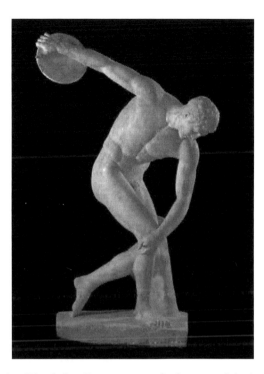

Figure 4. *The Townley Discobolus.* Roman copy of a bronze original of the 5th century BC by Myron. British Museum, London.

head was affixed looking down towards the right foot rather than positioned parallel to the ground and glancing slightly back towards the discus. It is difficult to determine what prompted this departure from an already extant exemplar, for even if the restorer did not have access to the earlier find, the descriptions in Quintillian and Lucian, upon which the attribution depends, seem reasonably clear about the position of the head. Here, it can only be speculated that archaeological authenticity was less of a concern than the desire to create a particular aesthetic effect. Indeed, when queried on the evident erroneous disposition of the head at the time of purchase, the Italian antiquarian Ennio Quirino Visconti made the somewhat eccentric claim that Albacini's repositioned head should be regarded as an improvement upon Myron's original.[15]

Given the frequently speculative nature of restorations at this time, this difference in the position of the head may seem a minor point. The distinction between the Palombara *Discobolus* and Townley version was, however, to have a bearing on the ways in which the various *Discoboli* were viewed, valued and, later in the twentieth century, deployed to signify distinctive national and political associations. For whilst the Palombara *Discobolus* acquired a status as the most authentic of the examples discovered in the late eighteenth century, it was the Townley version that gained greater public exposure when it entered the collection of the British Museum following the collector's death in 1805.[16] Here, it consistently occupied a prime viewing spot, usually as the focal point at the end of a corridor of rooms, and at one point, was even mounted on a specially constructed revolving pedestal.[17] Despite its erroneously positioned head, the Townley *Discobolus* thus rapidly came to occupy an important position within the museological, academic and wider public perception of antique art, becoming the enduring image of Myron's lost masterpiece.

Myron in Victorian Britain

The prominent place afforded it at the British Museum helped familiarise the wider public with the *Discobolus*. Here it was regularly sketched by art students and, in 1857, photographs of the work in the new medium of stereoscopy were produced and widely disseminated. By the later nineteenth century, Myron's work was also leaving its mark on contemporary sculptors. Thus, for example, Sir William 'Hamo' Thornycroft's small bronze *The Stone-Thrower* of 1881 (Figure 5) focuses on the precise moment of balance and repose before exertion in an attempt to represent the perfected and harmonious male nude body. Although not directly referencing discus throwing, the visual parallel with Myron's work is here explicit.[18] Other sculptors, including William Blake Richmond, similarly turned to Myron's precedent in their explorations of the nude male athletic form.[19] Frederic, Lord Leighton's ground-breaking work entitled *Athlete Wrestling with a Python* (Figure 6) has most frequently been discussed in conjunction with its overt reference to another famous antique precedent, the *Laocoön*. However, it could also be argued that in formal terms, Leighton's *Athlete* makes more than a passing reference to Myron's *Discobolus*. Both works highlight a twisted torso and an outstretched and tensed right arm, counterbalanced by a less physically strained left arm bent at the elbow. Further, both figures are bent at the knee with the weight squarely placed on the right leg whilst the left is supported only by the contact of the toes with the ground.

Figure 5. William 'Hamo' Thornycroft, *The Stone Thrower*, 1881. Bronze. Robert Bowman Gallery, London.

Figure 6.   Frederic, Lord Leighton, *Athlete Wrestling a Python*, 1877. Bronze, Tate, London.

Even the awkward joint between the head and the torso, with the face directed downwards recalls the artificial reconstruction of the Townley *Discobolus*, the model most familiar to Leighton. David J. Getsy has argued that perhaps the most striking and innovative aspect of Leighton's *Athlete*, however, is its 'concerted departure from the unitary, organizing viewpoint', something that surely puts it at odds with the *Discobolus*.[20] Certainly Myron's work is most effective when viewed from directly in front, as is made evident by the overwhelming tendency for the work to be presented in photographs and displayed in museums in this manner. The circularity of the implied movement of the discus thrower's arms is thus highlighted, imposing a simple and comprehensible geometric form upon the work. With Leighton, however, this circularity is extended to form a more centrifugal spatial conception. Yet, this does not necessarily undermine an association between Myron's work and that of Leighton. For here it is as if the *Discobolus* has been taken down from its plinth and its movements translated into a three-dimensional format, one not dissimilar to the physical spiralling motions that Garrett would later adopt in contrast to his more traditionally inspired Greek competitors. None of this is to claim that Leighton was attempting to quote or, indeed, reinvent Myron's work. It is, however, to acknowledge that the *Discobolus* retained a significant presence in the broader consciousness of an artistic community throughout the latter part of the nineteenth century.

This period also saw British sculptors departing from the stylistic conventions of exemplary eighteenth-century neoclassical works to produce a more 'mimetic rendering of the body in three dimensions'.[21] This more corporeal emphasis, inspired in part by the sculptural re-conceptualisations of Auguste Rodin's early work in

France as well as the presence of the naturalist sculptor Jules Dalou in London, did not seek to abandon the influence of the ancients. Rather it sought to synthesise these dual modes of representation, to add a sense of vitality to the harmony and repose so celebrated in antique works. And it is clear that Myron's *Discobolus* here had a key role to play. In 1894, the writer, critic and doyen of the Aesthetic movement, Walter Pater published an essay entitled 'The Age of Athletic Prizemen: A Chapter in Greek Art'. Here, Pater specifically praised the *Discobolus* for its 'still irresistible grace', describing it as a work to be admired both for its 'mastery of natural detail' and as 'a veritable counterfeit of nature'.[22] His emphasis on the notional 'realism' of Myron's work did not, however, preclude its simultaneous 'idealism': thus for Pater, Myron 'was in fact an earnest *realist* or *naturalist*, and rose to central perfection in the portraiture, the idealised portraiture, of athletic youth'.[23] Notably, it was Myron's capacity to represent physical movement that, for Pater, set him apart from his contemporaries as 'the beau ideal of athletic movement'.[24] Here, it is the duality of the moment captured in the *Discobolus*, the 'mystery of combined motion and rest, of rest in motion' that seems most to attract Pater's attention. The posthumous publication of this essay in Pater's 1895 volume *Greek Studies*, served further to reinforce the significance of Pater's views on Greek art, and the *Discobolus* in particular, not only for a British readership, but also in Europe.[25] This synthesis of naturalism and idealism, of simultaneous rest and motion (repose and vitality), was also recognised by the sculptural critic Edmund Gosse as a key element in the work of contemporary Victorian sculptors, which he dubbed the 'New Sculpture'.[26] It is perhaps no coincidence here that this concept was first articulated in 1894, the same year that Pater published his 'Athletic Prizemen' essay. And it might be added that this also coincided precisely with Coubertin's declaration at the Sorbonne Congress in Paris, of his plans to revive the Olympic Games. Here, both art and sport embraced classicism, albeit notably reworked for modern times and modern sensibilities. Once again the shadow of Myron's *Discobolus* loomed large over both practices.[27]

All of this takes us back to Athens in 1896 and Albert Meyer's official photograph of Robert Garrett. It should be acknowledged that Meyer's representation of a contemporary figure adopting a pose from antique statuary was hardly a unique undertaking in the late nineteenth century. To cite perhaps the most famous example of this practice, the German-born body-builder Eugen Sandow was regularly photographed throughout the 1880s and 1890s in the posture of such canonical classical precedents as the *Farnese Hercules* or the *Dying Gaul*.[28] Yet, despite its overt classical reference, Meyer's photograph of Garrett can be distinguished from other contemporary *tableaux vivants* derived from classicism precisely because it prioritises contemporary sports practice over celebrations of an idealised male physique. Garrett is chosen as a subject for this work on the basis of his victory in a particular competition rather than because of any conception of his physique as representative of Hellenistic ideals. Further, he is represented in an athletics costume that not only identifies his status as a modern sportsman, but also specifically as a competitor representing his nation state, as indicated by the stars and stripes emblazoned across his chest. This, it might be added, is in notable contrast to Meyer's photograph of 1896 marathon victor Louis Spiridon, posed in a timeless Greek national costume, rather than as an athlete. In this way, Meyer's representation of Garrett can be read as negotiating a complex signifying terrain. On the one hand, it quotes a popularly known classical precedent, yet simultaneously distances itself from this source. Executed in the technologically modern medium of photography, Garrett is here represented as a modern Olympic athlete adopting the pose of an antique bronze, known only through a later copy in marble. Garrett's head placement, it might also be noted, reiterates the erroneous restoration of the British Museum Townley version, adding yet another layer of removal between the modern subject and its original classical referent. Ultimately, Meyer's photograph of Garrett articulates a complex and intriguing set of tensions between the past and the present, between the ancient and the modern Olympic Games. It thus serves to foreground an important question regarding the revived Olympics of 1896: to what extent did the Games actually forge a link with the classical past, thus establishing a continuity between ancient and modern times, cultures and values, or simply deploy aspects of this ancient history as a means to justify the establishment of a modern sporting festival reflective far more of contemporary social, political and ideological concerns? In the latter configuration, the revival of the Games can be seen to conform to historian Eric Hobsbawm's notion of 'invented traditions'.[29] This tension would continue to trouble those both participating in, and those representing, the Games throughout the twentieth century. And the visual form of the *Discobolus* would return time and time again as a vehicle through which this problem might be negotiated.

Free-Style versus Greek-Style

On 1 May 1906, just over a decade after Garrett's victory at the inaugural Games in Athens, the Panathenaic stadium in Athens once more played host to an Olympic discus competition. This was on the occasion of the Intercalated Games, an event held on one occasion only, at the midway point between the official Olympic Games of 1904 and 1908.[30] Since the success of the first Olympic festival in 1896, Coubertin had fiercely resisted attempts by the Greek authorities to establish Athens as the permanent home to the Olympic Games.[31] However, after the debacle of the Games of 1900 in Paris and 1904 in St Louis, Missouri, both of which had been subsumed within greater international exhibitions and were widely regarded as failures, Coubertin was forced into a compromise by bringing the Games back to Athens.[32] These Games proved a great success and, as had been the case a decade earlier, the Greeks were again particularly keen to succeed in the discus competition. Their athletes, however, had been slow to adopt the spinning action they had first witnessed in Garrett's victory in 1896 and that was increasingly being deployed by other international athletes including the Hungarian, Rudolf Bauer and the American, Martin Sheridan (gold medal winners at the 1900 and 1904 Games, respectively). Instead, the Greek competitors still held the view that the best way to perform this sport was to adopt the posture of the *Discobolus*. Accordingly, a new event was introduced into the 1906 Games, so-called 'Greek-style' discus throwing, as distinct from 'Free-style' as Garrett's technique was now designated. In this competition, the athletes threw from a raised, square pedestal with the discus released from a standing position. The official rules for this new competition clarify how extensively the technique depended upon Myron's prototype:

The method of throwing is as follows:-

The thrower places himself on the pedestal with the feet apart, and holding the discus in either hand. He then grasps it with both hands and raises them without letting go the discus with either, extending the rest of his body at the same time in the same direction.

After that he turns the trunk to the right and bends sharply, so as to bring the left hand, which has now left hold of the discus, to the right knee, and the right hand, still holding the discus, as far back as possible. At this moment the right foot should be forward and both legs bent; the right foot rests full on the sole, and the left on the toes only. Then by a sharp and simultaneous extension of the whole body the thrower throws the discus forward.[33]

Although the introduction of this new event was clearly designed to improve the chances of the Greek athletes, it still failed to generate a native victor; Nicolaos Georgantas only managed to repeat his second place of 1904 in both the 'Greek-style' and 'Free-style' competitions. Nonetheless, the Greeks stuck to their guns and insisted that 'Greek-style' discus throwing also be included in the 1908 Games in London. Once again, the Greeks failed to record a victory, finishing only fifth and sixth. The *Official Report* of the London Games was notably scathing about the decision to retain the 'Greek-style' competition, claiming that it was 'unnecessary, for the same athlete won both the free and the restricted style and in neither case was a Greek, by whose nation the restricted rules were introduced, within the first four'.[34] The 'Greek-style' discus competition thus had a short life in Olympic history and had been abandoned by the time of the 1912 Stockholm Games. What this episode reveals, however, is the extent to which Myron's *Discobolus* continued to shape perceptions of the link between the ancient and the modern through the first decade of the modern Games. At the same time this tale highlights one of those strange moments in which life truly imitates art.

The Post-War *Discobolus*

The next significant reference to the *Discobolus* in Olympic visual culture came with the production of the official poster for the 1920 Games. Following the cancellation of the 1916 Games, originally scheduled to take place in Berlin, the IOC awarded the Games of 1920 to Antwerp, the second city of Belgium.[35] This gesture was very much in the spirit of solidarity with the nation whose invasion had been the catalyst for much of the fighting during the First World War. The official poster produced to promote these Games featured a monumental discus thrower towering above the cityscape of Antwerp and festooned with swirls of cloth representing the national flags of the competing nations (Figure 7). The original design for the poster predated the war, having been produced for a brochure as part of the city's original 1914 bid to hold the Games, and is listed in the *Official Report* as the work of Walter van der Ven.[36] Whilst the inclusion of a discus thrower inevitably invoked Myron's famous precedent, a dual reference was here made to a sculptural representation of a discus thrower produced a century earlier by Matthias Kessels.[37]

The decision to include a representation of Kessels' work in the Antwerp poster is an intriguing one. As a Maastricht-born sculptor, Kessels is conventionally identified as a Dutch artist, though at the time he produced his *Discus Thrower* much of modern day Belgium remained part of the broader United Kingdom of the Netherlands. Thus, from a Belgian perspective in 1920, Kessels could be identified either as a neighbour crossing the border or a son of the soil. However, enveloped by the swirling flags of the community of nations (which also add a touch of strategic modesty) and in the pro-internationalist context of the Olympic movement, Kessels' *Discus Thrower* signifies a link both to the past and to the present. On the one hand, in a post-war context the inclusion of a classical *Discobolus*, albeit one redefined in early nineteenth-century neoclassical form, clearly referenced the ancient Olympics.

Figure 7. Walter van der Ven and Martha van Kuyck, Poster for the 1920 Antwerp Olympic Games. © 2012 International Olympic Committee – All rights reserved.

This inevitably drew attention to the Ekecheiria, the military truce implemented, symbolically at least, at ancient Olympia during the period of the Games. As modern day Europeans knew only too well, this had certainly not happened during the recent conflict. On the other hand, the gathering of flags around an image of sport situated geographically in the city of Antwerp proposed a more conciliatory present, where nation states could compete on the playing fields rather than the battlefields of Flanders. As if to reinforce this rejection of military conflict, the shield and sword that form the coat of arms of Antwerp are here garlanded with flowers, the circular form of the shield now echoing that of the discus held in the hand of the frozen athlete. To foster further the explicit message of international peace and co-operation, the Belgian Olympic Committee produced 90,000 posters, translated into 17 different languages. A further 2,500,000 smaller versions were also produced and distributed internationally.[38] The Antwerp Games also witnessed the first release of doves of peace, and the first official declaration of the Olympic Oath. Further, the Olympic Games of 1920 were the first to be staged beneath the Olympic flag, with its five interlocking rings symbolising the union of the five continents. Designed by Coubertin himself in 1914, the flag has since stood as the Olympic movement's official symbol of international peace and co-operation.

Myron Recruited to the National Socialist Cause

German athletes did not compete at Antwerp in 1920. Whilst not officially banned from participating – this would have gone against the official constitution of the

IOC – Germany was simply not invited to take part, a strategic 'omission' that was repeated four years later for the Paris Games of 1924. It was not until the Amsterdam Games of 1928, a full decade after the end of the war, that German athletes were again able to compete for Olympic glory.[39] Once back in the fold, however, the German Olympic Committee wasted no time before proposing that the loss of the Games of Berlin 1916 be rectified by allowing the German capital to stage a future Olympic festival. In May 1931, the IOC thus declared that Berlin would play host to the Games of 1936. At this time, Germany was still governed by the shaky coalition that constituted the Weimar Republic. It was also on the eve of a major financial crisis. Within two years, the nation had undergone major changes and was led by Adolf Hitler's National Socialist German Workers' Party. All of this paved the way for what became the most politically controversial Olympic festival of the twentieth century and the most notorious redeployment of Myron's *Discobolus*.

Leni Riefenstahl's infamous cinematic account of the Berlin Games, ostensibly produced as a sports documentary, went way beyond the simple reportage that had characterised earlier Olympic film footage. At the time of its release, *Olympia* was widely praised, as nothing less than 'a poem, a hymn, an ode to beauty', even a veritable sport-symphony.[40] Perhaps the most significant innovation in *Olympia* was the inclusion of a narrative prologue to both parts of the film, and it was here that Myron's *Discobolus* came to play a starring role. In *Festival of Nations*, the first 15 min are taken up with a scene-setting montage of images, shot by cameraman Willy Zielke, that take the viewer from the sites of ancient Greece to the heart of modern Berlin. As the opening titles fade, the camera pans across a desolate and misty landscape strewn with broken columns, lingering over these fragmented architectural remnants now overgrown with weeds. The absence of any signs of humanity adds to a broad sense that a long-forgotten land is about to be brought back to life. The plaintive strings of Herbert Windt's Wagnerian soundtrack add a further sense of mystery and melancholy to the scene as the music accompanies the camera, and thus the spectator, moving slowly and deliberately through doorways and around corners to discover ever-new vistas of a neglected antiquity. The emphasis on architectural detail soon gives way to a focus on statuary. Famous monuments (including the Barberini Faun and the Medici Venus) are dramatically lit and evocatively captured by a moving camera that choreographs a Pygmalion-like resurrection of the ancient marbles. Here, the spectator is presented with the concept of re-awakening, a re-birth from a long dormancy, an idea explicitly articulated in what is perhaps the most famous sequence from Riefenstahl's *Olympia*. As the camera rotates around a plaster replica of Myron's *Discobolus* (acquired specially for the film production), the image of a near-nude male athlete, adopting the same posture, is superimposed on the classical model. Thus, the statue literally comes to life and performs, in slow and exquisitely choreographed motion, the physical rotations of a discus thrower in action (Figure 8).

The inclusion of Myron's *Discobolus* in Riefenstahl's epic was clearly intended to evoke the ancient Olympic Games, although the allusion is to a romanticised, rather than a historically specific, notion of the classical past. Here, the visual amalgamation of the ancient and modern athletes forges an explicit link between the classical Greek past and modern, National Socialist Berlin, thus claiming the latter as the natural inheritor of the former. More significantly, this connection is represented as direct, seamless and unmediated by other historical or cultural circumstances. For example, the fact that the German passion for all things Greek dates back to at least the eighteenth century, or that the revival of the Olympic Games might owe at least some

Figure 8.   Still from Leni Riefenstahl's *Olympia*, 1938. Leni Riefenstahl Produktion.

debt to the emergence of modern sports in Britain and France, is carefully edited out, both metaphorically and literally. In this context, Myron's *Discobolus* acts as a signifier of historical transference, notionally not only legitimating the revived Olympic festival, but also conferring ownership of this to the National Socialist regime. Indeed, Hitler's recognition of the importance of this symbol was significantly reinforced in 1938, the same year that Riefenstahl's film was released, when he secured the purchase, from the Italian Fascist leader Benito Mussolini, of the Palombara *Discobolus* for the Munich Glyptothek and the German nation.[41]

Riefenstahl's *Olympia* has gone down in history as a cinematic *tour de force*. Throughout the later twentieth century it has retained its status as an icon of documentary cinema, resulting in the award of numerous prizes. Yet, it is also, of course, a conflicted and contradictory product, an innovative, creative and compelling piece of cinematic theatre tainted by its implicit desire to celebrate some of the more problematic values associated with the National Socialist regime by whom, and for whom, it was essentially produced. Despite continued support for the film in some quarters, the appropriation of Myron's *Discobolus* in this most infamous of Nazi cultural products perhaps inevitably left its reputation tarnished, if only by association. Yet, this did not result in the *Discobolus* form being entirely neglected in the post-war era. Rather the visual symbol would undergo new appropriations as artists strove to renegotiate ways in which Myron's masterpiece could speak to the concerns of a new era and a new post-war generation.

After Riefenstahl

In 1946, the Edinburgh-born artist Eduardo Paolozzi, then still a student at the Slade School in London, produced a small, mixed-media collage that he entitled *Discobolus of the Castel Porziano* (Figure 9). The work juxtaposes three incongruous images: a female gymnast performing calisthenics, a Russian Suprematist teapot and a fragmented torso of Myron's *Discobolus* transformed into a strange clockwork machine driven by cogs and gears. This work was typical of much of Paolozzi's early work in collage. As a boy, he had been an avid collector of cigarette cards, which he acquired whilst working in the family shop, and later he incorporated many of these disposable images into his works. At this time, Paolozzi regarded himself as working very much within the surrealist tradition, culling and redeploying these multiple images from mass culture into strange juxtapositions. Here, however, Paolozzi's specific use of the *Discobolus* offers a complex and alternative engagement with Myron's iconic work, and one that might suggest ways that the National Socialist appropriation of the *Discobolus* served to destabilise its potential significance within broader cultural histories. Notably, Paolozzi focuses his attention not on the eighteenth-century discoveries of copies after Myron, such as the Palombara *Discobolus* acquired by Hitler in 1938 and the Townley version that could be seen in the British Museum. Rather his work represents a much more recent find, a Roman torso, after Myron, discovered at the Castel Porziano in 1906. And here, the fragmented and broken body of the Porziano *Discobolus* stands in stark contrast to the perfected image of male athleticism that had earlier inspired both Hitler and Riefenstahl. In the context of 1946, this fragmentation also inevitably recalled the destruction wrought upon both the physical body and, more metaphorically, society and culture by the Second World War, not least as the inclusion of mechanical components echoed the emphasis on machine-like prosthetics that had characterised

Figure 9. Eduardo Paolozzi, *The Discobolus of the Castel Porziano*, 1946. Collage, mixed media. Private coll. © Trustees of the Paolozzi Foundation, Licensed by DACS 2012.

the work of many artists associated with the Dada movement in the immediate wake of the previous global conflict. Further, this very physical imperfection is notably contrasted against the image of the female gymnast in the lower left who could have come from a frame in Riefenstahl's *Olympia*. This figure stretches and twists her torso in a manner not dissimilar to that performed by Myron's model, yet also extends her arm to form what could only be identified in 1946 as an explicit reference to a Nazi salute.

The Suprematist-inspired teapot certainly seems to be the most incongruous element within Paolozzi's collage, although its notional status as a consumer artefact may serve to confer a similar status on the female gymnast. The fact that the posture adopted by this figure echoes the handle and spout of the teapot only serves to reinforce this visual analogy. But what role might the *Discobolus* itself play here? Standing between these two signifiers of Nazi and Soviet culture, the *Discobolus* perhaps appears as the site of destruction, the metaphorical war-torn and ravaged landscape upon which a major cultural battle has been fought. And, it might be added, classical culture appears to have come out worst. It should be pointed out here that Paolozzi was no traditionalist, and his *Discobolus of the Castel Porziano* should certainly not be read as some explicit claim for the victimhood of classicism in a modern age. Yet, it does suggest the centrality of culture within the ideological debates of the 1930s and 1940s, something that would later intensify during the Cold War era. It might also be added that the fragmented *Discobolus*, as a relic of bygone age pushed into the background despite its very grandeur and stature, could also suggest the destruction of Italy's classical heritage, not least through Mussolini's particular brand of Fascism and its links to German National Socialism, as exemplified in the controversial sale of the Palombara *Discobolus* to Hitler in 1938. Transformed into a machine by the inclusion of mechanical parts, the *Discobolus* now appears more like a weapon of war than a work of art, whilst the fragmentation becomes suggestive of violent destruction rather than simply the ravages of time.

Paolozzi's own Italian heritage should not be overlooked here, either. Whilst no supporter of Italian Fascism, Paolozzi's familial links would likely have made him, at the very least, sensitive to the catastrophe that had befallen his homeland by 1946. Further, his own sense of alienation as the son of an Italian immigrant can only have been exacerbated during the war when, despite being born and raised in Scotland, he and his family fell victim to Britain's wartime internment policy. On 10 June 1940, when still just 16 years of age, Paolozzi, along with virtually all men of Italian origin, was arrested as an enemy of the state and spent three months in custody at Saughton prison.[42] During this period Paolozzi's father, grand-father and uncle, all of whom had also initially been interned, left Britain for Canada, but all were killed when their ship was torpedoed by a German submarine. The significance of this episode in Paolozzi's early life is not introduced here to suggest that his *Discobolus of the Castel Porziano* might somehow be read as a psychological response to early trauma. This would clearly be stretching a point. However, the notion that a mutilated and destroyed *Discobolus* might be read as potentially signifying the sense of loss and alienation in a post-Fascist Italy, not least as a consequence of Mussolini's flirtation with German National Socialism, should not be entirely discounted.

Paolozzi's deployment of collage, constructing his work from images culled from mass culture, thus exploits the widespread dissemination of iconic images such as the *Discobolus* whilst simultaneously displacing them with his own new mode of artistic production. And here the notional damage inflicted on the *Discobolus* might also be read as signifying the damage done to the reputation of the work in the eyes of a broader public. In the wake of the Fascist appropriation of classicism, Myron's *Discobolus* would likely struggle to regain a reputation untainted by its past association with Fascism.

Resurrecting the *Discobolus*

Nonetheless, immediately following the defeat of Germany, some concerted efforts were being made to rehabilitate Myron's work, to make it more meaningful for a modern age and to distance it from its association with the National Socialist regime. The post-war Italian government, for example, rapidly sought to 'repatriate' the Palombara *Discobolus*, reclaiming it as war booty, despite the fact that it had been legitimately purchased by the National Socialist regime. After some legal wrangling, the Palombara *Discobolus* was brought back to Rome where it was fêted like a returning hero. Following much publicity, the work was afforded pride of place as part of the Museo Nazionale collection, displayed prominently at the Baths of Diocletian.

In Britain too, the *Discobolus* underwent a process of resurrection, most notably in connection with the first Games of the post-Second World War era, held in London in 1948. Much like the Games of Antwerp 1920, the 1948 London Olympics were of necessity organised with little preparation time and on something of a shoestring budget. The Wembley Empire Stadium, unlike much of the rest of the city, had remained largely undamaged by the Blitz and was therefore able to stage most of the sporting events. Accommodation for athletes and officials was a more pressing problem and it was thus no coincidence that the 1948 Games were subsequently dubbed the 'Austerity Olympics'.[43]

The conditions of post-war austerity also notably impacted the production of the official poster for the London Games. Given the limited availability of both time and funds, no competition was held and the selection process was confined to a small number of proposals submitted to the Executive Committee.[44] The poster selected from these was the work of the commercial artist Walter Herz of the Heros Publicity Studios in London and featured a design that owed something of a debt to the Antwerp Olympic poster of 1920. Thus, Herz's poster (Figure 10) established the geographical location of the Games by featuring a famous London landmark, in this case the Houses of Parliament, as a visual backdrop. Before this, and similarly floating in an ambiguous space, he placed a monumental classical sculpture, thus establishing a link between the antique and the modern. Much as the Antwerp poster had selected Kessels' *Discus Thrower* as a work that carried connotations of a regional identity, Herz not only chose Myron's *Discobolus* as his foreground image, but more specifically the Townley version from the British Museum.

The prominence of Myron's *Discobolus* as a visual signifier for the first Olympic Games held since the Berlin Games of 1936 might well be read as a conscious riposte to Riefenstahl's *Olympia* and the wider appropriation of antiquity under National Socialism. Indeed, London notably retained the torch run from Olympia, a tradition that had effectively been invented in National Socialist Germany in 1936. Thus, at the London Games of 1948 the modern cinematic *Discobolus* of Riefenstahl's *Olympia* was returned to its rather more mundane status as a frozen athlete from a distant past, to be admired and even revered, but no longer to be the blueprint for a new race of *Übermenschen*.

18

Figure 10.   Walter Herz, *Poster for the 1948 London Olympic Games.* © 2012 International Olympic Committee – All rights reserved.

The *Discobolus* Out of Favour?

Despite the best efforts of the London 1948 Olympics to resurrect the *Discobolus* and reclaim it from its former association with Riefenstahl and the National Socialist regime, Myron's iconic work became increasingly side-lined during the second half of the twentieth century. As the Games themselves were transformed into a modern sports phenomenon distributed globally through the medium of television, the relevance of the classical origins of the Olympic movement came to play a more diminished role, not least as concepts of Olympic history focused increasingly, often exclusively, on the history of the modern Games. Further, the political tensions generated during the Cold War, the scandals regarding the amateur/professional debate and the problems of chemically enhanced performance all served in various ways to distance the modern Olympics from its classical heritage and its association with such iconic artefacts as Myron's *Discobolus*.

Yet, despite these multiple distractions, the *Discobolus* did not entirely disappear from visual culture. In 1983, for example, the Russian artist-duo Vitaly Komar and Alexander Melamid produced a work entitled *Discobolus* as part of their *Nostalgic Socialist Realism* series (Figure 11). Having originally established a reputation as so-called 'unofficial' artists in the Soviet Union during the 1970s, Komar and Melamid are perhaps best known for producing what they termed Sots Art, a unique and frequently ironic integration of ideas emanating from western Pop Art, Conceptualism and Soviet Socialist Realism.[45] After emigrating from the Soviet Union, they rapidly became an important part of the contemporary art scene in New York in the late 1970s. The *Nostalgic Socialist Realism* series, exhibited at the Ronald Feldman Gallery in New York in the early 1980s, perhaps best expresses Komar and Melamid's ironic engagement with official Soviet Socialist Realist style. In their striking adaptation of Myron's classical exemplar, the artists combine a use of a heightened realism, derived from official Soviet art conventions, with a series of aggressive paint splatters in garish colours. These physically expressive marks deliberately undermine the smooth surface of the underlying work. At the same time they make a clear reference to the gestural paintings of Jackson Pollock, whose Abstract Expressionist canvases of the 1950s were widely promoted during the Cold

Figure 11. Vitaly Komar and Alexander Melamid, *Discobolus (from Nostalgic Socialist Realism series)*, 1983. Oil on canvas. Private collection.

War era as evidence of the notional artistic freedoms of the West compared to the aesthetic confinement of imposed Socialist Realism. Komar and Melamid are not here claiming the superiority of one style over another. Rather they recognise and articulate, in visual terms, the interdependence between two notionally oppositional forms of expression. And it is surely no coincidence that this reference to the oppositional claims regarding artistic culture should be articulated through the image of Myron's *Discobolus* just three years after the United States had boycotted the Moscow Olympics of 1980 and a year ahead of the planned Los Angeles Games of 1984. Although at this stage, the Soviet Union was yet to take decisive action concerning its subsequent boycott of the 1984 Games, criticisms of preparations in Los Angeles had made regular appearance in the Soviet press from 1980 onwards and tensions between the two super-powers were at a high point.[46] It should be added, however, that these gestural marks also carry another important significance. In New York in the early 1980s, graffiti-art was gradually making a transition from the street to the gallery, as artists including Jean-Michel Basquiat and Keith Haring came to the fore.[47] In *Discobolus*, Komar and Melamid's overlay of gestural marks clearly allude to a graffiti-like transgressive act, not least through the addition of a moustache to the face of the athlete, and an ejaculating penis. Yet, perhaps more importantly, their work also incorporates a Nazi armband which simultaneously explodes into bright red blood-like splatters reminiscent of X-rated video nasties. Here, the violent transformation of Myron's work serves to reinforce the continuing links between Myron's *Discobolus* and its appropriation under National Socialism, even as a link is forged with trends in contemporary art. For Komar and Melamid, it would seem, the *Discobolus* remained tainted by its past associations.

The *Discobolus* in China

In recent years, the *Discobolus* has begun to make something of a comeback in visual culture, not least in association with the Beijing Olympics of 2008. As the first Games to be held in Communist China, the Beijing Games transformed China's engagement not only with the Olympic movement but also with the West more generally. The sporting achievements of China's athletes, winning 51 gold medals compared with only 36 for the United States and 23 for Russia, have certainly forced the previously dominant sporting nations of the world to sit up and pay attention. Similarly, cultural successes such as the spectacular Opening Ceremony and Ai Weiwei's highly imaginative Beijing National Stadium, colloquially known as the Bird's Nest, have contributed to a broader expansion of interest in contemporary Chinese art, architecture and design.

Whilst the Olympic Games were still in preparation, the Chinese sculptor Sui Jianguo notably appropriated the form of Myron's *Discobolus* in his work, effectively giving the antique sculpture relevance for the emergence of China on the world stage. Sui, a Professor of Sculpture at the Central Academy of Fine Arts in Beijing, is currently recognised as one of the most influential artists in China and his works have been extensively exhibited both within his home nation and in the international arena. In the late 1990s, whilst on an Arts Fellowship in Australia, Sui produced the first of his works based on the Mao suit, a hollow metal jacket in the form of an empty shell that simultaneously fetishises and critiques the uniformity of society and culture under Mao. Over the next decade, he produced countless versions of these suits in both small and monumental scale and in a variety of media and colours. By the late 1990s, Sui developed this interest by producing versions of famous sculptures clothed in the famous Mao suit. These included versions of Myron's *Discobolus* (Figure 12). Sui was doubtless inspired by China's continuing attempts throughout the 1990s to host the Olympic Games: it was only narrowly defeated in its bid to secure the millennium Games of 2000, and soon thereafter launched its proposal for 2008. By clothing Myron's athlete in the infamous Mao suit, Sui makes an ironic comment on contemporary Chinese society. On the one hand, the Olympic bid reflected China's ambitions to be a bigger player on the world stage, discarding a past associated with Mao's Cultural Revolution and the Great Leap Forward. On the other, Sui argued, the nature of contemporary Chinese society and culture simultaneously suggested a metaphorical continuity with this past, symbolised by the retention of the outer trappings of Mao's suit which both restricts and restrains the Chinese people. Sui's life-size *Discobolus* thus implies a duality of freedom and oppression, expressed through the form of the Western antique figure most famous for this freedom of physical movement, here confined in clothes utterly unsuited to his actions.

Following the announcement that Beijing would host the Games of 2008, Sui's Mao-suited *Discobolus* reappeared in several manifestations at contemporary art shows throughout the world, as well as a major retrospective exhibition that toured China.[48] During the Games themselves, his works were also exhibited in Times Square in Hong Kong and here, alongside his earlier Mao-suited *Discobolus*, Sui exhibited a new work entitled *The New Disco-bolus*. This work features a dozen

Figure 12.   Sui Jianguo, Discobolus, c. 2004. Painted bronze. Private collection.

Figure 13. Sui Jianguo, *The New Disco-bolus*, 2008.

identical discus throwers, all adopting the pose of Myron's *Discobolus*, arranged in two rows (Figure 13). Unlike his previous works on this theme, however, *The New Disco-bolus* does not simply replicate Myron's athlete. Rather it presents Chinese businessmen in western suits arranged in a formation that alludes both to dance (hence the hyphenated separation of '*Disco*') and military ranks. In this way, *The New Disco-bolus* recalls, if on a smaller scale, China's most famous ancient sculptural work, the second century BC *Terracotta Army*. Sui has thus both referenced and transformed Myron's work into a modern army of businessmen about to take the world by storm. The adoption of the *Discobolus* pose further implies that it is the Olympic Games that have facilitated this opportunity for a new global trade invasion. That the work was installed in a shopping mall at the heart of China's thriving tiger economy for the duration of the international Olympic festival only serves to reinforce this unambiguous message.

Sui's engagement with the *Discobolus* at the time of the Beijing Olympics also references one last context in which Myron's antique work continues to cast its shadow over visual culture. For whilst Sui's work was drawing crowds in Times Square, the Townley version of Myron's *Discobolus* was itself on display at the Hong Kong Heritage Museum as part of a British Museum travelling exhibition entitled *The Ancient Olympic Games*.[49] The presence of Myron's *Discobolus* in China at this time reflected the cultural collaboration between China and Britain at the moment when the Chinese authorities were about to hand over the Olympic flag to London in preparation for the next Games. And indeed, after its tour of Asia, the Townley *Discobolus* will itself be returning to its London home in time to be displayed in a place of honour in the British Museum. Here, it will continue to cast its shadow over the festival of the 30th Olympiad at the London 2012 Games, and indeed beyond.

Acknowledgement
Research for this article was funded by the Leverhulme Trust.

23

Notes on contributor

Mike O'Mahony is a Senior Lecturer in History of Art at the University of Bristol. He has published widely on the representation of sport in art and visual culture and is the author of *Sport in the USSR: Physical Culture – Visual Culture* (2006) and *Olympic Visions: Images of the Games through History* (2012).

Notes

1. For example, Phillips, O'Neill and Osmond, 'Broadening Horizons in Sport History'; Guttmann, *Sports and American Art*; Huggins and O'Mahony, *The Visual in Sport*; O'Mahony, *Sport in the USSR*; O'Mahony, *Olympic Visions*.
2. For a brief account of the history of Myron's *Discobolus*, see Haskell and Penny, *Taste and the Antique*, 199–202.
3. Wallachinsky and Loucky, *Complete Book of the Olympics*, 227.
4. Quoted in Llewellyn Smith, *Olympics in Athens*, 166–7.
5. Garrett was victorious in the shot put, finished second in the long jump and equal-second in the high jump.
6. Sloane was a founder member of the International Olympic Committee (IOC) and the first President of the United States Olympic Committee (USOC).
7. Mandell, *First Olympic Games*, 115.
8. Mandell, *First Olympic Games*, 127.
9. *Official Report, Athens 1896*, 64.
10. Richardson, 'The New Olympian Games', 276.
11. *Official Report, Athens 1896*, I 64 and II 65.
12. These are Quintillian's *Institutio Oratoria* 2.13.10 (c. 95 AD); Lucian's *Philopseudes* 18 (c. 150 AD); Philostratus' *Imagines* (c. third century AD); and Pliny's *Naturalis Historia* 34.19.57–8.
13. Once this had been identified as a copy of the *Discobolus*, other copies after Myron were identified in various media, including Greek vases, small statuettes and even decorations for gem stones. For a detailed account of the various *Discoboli* forms identified to date, see Thliveri, *Evidence for the Discobolos*.
14. In a letter to Townley, Jenkins made the highly doubtful claim that the head had been found alongside the body and that 'there was never the slightest doubt of its authenticity'. See Jones, *Fake?*, 140.
15. Jones, *Fake?*, 140.
16. Cook, *Townley Marbles*, 59–62.
17. Jenkins, *Archaeologists and Aesthetes*, 136.
18. Beattie, *New Sculpture*, 149. In 1906, when Athens staged the Intercalated Games, stone throwing was one of the major field events in which 16 athletes from 8 nations competed. Athletes threw a weight of 6.35 kg. The event was won by the Greek athlete Nicolaos Georgantas, who also finished second in the discus competition. Wallachinsky and Loucky, *Complete Book of the Olympics*, 282.
19. Richmond's *An Athlete* of 1879 notably referenced another famous lost work by Myron, dedicated to the victorious runner Ladas.
20. Getsy, *Body Doubles*, 31.
21. Getsy, *Body Doubles*, 1.
22. Pater, 'Age of Athletic Prizemen', 122.
23. Pater, 'Age of Athletic Prizemen', 123.
24. Pater specifically compared Myron's work to Polycleitus' *Diadumenus*, which he described as 'the beau ideal of athletic repose'. His term 'beau ideal' is here deployed to paraphrase the eighteenth-century antiquarian Johann Joachim Winckelmann.
25. For an account of the broader reception of Pater's work, see Bann, *Reception of Walter Pater*.
26. Gosse, 'New Sculpture' 138–42, 199–203, 277–82, 306–11.
27. In January 1893, Myron's *Discobolus* also made a striking appearance on the London stage as part of the stage décor (designed by Sir Lawrence Alma-Tadema) in Sir Herbert Beerbohm-Tree's dramatization of *Hypatia*, a tale of love and conflict set in Alexandria during the last days of the Roman Empire. See Liversidge, '*Hypatia* at the Haymarket'.

28. Chapman, *Sandow the Magnificent*, 33–4.
29. Hobsbawm and Ranger, *Invention of Tradition*, 263–308.
30. Though regarded by the competitors as official Olympic Games, the IOC subsequently declared the Games of Athens 1906 unofficial, and they are often overlooked in Olympic histories.
31. Llewelyn Smith, *Olympics in Athens*, 200.
32. For accounts of the Paris and St Louis Games, see Drevon, *Jeux olympiques oubliés* and Matthews, *America's First Olympics*.
33. *Official Report, London, 1908*, 96.
34. Ibid.
35. For a history of how Antwerp secured the Olympic Games of 1920, see Renson, *The Games Reborn*.
36. *Official Report, Antwerp, 1920*, 17. Margaret Timmers has claimed that the original conception of the poster was the work of van der Ven's wife, Martha van Kuyck. Timmers, *A Century of Olympic Posters*, 31.
37. In 1880, a bronze copy of this marble original had also been cast and put on display in the gardens of the Palais des Academies, in Brussels.
38. *Official Report, Antwerp, 1920*, 17–18.
39. Guttmann, *The Olympics*, 38.
40. Hinton, *Films of Leni Riefenstahl*, 47.
41. Haskell and Penny, *Taste and the Antique*, 202.
42. Spencer, *Eduardo Paolozzi*, 50.
43. For accounts of the London 1948 Games, see Hampton, *The Austerity Olympics* and Phillips, *The 1948 Olympics*.
44. Timmers, *A Century of Olympic Posters*, 56.
45. For an account of the work of these artists, see Ratcliff, *Komar and Melamid*, 59–64.
46. Mertin, 'Soviet Union and the Olympic Games', 243–4.
47. Ratcliff, *Komar and Melamid*, 144.
48. The work even made an appearance in Athens during the 2004 Olympics, as part of an exhibition entitled *Olympic Cities: Gods Become Men* at the Frissiras Museum of Contemporary Art.
49. The *Discobolus* had earlier been exhibited at the Shanghai Museum prior to the opening of the Beijing Games.

References

Bann, S., ed. *The Reception of Walter Pater in Europe*. New York: Thoemmes Continuum, 2004.
Beattie, S. *The New Sculpture*. London: Yale University Press, 1983.
Chapman, D. *Sandow the Magnificent: Eugen Sandow and the Beginnings of Bodybuilding*. Urbana and Chicago: University of Illinois Press, 1994.
Cook, B. *The Townley Marbles*. London: British Museum Publications, 1985.
Drevon, A. *Les jeux olympiques oubliés: Paris 1900*. Paris: CNRS Éditions, 2000.
Getsy, D. *Body Doubles: Sculpture in Britain 1877–1905*. London and New Haven: Yale University Press, 2004.
Gosse, E. 'The New Sculpture: 1879–1894'. *Art Journal* 56 (1894): 138–42, 199–203, 277–82, 306–11.
Guttmann, A. *Sports and American Art from Benjamin West to Andy Warhol*. Amherst and Boston: University of Massachusetts Press, 2011.
Guttmann, A. *The Olympics: A History of the Modern Games*. Urbana and Chicago: University of Illinois Press, 1992.
Hampton, J. *The Austerity Olympics: When the Games Came to London in 1948*. London: Aurum Press, 2008.
Haskell, F. and N. Penny. *Taste and the Antique: The Lure of Classical Sculpture 1500–1900*. New Haven: Yale University Press, 1981.
Hinton, D. *The Films of Leni Riefenstahl*. Lanham, Maryland: Scarecrow Press, 2000.
Hobsbawm, E. and T. Ranger, eds. *The Invention of Tradition*, Cambridge: Cambridge University Press, 1983.

Huggins, M. and M. O'Mahony, eds. *The Visual in Sport*. London and New York: Routledge, 2011.

Jenkins, I. *Archaeologists and Aesthetes in the Sculpture Galleries of the British Museum 1800– 1939*. London: British Museum Publications, 1992.

Jones, M. *Fake? The Art of Deception*. Berkeley and Los Angeles: University of California Press, 1990.

Liversidge, M. "'Living Alma-Tadema Pictures": Hypatia at the Haymarket'. In *Making Sense of Greek Art: Ancient Visual Culture and its Receptions*, ed. V. Coltman, 155–78. Exeter: University of Exeter Press, 2012.

Llewellyn Smith, M. *Olympics in Athens 1896: The Invention of the Modern Olympic Games*. London: Profile Books, 2004.

Mandell, R. *The First Modern Olympics*. Berkeley, Los Angeles, London: University of California Press, 1976.

Matthews, G. *America's First Olympics: The St. Louis Games of 1904*. Columbia: University of Missouri Press, 2005.

Mertin, E. 'The Soviet Union and the Olympic Games of 1980 and 1984: Explaining the Boycotts to their People'. In *East Plays West: Sport and the Cold War*, ed. S. Wagg and D. Andrews, 235–52. London and New York: Routledge, 2007.

Official Report. Olympic Games. Antwerp, 1920.

Official Report. The Fourth Olympiad. London, 1908.

Official Report. The Olympic Games, BC 776–AD 1896. Athens, 1896.

O'Mahony, M. *Olympic Visions: Images of the Games through History*. London: Reaktion Books Ltd., 2012.

O'Mahony, M. *Sport in the USSR: Physical Culture – Visual Culture*. London: Reaktion Books Ltd., 2006.

Pater, W. 'The Age of Athletic Prizemen'. In *Greek Studies: A Series of Essays*, ed. Charles L. Shadwell. London: Macmillan, 1895.

Phillips, B. *The 1948 Olympics: How London Rescued the Games*. Cheltenham: SportsBooks Ltd., 2007.

Phillips, M., M. O'Neill, and G.Osmond. 'Broadening Horizons in Sport History: Films, Photographs and Monuments'. *Journal of Sport History* 34, no. 2 (2007): 271–93.

Ratcliff, C. *Komar and Melamid*. New York: Abbeville Press, 1988.

Renson, R. *The Games Reborn: The VII Olympiad, Antwerp 1920*. Leuven: Pandora-Snoeck-Ducaju and Zoon, 1996.

Richardson, R. 'The New Olympian Games'. *Scribner's Magazine* XX (1896): 267–86.

Spencer, R., ed. *Eduardo Paolozzi: Writings and Interviews*. Oxford: Oxford University Press, 2000.

Thliveri, H. *Evidence for the Discobolus of Myron and its Place in Ancient Greek Art*. PhD diss., University of London, 1996.

Timmers, M. *A Century of Olympic Posters*. London: V&A Publishing, 2008.

Wallachinsky, D. and J. Loucky. *The Complete Book of the Olympics*. London: Aurum Press, 2008.

Modern Pentathlon at the London 2012 Olympics: Between Traditional Heritage and Modern Changes for Survival

Sandra Heck

Ruhr-University Bochum, Germany

In London, in 2012, the modern pentathlon (fencing, swimming, horse riding, shooting and running) celebrated its centenary. In its 100 years of Olympic history several rule changes have taken place. Directly after its Olympic debut in Stockholm in 1912, the International Olympic Committee headed by Pierre de Coubertin evaluated the event and criticised the shortcomings between the supposed idea behind the sport and its implementation. After Coubertin's death, the sport continued to develop; recently running and shooting have been joined in a so called combined event. In all cases, the presidents of the Union Internationale de Pentathlon Moderne (UIPM) argued the associated rule changes by referring to the original idea of the modern pentathlon. The sport's insecure future after the Games in Rio in 2016 provides sufficient reason to investigate the discrepancy between the marketing strategy of the UIPM and the ideological origins of the modern pentathlon. It finally allows an analysis of select historical rule changes that fitted the original idea behind the events and those that served purely modern strategies of survival. Thus, the topic also stands as an example of the policies of a contemporary international sports federation that uses (select parts of its) history and (invented) traditions as strong and successful marketing tools.

Recent discussions on the deletion of wrestling from the Olympic sports programme in 2020 have once more raised the topic of the questionable importance of keeping the modern pentathlon in the Games. Composed of fencing, swimming, horse riding, shooting and running, it has continuously been an Olympic sport since the Games in Stockholm in 1912. Even though the combined event celebrated its Olympic centenary last year in London, it still takes a bit of a backseat in modern sports circles. It is just as difficult to attract spectators as it is to attract athletes to the sport, and thus, it is widely disadvantaged in broadcasting. As a further consequence, (most recently, since the 1990s) the event has frequently been seen as being at risk of being deleted from the Olympic sports programme. The crucial point is that several other, new sports would like to achieve Olympic status, but the number is limited. Thus, in the history of the Olympic Games some sports have been already deleted from the programme, while others have been added.[1]

Despite its 100-year Olympic history, the characteristics of the modern pentathlon are still relatively unknown today. The designation of the event as 'modern' and its composition of five relatively opposed disciplines seem somewhat bizarre. The Greek word 'pentathlon' rather promises strong links to the ancient Games, and this heritage has served as a long-term guarantee that the event would remain in the Olympic programme. A second point in its favour is that the *Union Internationale de Pentathlon Moderne* (UIPM) strongly promotes the idea that Pierre de Coubertin was the creator of the sport.[2] Both these arguments have contributed to the continuous appearance of the modern pentathlon in the Olympic Games programme. This leads to the central point of this article, which aims at contrasting the ideals behind the first Olympic modern pentathlon in 1912 with the most recent implementation in London in 2012.

As literature on the history of the event is rare and as the federation does not have public archives,[3] information is mainly taken from Coubertin's writings found in the International Olympic Committee (IOC) Archives in Lausanne, Switzerland, and from recent articles on the policy of the UIPM. First, select aspects of today's modern pentathlon regulations are presented in their historical evolution.[4] Second, the current situation is compared to select original objectives pursued in the implementation of a modern form of Olympic pentathlon in 1912. Finally, the results allow us to distinguish between components of 'traditional heritage' on the one hand and of 'modern changes for survival' on the other. The insecure future of the event after the Games in Rio in 2016 gives a special cause to investigate the UIPM's marketing strategy with regard to the use of the sport's ideological origins. It finally allows us to differentiate between select historical rule changes that fitted the original concept behind the event and those that served purely as modern survival strategies. Thus, the topic also serves as an example of the policies of a contemporary international sports federation that uses (select parts of its) history and (invented) traditions as strong and successful marketing tools. By doing so, it reveals modern sporting decisions in a different light and finally proves how well the modern pentathlon of London 2012 still fitted the original objectives, which 100 years earlier led to its inclusion in the Olympic Games programme.

Shortened, Mediatised and Disarmed: The Characteristics of the Modern Pentathlon at the London Olympics in 2012 and their Evolution

The men's modern pentathlon was held on 11 August 2012 in London's Greenwich Park followed by the women's event a day later.[5] Each event was contested by 36 athletes. Modern Pentathletes have struggled to remain a part of the Olympic Games programme, especially as 10 years earlier, at the 114th IOC Session in 2002, the IOC had decided to limit the number of Olympic sports to a maximum of 28. Thereafter, criteria for the choice of sports were developed and ratified by the IOC Session in 2004. These criteria embraced the 'history and tradition' of the sport, the 'universality', the 'popularity', the 'image', the 'athletes' health', the 'development of the International Federation' (IF) and the 'costs'.[6] Thus, five new sports, golf, karate, rugby union, roller sports and squash, were taken into consideration for the Olympic Games of London 2012. However, neither of the two finalists, karate and squash, achieved the required two-thirds vote. Contrastingly, baseball and softball were excluded from the official programme so that in London only 26 sports were performed, among them still, the modern pentathlon.[7]

In 2012, both the male and the female modern pentathletes started with the epée fencing, followed by the 200-m freestyle swimming, show jumping (riding course of 350–450 m length consisting of 12 obstacles) and ending with the combined event (pistol-shooting and cross-country running over a total of 3000 m). The implementation of the so-called combined event had been decided by the UIPM at the end of 2008 and was part of the Olympic event in London for the very first time. It is similar to the biathlon that connects cross-country skiing with shooting and promises greater public interest.[8] This recent addition also reduces the competition time for both athletes and spectators and thereby aims to improve attraction. As a consequence, some journalists suggested renaming the sport the 'Tetrathlon' because of the reduced number of individual competitions.[9] This proposition was not, however, attractive to the UIPM because of the ancient tradition of the 'pentathlon'. From the athletes' perspective the new combined event initially caused criticism, mainly because it created new requirements in terms of performance and training. The German modern pentathlete Lena Schöneborn, female gold medallist of Beijing 2008, perceived it as a compromise: 'Die Athleten wollen ja auch, dass ihr Sport populär ist. Deswegen nimmt man bestimmte Sachen in Kauf. Auch wenn sie nicht so toll sind.'[10] The new format finally convinced all sceptics in the federation, as its less dangerous character provided the opportunity for the event to be part of the Youth Olympic Games of Singapore in 2010.[11] On the other hand, it remains questionable how far the athletes and their sport should generally go to conform with what their federation perceives as another means of survival.

The three other disciplines of the modern pentathlon have changed only slightly over the years. In 1988, the cross-country horse riding was transferred into a stadium show jumping competition. This facilitated the organisation and allowed spectators to follow the whole discipline live on site. Moreover, in Sydney 2000, the swimming distance was shortened from 300 to 200 m and the cross-country race from 4000 to 3000 m. Also, since the Olympic Games of Atlanta in 1996, all the five contests take place in one day only. In 1984, the event had already been compressed from a five- into a four-day schedule (the fourth day beginning with shooting and concluding with running).[12]

The newest development, however, which had its Olympic debut – just like the combined event – in 2012, too, was the laser shooting.[13] Previously, in 1996 in Atlanta, the .22 calibre rapid-fire pistol competition had already become a 10-m air pistol event. The shooting with multimedia pointers (instead of air guns) was decided upon in 2010, and tested at the Youth Olympic Games in Singapore.[14] In contrast, the laser technology was not used by the shooters in any Olympic discipline, just in the training of the junior athletes.[15] The implementation in the modern pentathlon is, however, supposed to reduce both costs and noise, to facilitate travel and to increase the safety and acceptance (using a gun for sport had created problems in certain countries in the past).[16] UIPM President Klaus Schormann is absolutely convinced of this innovation: 'Wir schreiben damit schon ein bisschen Geschichte.'[17] The company that invented the laser technology for the modern pentathlon in 2011 cancelled its cooperation with the federation and accused its members of breaching the contract in several points.[18] However, this had no influence on the continued use of this shooting technology in modern pentathlon competitions. In 2012, David Svoboda from the Czech Republic and Laura Asadauskaitė from Lithuania managed the new requirements most successfully and took the gold medals.

To sum up, beginning in the late 1980s and reinforced in the last four years several changes have been implemented in the modern pentathlon regulations. Those changes were enforced by the UIPM, after the event had been previously governed by the IOC until 1948.[19] Although the five disciplines generally remained the same, the specifics and the scheduling shifted over the years. The common purpose, however, was always to 'modernise' the sport. Klaus Schormann remembers a defining moment: 'When we had a discussion with the International Olympic Committee in 2002, to survive in the Olympic programme, I promised [IOC President] Jacques Rogge we would work hard to modernise.'[20] Modernising means increasing the attraction for both the media and the spectators, making it more accessible for new, young athletes and hence saving its position as an Olympic sport. This strategy has worked quite successfully until very recently. At the

IOC meeting in Mexico City in November 2007, for instance, the IOC members clearly bolstered the modern pentathlon as important part of the Olympic Games programme.

The future of the sport also strongly depended on the quality of its media presentation in London, which is why the UIPM specially monitored media activities during the period of the Games (11–12 August 2012).[21] It emerged that when focusing just on the UK, China, Lithuania, Brazil, Czech Republic and Russia, a total of 637 online articles were written, read by around 110 million people. In comparison to the World Cup Final one year before when 73 media had been accredited,[22] in London 2012 the number was more than five times as high (366 accreditations).[23] During the two-day event, 124,256 visitors of the official website and 14,553 additional Facebook fans could be identified, proving once more the importance of the Olympics for the image of the sport. With regard to television, the modern pentathlon was watched in 170 countries, including 54 live broadcastings. Thus, according to the UIPM statistics the event increased its visibility through different media in 2012.

Nevertheless, in comparison to other more popular sports the number of press reactions to the modern pentathlon in 2012 still emphasised the sport's minor position, even in the year of its centenary. According to the author's own analyses, the sport did not become the subject of media focus in the USA nor in Great Britain, France or Germany.[24] Critical comments generally remained rare and it was the portraits of chosen athletes [25] or the presentation of national results that dominated.[26] This positive portrayal was of course favourable for the federation that is struggling to keep its sport an Olympic sport, but it was not reflecting an objective, critical journalism. With regard to the number of 'deserving sports', only few journalists clearly expressed their astonishment that the Olympic programme supports sports that in fact 'nobody watches'.[27] Despite the new developments, the rules generally remained uncriticised by the press. Only in the US–American journal *The Atlantic* could one read for instance that 'the rules are as Byzantine as the scoring system', and that the new laser guns are 'more Star Wars than Peloponnesian' and 'may pull in a handful of extra viewers, if only for the sake of novelty'.[28] In other publications like in *The New York Times* or the British newspaper *The Independent*, only certain sentences or titles contained slight comments, however, which were largely in the same vein as those of previous years.[29] The rest of the above-mentioned articles – just like the majority of press reactions – were neutral in their description of the new developments.[30] Surprisingly enough, some articles even concentrated on the 'old' disciplines of the event instead of evaluating the recent changes.[31] Nevertheless, showing a willingness to modernisation was a core strategy of the federation in order to fit the IOC's criteria for Olympic sports.[32]

Furthermore, the UIPM used a second powerful strategy by highlighting their sport as traditional and pointing out its rich Olympic history. However, this historical adaptation is quite selective, concentrating on the ancient heritage and Coubertin's power as its inventor, with the military origins of the sport usually being neglected. In 2010, on the occasion of the World Championships in Chengdu/China, for instance, a newly constructed competition venue was particularly devoted to Coubertin. Jacques de Navacelle, Coubertin's great nephew, had previously approved the use of the famous name. For the UIPM Secretary General at that time, Joël Bouzou, there is no doubt that the modern pentathlon in the twenty-first century corresponds more than ever to Coubertin's ideals and is hence moving in the right direction: 'I think Pierre de Coubertin, from where he is, is very proud of us. We are not only the sport showcasing the complete athlete and highlighting all the different skills, we are also very modern through the new combined event, the laser shooting and such a wonderful multi sport complex in China when sport becomes not only a competition and an entertainment, but also permanent education and a mix of all populations of the world in mutual respect and understanding.'[33]

Several of the previously presented rule changes have likewise been accounted for by putting Coubertin's original aims into practice. Besides the military training and other national roots, it was principally Coubertin who gave the modern pentathlon its ideological background. Do the traditional ideals attributed to the modern pentathlon today correspond to the historical reality? And just how far are the current rule changes linked to the original objectives dedicated to the modern pentathlon of the early twentieth century?

Reforms of the Modern Pentathlon Regulations in the Light of Coubertin's Original Ideals

Directly after the Olympic debut of the modern pentathlon in 1912, the IOC members, most of all their President Coubertin, evaluated the event and criticised the gap between the idea supposedly directing the sport and its implementation. Possibly the recent rule changes have brought the event closer to those original objectives, or possibly even led to a greater modernisation and alienation. With regard to the relationship of the current UIPM strategy to the original objectives of the modern pentathlon, three different categories can be identified: (a) invented traditions,[34] (b) implemented original ideas and (c) contradictions. In each case, examples of the named strategy of the federation are given to underline the hypothesis.

Inventing a Tradition: The Ancient Model

The timeline in the history section of the UIPM homepage mentions first of all the 'Greek Olympic Games Pentathlon'[35] and thereby puts the modern event in its place in a thousand-years-old Olympic tradition. The names are obviously related but the concrete disciplines differ. The ancient pentathlon, which included a run, a long jump, a javelin throw, a discus throw and wrestling, was more closely connected to other modern Olympic combined events. Within the modern Olympic Games movement, the Intercalated Games in 1906 re-introduced, for instance, the ancient form of the pentathlon.[36] Six years later, when the modern pentathlon had its Olympic debut, a second pentathlon, the so-called 'Swedish Pentathlon' was also based on the ancient model but replaced the wrestling with a second run (1500 m). As this athletic pentathlon was cancelled after 1924 – later enlarged to a heptathlon – it did not remain part of the public memory.[37] The modern pentathlon prevailed and its federation continued using the ancient model as means of promotion.

Stronger than the significance of its title, however, is the ideological relationship between the ancient and the modern form of the event. The pentathlete of ancient times and the early modern pentathlete were both strongly connected to military service and hence to war preparation. However, this link is not mentioned in the historical overview of the federation at all and thus generally remains unconsidered. To present the modern pentathlon as a military – or to be more precise former military – sport is probably not expected to attract great attention. In contrast, in the time leading up to World War I, the links between sport and military were much stronger and socially acknowledged.[38]

The UIPM rather reminds us of the promotionally effective aspects for instance that 'admiration for the Ancient Pentathlon was fully shared by the founder of the Modern Olympics, Baron Pierre de Coubertin'.[39] Using ancient tradition to legitimise the Olympic status of the modern pentathlon is indeed not new. Coubertin himself used this romantic link as both inspiration and positive advertisement and was quite successful with this strategy at the beginning of the twentieth century. It was not a difficult task to boost interest in the ancient Games, as many people were already enthusiastic about Philhellenism.[40] From an early stage, Coubertin emphasised that the 'form' had to be adapted to modern times, even if the 'spirit' generally remained the same.[41] He proclaimed 'la formation de l'all-round man',[42] which was true both for ancient and for modern times. After the 1906 Intercalated Games in Athens, it became, however, evident that he rather searched for possibilities to frustrate the Greeks' attempt to establish their own Olympic Games movement and so he aimed therefore at creating a modern pentathlon that contrasted to the Greek one of 1906 which had been more obviously strongly connected to the ancient model. As a further consequence, this made room for the implementation of the above-mentioned 'Swedish', classical, pentathlon in 1912 which remained more closely related to the ancient model: 'Il y a eu deux pentathlons: le moderne' – le mien – dont les débuts ont été très brillants et le classique [...].'[43]

Thus, even in 1912 the 'modern' (in terms of that time) aspects of the Olympic modern pentathlon were more prominent than its ancient forerunner. That is one reason why the event was composed of a new combination of disciplines.[44] These disciplines contrasted both to the ancient pentathlon, to its re-establishment in 1906 and to the rather athletic-oriented Swedish pentathlon of 1912. This distinction between Greek, Swedish and other forms of pentathlon lost its importance over the years but even though the ideological circumstances are different today, the nostalgic touch of the Ancient Olympic Games still attributes a positive, valuable character to the modern pentathlon. This positive image is also transported through the ongoing creation of links to the supposed 'founding father', Coubertin.

Implementing Coubertin's Original Ideas: The One-Day Format and the Combined Event

Another strategy used to legitimise current changes in the modern pentathlon regulations corresponds to the educational background Coubertin had dedicated to this sport. This argumentation is likewise problematic, as the athletic and social ideals have significantly changed over the years and hence also the perspectives in which the modern pentathlon is viewed. At the beginning of the twentieth century, Coubertin stated: 'Et le Pentathlon moderne dont personne ne voulait en 1909 quand j'en annonçai la fondation, recueillit en 1912 à Stockholm des suffrages unanimes et suscite de tous côtés des imitations. Chacun veut faire de ses fils des "débrouillards" [...].'[45] Débrouillardism as a philosophy of life does not fit today's society, which increasingly requires specialists in certain tasks trying to refine them to a maximum.[46] Nevertheless, select issues of Coubertin's original ideas are still nowadays promoted, creating a feeling of a traditional and hence valuable issue; not as nostalgic as the link to the ancient Games, however, but nevertheless slightly more closely related to the reality of the modern Olympics.

The lengthy duration of the competition and the different rules of the five disciplines demonstrate a major difficulty for the promotion of the sport in the twenty-first century. They hinder the transparency of the sport for the spectator and make it less suitable for television. That is why the competition time has continuously been shortened until it reached the present one-day format. This clearly corresponds to Coubertin's idea and has been promoted as such: 'Le créateur de ce Pentathlon qui fut inauguré à Stockholm, lors de la Vᵉ Olympiade, est le premier à reconnaître que [...] les cinq épreuves qui le composent devraient se succéder sans interruption, l'athlète passant de l'une à l'autre sans autre sans interruption, l'athlète passant de l'une à l'autre sans autre arrêt que celui nécessité par une sommaire modification de costume. On y viendra sans doute.' [47]

The combined event, which connects the cross-country run with the shooting, is another step towards shortening the competition time and inter-relating the disciplines. The idea of the uninterrupted discipline sequence was probably linked to the legend of origin based on the adventures of a military officer: 'On vient de nous parler de l'officier en campagne'. Qu'il parte donc en bicyclette, qu'il tire, qu'il saute à cheval, qu'il continue à pied et qu'enfin, tout habillé, il se jette à l'eau, voilà une salutaire copie de la guerre et des obligations qu'elle peut imposer à un homme.' [48] As the origin of the story is unknown and cannot be reconstructed through archive material, the initial inspiration is not clear. Either Coubertin's ideas led to the creation of the military legend or the legend inspired Coubertin, who just aimed to implement it.[49]

However, the one-day-format and the combined event represent only two aspects of the legend. The military links have meanwhile generally been given up. With the success of Lars Hall, the first non-military gold medal winner of the modern pentathlon in Helsinki 1952, the sport entered a new 'civilian' era. Previously, the sport had almost exclusively been practised by military officers.[50] Coubertin's aim to invite officers to train in running and swimming while encouraging the lower social classes to take up horse riding had thereby lost its social cause.[51] Coubertin's wishes were originally based on the military-masculine 'zeitgeist' of the early twentieth century. As the modern pentathlon no longer has a function in terms of the (para-)military preparation, one of the most important principles of legitimisation has gone. When considering the history of the sport, this context cannot be ignored, which also means that Coubertin's ideas cannot function in terms of today's identity. Modern warfare and military fitness training are no longer dependent on the skills developed by the practice of the modern pentathlon, so that putting into practice the demands that Coubertin championed in 1912, thus contradicts one of his own major arguments: adaptation to the time and its respective socio-cultural circumstances.

On the other hand, not all of Coubertin's points of concern were finally taken by the UIPM as reasons for rule changes in the future. For instance, Coubertin had also suggested replacing shooting with his favourite sport rowing, which was never taken into consideration.[52] Moreover, in the course of the time, parts of Coubertin's original ideas not only became outdated but were superseded by changes in military and wider practices.

Opposing the Original Idea: Modernisation through Gender Equity and New Technologies

With the inclusion of a woman's competition in Sydney 2000, the UIPM finally departed from Coubertin's heritage. When, 88 years ago, the Swedish Olympic organising committee had to handle a woman's application for the modern pentathlon in 1912, he gave a clear hint to his preferred answer: 'As to the modern pentathlon I am personally opposed *to the admittance of ladies* as competitors in the Olympic Games. But as they are this time admitted as tennis players, swimmers, etc. I do not see on what ground we should stand to refuse them in the Pentathlon. However, I repeat that I greatly *regret the fact*. Therefore, I leave to you to decide and if you refuse or accept the engagement, I shall agree with you.'[53] Finally, despite the lack of a particular rule, British Helen Preece's request in 1912 was confronted with a unanimous hostile refusal.[54] After this bad experience, no woman tried to enter the modern pentathlon again for decades. Even 16 years later, Coubertin emphasised that he was indeed ready for changes but not in regard to the women's question: 'Personnellement, je voudrais voir le Pentathlon moderne ramené aux directives que j'avais posées en le créant. Quant à la participation des femmes aux Jeux, j'y demeure hostile. C'est contre mon gré qu'elles ont été admises à un nombre grandissant d'épreuves.'[55] The international and national federations underlined this position by delaying the involvement of women in the Olympic modern pentathlon until Sydney 2000.

A similar break and thereby a clear step towards modernity was reached by the invention of the laser pistol. Already in 1996 the federation had not been shy to exchange the weapon that had originally been used in 1912. However, as neither of those technologies (the 10-m air pistol of 1996 nor the laser pistol of 2012) existed during Coubertin's time he actually did not have such a choice. In contrast, the transfer of the cross-country horse riding competition into a stadium show jumping competition in 1988 would have been possible in the early Olympics as both sports then existed. The cross-country horse riding was clearly more closely related to the legend of origin with the officer galloping his way through the enemies' territory; however, in this case the move towards a modern, spectator-attractive format was also obviously dominating the decision of the federation.[56]

Building the Future: The Modern Pentathlon after Rio 2016

As there are generally more sports recognised by the IOC than are included in the official Olympic programme, these sports may apply for inclusion in future Olympics through a recommendation by the IOC Olympic Programme Commission. This leads to a decision of the IOC Executive Board and finally to a vote of the respective IOC Session.[57] As a result, the IOC Executive Commission has recently, in February 2013, re-evaluated all current Olympic sports according to criteria such as broadcasting rates, finances, tickets sold, world-wide diffusion, popularity and engagement in the anti-doping-campaign.[58] Again the modern pentathlon seems to survive, but the wrestling is in danger of being excluded in 2020. Nevertheless, also the place of the modern pentathlon is for the moment only guaranteed until the Olympic Games of Rio de Janeiro, Brasil, in 2016.[59] For sports like the modern pentathlon that primarily define themselves in terms of their continued Olympic presence and depend on the related financial benefits, remaining in the Olympic programme is essential for their future.[60]

Despite all efforts, the modern pentathlon remains a minor sport in the twenty-first century. It is still harder and more expensive to train for five disciplines (including equipment for horse riding, fencing and shooting) in five different venues than it is to focus on one sport only. Even though the diversified training has positive effects on both co-ordination and endurance, it remains time-consuming. As it is not a sport for the masses, it is in the eyes of the general public often confused up with the athletic combined events (the heptathlon or the decathlon) and even the five disciplines or the best modern pentathletes in most countries are unknown. Moreover, from the athletes' point of view there is no promise of high income – even for the elite sportsmen and women – as is the case in many other modern Olympic sports. With regard to Beijing 2008, for instance, German Lena Schöneborn's Olympic gold medal in the modern pentathlon contributed very little to increase the national visibility of the sport, especially because she failed to appear again four years later. In other countries, the modern pentathlon lives a shadow existence behind sports that are more easily merchandised and socially more widespread. In Sweden, however, due to its rich history of national success, the modern pentathlon is still comparatively popular, but even there the national federation fights to find new athletes of the right calibre.[61] That is probably one reason why the event's presence in the

Olympic programme is currently only secure for another four years, up to the Olympic Games in 2016.[62] There, in Rio de Janeiro, once again 28 sports will form the Olympic sports panel as the IOC voted 2009 in Copenhagen to include golf and rugby union.[63]

At the 125th IOC Session, to be held in Buenos Aires, Argentina, in September 2013, the IOC is to decide the future of the Olympic programme after Rio.[64] Once more the modern pentathlon will be discussed and partly measured by the results of the efforts made to modernise the sport. Thus, the UIPM's struggle for survival goes on. The modern pentathlon has also in 2012 not yet reached its final appearance and possibly never will. It is, just like the Olympic movement in general, in a continuous process of change, interacting with the social development and the requirements of a particular culture. To secure modern pentathlon's future after Rio 2016, the UIPM is depending on a positive image, not on a detailed-oriented re-appraisal of the past. At the recent UIPM Congress in October 2012, it has been agreed for instance to 'change the combined event to have 4 shooting series (instead of 3), and 4 running laps of 800 m (instead of 3 running laps of 1000 m) and the maximum time to secure the 5 green lights on each shooting series has been reduced from 70 s to 50 s'. The aim is to increase the 'drama and excitement' of the laser shooting in the combined event.[65]

Further ideas for new changes after London already exist. One concrete aim for 2016 and 2020 is, for instance, to perform the swimming in a temporary pool and also the fencing with the other disciplines in one common sports complex.[66] This would minimise the travels between venues and additionally reduce the competition time and thereby also increase the attraction for broadcasting. Schormann calls this 'mit der Zeit Schritt halten'.[67] If commerce advances to the new Olympic idea, it probably seems to be the right strategy to 'modernise' or 'mediate' the modern pentathlon continuously and thus to recommend it as a telegenic, marketable sports attraction. In this context, image videos and the intense use of social media (Twitter and Facebook) are just another proof that the UIPM is aware of the signs of the time.[68]

As the spectator and hence the media generally play a dominant role today, the need for creating mediagenic formats has increased.[69] If they are congruent with the history of the modern pentathlon it underlines and hence facilitates the decision for rule change; if they differ, Coubertin's general claim for keeping up with the times still fits. Thus, whatever the invention, a historical legitimation is always possible. This has of course nothing to do with an extensive reconciliation of the past; however, as long as surviving in the Olympic programme remains a priority this attitude will probably not change, not even in a historical year like the centenary in 2012. Whether the modern pentathlon will succeed in its balancing act between tradition and modernity, it will become apparent with the development of audiences and media exposure and ultimately in the forthcoming IOC decision about the future Olympic sports. Several new popular and indeed 'modern' sports are already attempting to obtain a position within the Olympic Games programme[70] and other 'traditional' sports might be accused of not keeping up with the times.[71] Thus, the struggle between Olympic traditions and concessions to modernity goes on.

Despite the innovations of 2012 some observers of the modern pentathlon talk about a 'crises of identity'.[72] Criticisms are especially addressed to the assumed 'elitist and outdated' character of the sport.[73] The continuing lack of public interest could indeed emerge as modern pentathlon's destiny after 2016. Other sampled sports, which are already recognised as part of the Olympics, such as the triathlon or the biathlon, have had greater success from a marketing point of view.[74] Although the modern pentathlon met the required minimum distribution for Olympic sports in 75 countries on four continents as early as 2000, the number of participants remains relatively low.[75] The biathle, a combination of running and swimming, which is also headed by the UIPM, is likewise relatively unknown. Since it is easier to learn, however, and thus reaches more sport enthusiasts than the modern pentathlon, its affiliation with the UIPM met its purpose at least on the national level and in the short term.[76] However, at international level the biathle is still not sufficiently widespread and therefore far from being assured of taking one of the treasured places in the Olympic programme.

For the moment the governing body of the modern pentathlon has still time to think about further developments of their sport. Despite the remaining criticism, Bouzou is confident that the modern pentathlon will stay in the programme: 'We already have positive support from the IOC. The sport has to and will remain in the Olympic Games. The spectacle we saw [in London in 2012] is the best message we can send to the critics.'[77] Since 2001, the sport has generally found a supporter in Count Jacques Rogge. His term of office, however, will end soon in 2013. At the previously mentioned 125th IOC Session in September not only the new host city will be elected, but also two further important decisions will be made: A new IOC President will be elected and the possible addition of new sports for the 2020 Games will be discussed.[78] If the nomination of new sports meets with a President in favour of renewing the sports programme, the future of the Olympic modern pentathlon might become bleak.

Conclusion

The centenary of the modern pentathlon is generally an appropriate moment for a retrospective view. Ideals that were related to the first Olympic modern pentathlon in 1912 have been presented in this paper and compared with the event at the Olympic Games in London 100 years later. It emerged that the current marketing strategy of the UIPM generally embraces three different lines: the invention of traditions, the implementation of Coubertin's ideas and pure modernisations. By giving concrete examples for each of the three strategic lines it could be proved that the modern pentathlon in London 2012 was indeed a mixture of 'traditional heritage' on the one hand and of 'modern changes necessary for survival' on the other. Some nostalgic, historical elements were intentionally promoted by the UIPM (such as the relationship to the ancient pentathlon for instance), some were neglected (e.g. the inclusion of rowing as a pentathlon discipline) and others seemed too far removed from today's social value system (such as the exclusion of women). But the UIPM was not only focusing on the past when representing its sport. Some modern inventions like the laser pistol have recently been implemented to underline a clear step towards modernity.

For some this manner of presentation seems inconsequent and one-sided, such as from the scientific point of view several historical aspects are neglected. For others it is just clever and exemplary for the policy of a contemporary international sports federation that uses select parts of history and (invented) traditions as strong and successful marketing tools. Indeed, it has to date successfully managed to continually secure the place of the modern pentathlon in the Olympic programme. This is even more surprising as the claim to continue to redeem Coubertin's ideals is actually anachronistic. Today the ancient pentathlete serves less as a model than the débrouillard of the nineteenth century. Both have rather developed as romanticised relics of an almost forgotten era. Certainly, devotees can be found today of the cultivation of traditions, but great and widespread enthusiasm cannot be aroused in this way. That is why it is indeed wise to drive on two tracks, alluding to the rich past but also keeping up with the times. Leaving Coubertin's specific discipline preferences totally aside and just retaining him as the inventor of the event would possibly even provide greater room for timely transformation in the future. With an eye on the coming IOC decision for the Games of 2020, however, the struggle for Olympic survival and the fair balance between tradition and modernity continues.

Notes on Contributor

Sandra Heck holds a PhD from the Ruhr-University Bochum. She is a sport historian with a special interest in Olympic and military history. In particular she studies the themes of combined sports, French-German sport relations and sporting environments.

Notes

1. Welch, "Admission to the Programme," 332.
2. Compare the history section of the official homepage of the UIPM ("History").
3. The German, French and Swedish modern pentathlon federations have, respectively, confirmed that no documents are archived for the early period before 1924. Moreover, the meeting minutes of the UIPM and of the DVMF (Deutscher Verband für Modernen Fünfkampf) (German Federation for Modern Pentathlon) are not accessible (compare the private email of the DVMF, February 26, 2010).
4. The study is not aiming to present all rule changes that took place in the history of the modern pentathlon. The scoring, for instance, was originally based on a points-for-place system with the lowest score winning, but since 1956, the competition has been scored by using point's tables for each of the five events. Compare Heck, "Pentathlon Moderne," 102.
5. Surprisingly, it was only the fourth time in the history of the Olympic Games that a female concurrence of the modern pentathlon was organised. In the 1970s after the female movement had gained ground, the first women's world championships in the modern pentathlon were organised in 1981. However, it lasted until the Olympic Games in Sydney in 2000 that women competed against each other in the five events and hence broke down one of the last male Olympic domains. See Heck, "Breaking Down the Sex Barrier," 318–38 or Heck, "Der lange Kampf der 'Neo-Amazonen'" (ZDF Sport Online, July 6, 2012). http://sport.zdf.de.
6. IOC, "Olympic Programme," 1.
7. The exclusion of baseball and softball was decided at the 117th IOC Session in Singapore in 2005 ["They'rrre out! Olympics drop Baseball, Softball" (The Associated Press, July 9, 2005). http://nbcsports.msnbc.com/id/8504326/site/21683474/].
8. Ince, "Der Moderne Fünfkampf will modern werden" and UIPM, "Rules for Combined Event Running and Shooting".
9. J. Branch, "Modern Pentathlon Gets a Little Less Penta" (New York Times, November 26, 2008). http://www.nytimes.com/2008/11/27/sports/olympics/27pentathlon.html?_r=1& scp=4&sq=%22John%20Branch%22&st=cse and A. Gardner, "Modern Pentathlon to Become Four-event Discipline" (The Guardian, November 24, 2008). http://www.guardian.co.uk/uk/2008/nov/24/olympics-modern-pentathlon-combined-shooting-running.
10. C. Spiller, "Die Kunst, vom Sport zu leben" (Zeit online, July 23, 2012). http://www.zeit.de/sport/2012-07/schoeneborn-lena-olympiasieg-fuenfkampf/komplettansicht. Translation (all translations are done by the author): "The athletes indeed also want that their sport is popular. So one takes certain things into account. Even if they are not that great."
11. H.-P. Seubert, "Klaus Schormann glaubt an einen Volltreffer" (Echo Online, May 26, 2010). http://www.echo-online.de/sport/mehrsport/Klaus Schormann-glaubt-an-einen-Volltreffer;art2399,906303.
12. To create a more dramatic finish, the leader after four events started first in the running and each competitor followed at a handicapped lag. As a result of this, the order of finish in the run was the order of finish for the entire competition. Compare Heck, "Pentathlon Moderne," 102.
13. K. Sturm, "Fünfkämpfer schießen jetzt mit Laser" (Frankfurter Rundschau). Accessed October 14, 2012. http://www.fr-online.de/sport/pentathlon-fuenfkaempfer-schiessen-jetzt-mit-laser,1472784,4464352.html.
14. "Fünfkämpfer schießen in London 2012 mit Laser."
15. "Laserstrahl statt Patrone: Premiere im Modernen Fünfkampf" (Westfälische Nachrichten, August 10, 2012). http://www.wn.de/Welt/Sport/Olympia-2012/2012/08/Olympia-2012-Laser

strahl-statt-Patrone-Premiere-im-Modernen-Fuenfkampf [The same article can be found on the same day in the *Frankfurter Rundschau*].

16. O. Williams, "Laser Guns in Shooting Event Backed by Pentathlon Chief" (*BBC*, April 13, 2010). http://news.bbc.co.uk/sport2/hi/ modern_pentathlo.

17. "Laserpistolen beim Fünfkampf." Translation: "We thereby even write a bit of history." Compare also H.-P. Seubert, "Klaus Schormann glaubt an einen Volltreffer" (*Echo Online*, May 26, 2010). http://www.echo-online.de/sport/mehrsport/Klaus-Schormann-glaubt-an-einen-Volltreffer;art2399,906303.

18. Verband für Modernen Fünfkampf NRW. "IQ-Shooting kündigt Vertrag mit der UIPM."

19. Heck, "L'institutionnalisation d'une idée," 229–41.

20. Klaus Schormann in an interview with BBC Sport [O. Williams, "Laser Guns in Shooting Event Backed by Pentathlon Chief" (*BBC*, April 13, 2010). http://news.bbc.co.uk/sport2/hi/ modern_pentathlo].

21. UIPM, *UIPM 2012 Media Statistics*. Other independent studies on the media coverage of the modern pentathlon in 2012 do not exist in the knowledge of the author.

22. UIPM, *2011 Modern Pentathlon Media Key Facts*.

23. UIPM, *UIPM 2012 Media Statistics*.

24. The press sample includes chosen newspapers from the four mentioned countries, respectively, published in English, French or German language. The period embraces the four weeks before and after the Games as well as the coverage during the event and shall exemplary – without making a claim to be complete – give an insight in the media coverage of the modern pentathlon in 2012.

25. "Schöneborn fällt weiter zurück" (*FAZ.NET*, August 12, 2012). http://www.faz.net/aktuell/m oderner-fuenfkampf-schoeneborn-faellt-weiter-zurueck-11853292.html; R. McLeod, "London 2012: Pentathlete Mhairi Spence spurred on by Beijing miss" (*BBC Scotland*, July 25, 2012). http://www.bbc.co.uk/sport/0/olympics/18985496; G. Bardou, "Cazé, c'est raté!" (*Sports.fr.*, August 12, 2012). http://www.sports.fr/jo-2012/pentathlon-moderne/articles/jo-2012-amelie-caze-passe-a-cote-342396/?coverpentathlon-moderne; and Y. Cochennec, "Jeux olympiques: le pentathlon reste moderne" (*Slate.fr.*, August 12, 2012). http://www.slate.fr/life/59643/jeux-olympiques-pentathlon-moderne-amelie-caze.

26. This was true for articles in the French *L'Équipe* and the German *Spiegel*. Compare also "Modern Pentathlon: Svoboda Wins as Woodbridge Misses Out" (*BBC*, August 11, 2012). http://www.bbc.co.uk/sport/0/ olympics/18912786.

27. E. Helfers, "The Glorious Irrelevance of Modern Pentathlon" (*The Atlantic*, August 9, 2012). http://www.theatlantic.com/entertainment/archive/2012/08/the-glorious-irrelevance-of-modern pentathlon/260899/.

28. Ibid.

29. Compare, for instance, M. Pilon, "Modern Pentathlon, a Day of Madness" (*The New York Times*, August 11, 2012). http://www.nytimes.com/2012/08/12/sports/olympics/modern-pentathlon-brings-a-day-of-madness-to-olympics.html?pagewanted=all&_r = 0 ("one of the more bizarre and gruelling Olympic events") and C. Cooper, "Welcome to the Modern Pentathlon: The Oddest Test of a Complete Athlete" (*The Independent*, August 11, 2012). http://www.independent.co.uk/sport/olympics/news/welcome-to-the-modern-pentathlon-the-oddest-test-of-a-complete-athlete-8031967.html.

30. Some articles only copy the texts provided by the press agencies. Compare for instance "Laserstrahl statt Patrone: Premiere im Modernen Fünfkampf" (*Westfälische Nachrichten*, August 10, 2012). http://www.wn.de/Welt/Sport/Olympia-2012/2012/08/Olympia-2012-Laser strahl-statt-Patrone-Premiere-im-Modernen-Fuenfkampf [The same article can be found on the same day in the *Frankfurter Rundschau*].

31. Robertson and Lyall, "For Pentathletes, All Business on the First Date."

32. Through modernisation especially the 'popularity' and the 'image' of the modern pentathlon but also its 'universality' and 'costs' are addressed. IOC, "Olympic programme," 1.

33. M. Pound, "World Chapionships [sic!] Facilities to be Named Pierre de Coubertin Modern Pentathlon Centre" (*Sports Features Communications*, September 5, 2010). http://www.sports features.com/presspoint/pressrelease/51593/2010-world-chapionships-facilities-to-be-named-pierre-de coubertin-modern-pentathlon-centre.

34. Hobsbawm and Ranger, *The Invention of Tradition*.

35. Compare the official homepage of the UIPM ("History").

36. "Artikel 37. V. Pentathle Hellénique." See also Diem, "Die olympischen Spiele 1906," 86.
37. Becker, "Die Wiederbelebung des 'Hellenischen Fünfkampfes' 1886 im I. Wiener Turnverein", 172.
38. Mason and Riedi, *Sport and the Military*; Spivak, *Éducation physique, sport et nationalisme en France du second empire au front populaire*; Tauber, *Vom Schützengraben auf den grünen Rasen*; Waquet, "Le football des Poilus," 33–53.
39. Ibid.
40. Malter, *Der Olympismus Pierre de Coubertin's*, 9–10; Grupe, "Olympismus und olympische Erziehung", 227–9. The positive assessment of the Hellenistic period mainly refers to the German historian Johann Gustav Droysen (1808–1884) who designated the Hellenism as modern era of the antiquity (Droysen, *Geschichte des Hellenismus*; also in the twentieth century this opinion was widely shared).
41. de Coubertin, "Why I Revived the Olympic Games," 110–5.
42. de Coubertin, "Ce que nous pouvons maintenant demander au Sport," 21. Translation: "the formation of the all-round man."
43. de Coubertin, *Mémoires olympiques*, 125. Translation: "There were two kinds of pentathlon: the 'modern' – my one – which had an excellent start and the 'classical' [. . .]."
44. The further reasons for the choice of the five disciplines are not in the focus of this article. For further insight on this topic, see for instance Heck, "When Workmen Shoot, Fence, and Ride," 1–13.
45. de Coubertin, "Olympisme et utilitarisme", 72. Translation: "And the modern pentathlon which nobody wanted when I proclaimed its foundation in 1909, was unanimously welcomed in Stockholm in 1912 and even led to many copies everywhere. Everyone wants to turn his sons into débrouillards [. . . . . .]."
46. Heck, "Making Débrouillards," 139–57.
47. de Coubertin, *Pédagogie sportive*, 91–2. Translation: "The creator of this Pentathlon, which has been introduced in Stockholm at the 5th Olympics, was the first to recognize that it [. . .] would be better [. . .] that [. . .] the five samples of which it consists would follow each other without pause so that the athlete passes from one to the other without another stop as it results from the changing of the costume. No doubt that one will still achieve this."
48. de Coubertin, "Chronique du mois," 131. Translation: "It has just been talked about an 'officer in campaign'. That he rides his bike, that he shoots, that he jumps with a horse, that he keeps walking and finally that he jumps vested into the water, that's a healthy copy of the war and of the obligations that may the war impose to a man."
49. Compare Köris, *Moderner Fünfkampf*, 13.
50. Heck, "Modern Pentathlon and the First World War," 410–28.
51. Heck, "When Workmen Shoot, Fence, and Ride," 1–13.
52. In regard to the rowing compare also de Coubertin, *Mémoires olympiques*. Translated in Carl Diem-Institut, *Olympische Erinnerungen*, 116; de Coubertin, *Pédagogie sportive*. Translated in Mallwitz, 1928, 56.
53. Letter from Coubertin to Hellström. Riksarkivet Stockholm [Original underlined and in English language]. Compare also Mallon and Widlund, *The 1912 Olympic Games*, 232.
54. Heck, "Modern Pentathlon and Symbolic Violence," 45–67.
55. "Coubertin à tous les athlètes et participants aux jeux olympiques, assemblés à Amsterdam pour la célébration de la IXme olympiade." In The Netherlands Olympic Committee, *The Ninth Olympiad being the Official Report of the Olympic Games of 1928 Celebrated at Amsterdam*, 12. Translation: "Personally, I would like to see the modern pentathlon brought back to the guidelines that I had asked for when creating it. Regarding women's participation in the Games, I remain hostile. It is against my will that they were admitted to a growing number of events."
56. This is also true for the shortening of the length of the swimming and running course.
57. Compare for instance the example of mountain biking: Savre, Saint-Martin and Terret. "An Odyssey Fulfilled," 121–36. Compare also E. Helfers, "The Glorious Irrelevance of Modern Pentathlon" (*The Atlantic*, August 9, 2012). http://www.theatlantic.com/entertainm ent/archive/2012/08/the-glorious-irrelevance-of-modernpentathlon/260899/.
58. A. Wells, "Olympics 2020: IOC Removes Wrestling from Olympic Program" (*Bleacher Report*, February 12, 2013). http://bleacherreport.com/articles/1526010-olympics-2020-ioc-

removes-wrestling-from-olympic-program DOSB, "Ringer bangen um ihren olympischen Status."

59. Compare the private email of the UIPM Headquarters, February 28, 2009.
60. Lyberg, "I Cannot Say Anything Else But the Truth!," 11. Compare also Pound, "The Future of the Olympic Movement," 5.
61. Stockholm and Uppsala are today the two centres of the Swedish modern pentathlon (compare the private email of Göran Bylund, sports director of the modern pentathlon in the Swedish Combined Event Federation, May 11, 2012). Currently, there are, however, no Swedish modern pentathletes in the top five ("Ranking." Official homepage of the UIPM ("History").
62. Compare the private email of the UIPM Headquarters, February 28, 2009.
63. "Golf, Rugby Added for 2016 and 2020" (*The Associated Press*, October 9, 2009). http://sports.espn.go.com/oly/news/story?id=4545111.
64. DOSB, "Thomas Bach: Ringen hat weiter eine Chance auf Olympiastatus."
65. UIPM, *2nd Day Congress Summary*.
66. "London 2012 – 'Star Wars' bei den Fünfkämpfern" (*Yahoo! News Network*, August 31, 2012). http://de.eurosport.yahoo.com/01092010/73/london-2012-star-wars-fuenfkaempfern.html.
67. "Fünfkämpfer schießen in London 2012 mit Laser." Translation: "keeping up with the times."
68. Compare the Official Modern Pentathlon Channel on YouTube as well as the Twitter and Facebook account of the UIPM Headquarters. The YouTube channel has currently 321 subscribers [October 14, 2012], the UIPM Twitter account has currently 1756 followers and the official Facebook page "Modern Pentathlon" 45,145 likes [both on October 12, 2012].
69. Compare Chappelet and Bayle, *Strategic and Performance Management of Olympic Sport Organisations*; Irwin, Sutton and McCarthy, *Sport Promotion and Sales Management*; Billings, "Olympic Media: Inside the Biggest Show on Television."
70. To the emerging sports belong most of all baseball, softball, rugby, golf, inline skating, squash and karate. Compare, for instance, A. Schirmer, "Kampf der Sportarten: Skaten, Rugby und Golf wollen olympisch werden" (*news.de*, June 15, 2009). http://www.news.de/sport/843651108/skaten-rugby-und-golf-wollen-olympisch-werden/1/.
71. See for instance the excerpt of the article by B. Lendon, "Wrestling may be cut from Olympic Games" (*CNN (Cable News Network)*). Accessed February 22, 2013. http://edition.cnn.com/2013/02/12/sport/olympics-wresting: "The Executive Board of the International Olympic Committee announced Tuesday [February 12, 2013] that it has recommended dropping wrestling from the Summer Games beginning in 2020. Wrestling will now join the seven shortlisted sports – baseball/softball, karate, roller sports, sport climbing, squash, wakeboarding and wushu [...]."
72. E. Helfers, "The Glorious Irrelevance of Modern Pentathlon" (*The Atlantic*, August 9, 2012). http://www.theatlantic.com/entertainment/archive/2012/08/the-glorious-irrelevance-of-modern pentathlon/260899/ .
73. "Modern Pentathlon Revels in Final-day Spotlight."
74. Schwier, "Doing the Right Things," 7–13. Attempts in 1989 to incorporate the triathlon as a sport in the former UIPMB (Union Internationale de Pentathlon Moderne et Biathlon) failed because the association sought full control of the sport, the triathlon followers, however, preferred an autonomous organizational structure (Bernhardt, "The History of Triathlon").
75. IOC, *Olympic Charter*, 66. Compare also Savre, Saint-Martin and Terret. "An Odyssey Fulfilled," 121.
76. The opening to the popular sport brought the DVMF in 2006 namely a huge increase in the membership statistics in the amount of 959% (from 5600 to 59,000 memberships) (DOSB, *Demographische Entwicklung in Deutschland*, 14).
77. "Modern Pentathlon Revels in Final-day Spotlight – London 2012 – Modern Pentathlon."
78. IOC, "The Programme of the Games of the Olympiad," 2.

References

'Artikel 37. V. Pentathle Hellénique'. In Comité des Jeux Olympiques à Athènes (1905). (ed.). 'Jeux Olympiques Internationaux à Athènes 1906: Règlements – Première Partie, 25–26. No. 5 Correspondances officielles du COJO Stockholm 1912 avec le CIO', Coubertin et CNO, Fo35 13o99. CIO JO-1912S – MICRO: Microfilms des archives du COJO des Jeux Olympiques d'été de Stockholm 1912: correspondance, procès-verbaux, formulaires et résultats, 1908–1913, ID 46582, 9919. Mikrofiches: MI-1/ JO-1912 S – Microfilms – Archives COJO – 9919. IOC Archives Lausanne.

Becker, H. "Die Wiederbelebung des 'Hellenischen Fünfkampfes' 1886 im I. Wiener Turnverein." In *The Olympic Games through the Ages: Greek Antiquity and Its Impact on Modern Sport.* (Proceedings of the 13th International HISPA Congress Olympia/Greece. May 22–28, 1989), edited by R. Renson, M. Lämmer, J. Riordan, and D. Chassiotis, 166–175. Athen: Hellenic Sports Research Institute, 1991.

Bernhardt, G. "The History of Triathlon – Part II: Putting the Wheels in Motion." Accessed April 22, 2012. http://www.triatlonca.org/ diversos/History%20of%20Tri %20II.pdf

Billings, A. C. "Olympic Media: Inside the Biggest Show on Television." *Routledge Critical Studies in Sport*, 186 pp. London, New York: Routledge, 2008.

Chappelet, J. L., and E. Bayle. *Strategic and Performance Management of Olympic Sport Organisations.* Champaign, IL: Human Kinetics, 2005.

de Coubertin, P. "Ce que nous pouvons maintenant demander au Sport." *Conférence faite à l'Association des Hellènes Libéraux de Lausanne, le 24 février 1918*, 1–22. Lausanne: Edition de l'Association des Hellènes Libéraux de Lausanne, 1918.

de Coubertin, P. "Chronique du mois: Variante pour le Pentathlon." *Revue Olympique*, no. 92 (1913): 130–131.

de Coubertin, P. *Mémoires olympiques. Lausanne: Bureau International de Pédagogie Sportive, 1931.* Translated in Olympische Erinnerungen, ed. Carl-Diem-Institut. Wiesbaden: Limpert, 1996.

de Coubertin, P. "Olympisme et utilitarisme." *Revue Olympique*, no. 89 (1913): 68–73.

de Coubertin, P. *Pédagogie sportive. Paris: Crés, 1922.* Translated in Sportliche Erziehung, ed. Arthur Mallwitz. Stuttgart: Dieck, 1928.

de Coubertin, P. "Why I Revived the Olympic Games. Translated by Helen Chisholm." *Fortnightly Review* LXXXIV (July 1908): 110–5.

Deutscher Olympischer Sportbund (DOSB), ed. *Demographische Entwicklung in Deutschland: Herausforderung für die Sportentwicklung: Materialien – Analysen – Positionen.* Frankfurt a. M.: DOSB, 2007.

Deutscher Olympischer Sportbund (DOSB). "Ringer bangen um ihren olympischen Status." February 12, 2013. http://www.dosb.de/de/olympia/olympische-news/detail/news/olympia_aus_fuer_das_ringen/

Deutscher Olympischer Sportbund (DOSB). "Thomas Bach: Ringen hat weiter eine Chance auf Olympiastatus." February 18, 2013. http://www.dosb.de/de/olympia/olympische-news/detail/news/thomas_bach_ringen_hat_weiter_eine_chance_auf_olympiastatus/

Diem, C., Die olympischen Spiele 1906, quoted in Lennartz & Teutenberg, Die Olympischen Spiele 1906 in Athen, 86.

Droysen, J. G. [original published in 1843] *Geschichte des Hellenismus.* Cambridge: Cambridge Library Collection, 2011.

Fünfkämpfer schießen in London 2012 mit Laser. *T-Online.* August 23, 2010. http://sport.t-online. de/olympia-2012-fuenfkaempfer-schiessen-in-london-mit-laser-/id_42619164/index

Grupe, O. "Olympismus und olympische Erziehung: Abschied von einer großen Idee?" In *Olympischer Sport: Rückblick und Perspektiven*, edited by O. Grupe, 223–243. Schorndorf: Hofmann, 1997.

Heck, S. "Breaking Down the Sex Barrier: The Emancipation of Female Modern Pentathlon in West Germany (1967–1981)." *The International Journal of the History of Sport* 29, no. 2 (2012): 318–338.

Heck, S. "L'institutionnalisation d'une idée. Le pentathlon moderne du programme olympique à une fédération internationale." In *Histoire(s) de la performance du sportif de haut niveau*, edited by T. Bauer, and D. Gomet, 229–241. Paris: INSEP, 2011.

Heck, S. "Making Débrouillards: The Modern Pentathlon and the Pursuit of Completeness." *Olympika: The International Journal of Olympic Studies* XIX (2010): 139–157.

Heck, S. "Modern Pentathlon and Symbolic Violence – a History of Female Exclusion from Stockholm 1912 to Paris 1924." *International Review on Sport and Violence* no. 4 (2011): 45–67.

Heck, S. "Modern Pentathlon and the First World War – When Athletes and Soldiers Met to Practise Martial Manliness." *The International Journal of the History of Sport* 28, no. 3–4 (2011): 410–428.

Heck, S. "Pentathlon Moderne." In *Dictionnaire Culturel du Sport*, edited by M. Attali, and J. Saint-Martin, 102. Paris: Armand Colin, 2010.

Heck, S. "When Workmen Shoot, Fence, and Ride – Modern Pentathlon and the Promise of Social Integration at the Beginning of the 20th Century." *Stadion* 37 (2010): 1–13.

Hobsbawm, E. J., and Ranger, T., eds. *The Invention of Tradition*. Cambridge: Cambridge University Press, 2003.

Ince, H. "Der Moderne Fünfkampf will modern werden." March 25, 2009. http://www.tagesspiegel. de/sport/moderner-fuenfkampf-der-moderne-fuenfkampf-will-modern-werden/1481302.html

International Olympic Committee (IOC), ed. *Olympic Charter*. In force as from September 3, 1997 Lausanne: International Olympic Committee, 1997.

International Olympic Committee (IOC), ed. "Olympic Programme." *Factsheet: The Sports on the Olympic Programme*, 1–7. February 2008.

International Olympic Committee (IOC), ed. "The Programme of the Games of the Olympiad." *Factsheet: The IOC Sessions*, 1–9. http://www.olympic.org/Documents/Reference_documents_ Factsheets/IOC_Session.pdf Update – July 2012.

Irwin, R. L., W. A. Sutton, and L. M. McCarthy. *Sport Promotion and Sales Management*. Champaign, IL: Human Kinetics, 2002.

Köris, S. *Moderner Fünfkampf*. Ahrensburg bei Hamburg: Czwalina, 1984.

Laserpistolen beim Fünfkampf. June 3, 2010. http://www.spox.com/de/sport/mehrsport/leichtathleti k/1006/News/ein-hauch-von-star-wars-in-berlin-moderner-fuenfkampf-laserpistolen.html

Letter from Coubertin to Hellström. May 20, 1912 [Original in English with underlining]. Kommitténs för modern femkamp handlingar (Ö II l). Stockholmsolympiaden 1912 (SE/ RA/730226). Riksarkivet Stockholm.

Lyberg, W. "I Cannot Say Anything Else But the Truth!: Interview With the President of the IOC, Samaranch." *Journal of Olympic History* 5, no. 2 (1997): 10–15.

Mallon, B., and T. Widlund. *The 1912 Olympic Games: Results for All Competitors in All Events, with Commentary*. Jefferson/North Carolina: McFarland & Co., 2002.

Malter, R. *Der Olympismus Pierre de Coubertin's: eine kritische Studie zu Idee und Ideologie der modernen Olympischen Spiele und des Sports*. Köln: Barz und Beienburg, 1969.

Mason, T., and E. Riedi. *Sport and the Military: The British Armed Forces 1880–1960*. Cambridge: Cambridge University Press, 2009.

Modern Pentathlon Revels in Final-day Spotlight – London 2012 – Modern Pentathlon. August 12, 2012. http://www.olympic.org/content/news/media-resources/manual-news/2012/london2012/ 12/round-up-modern-pentathlon-revels-in-final-day-spotlight--london-2012/

Netherlands Olympic Committee, ed. *The Ninth Olympiad being the Official Report of the Olympic Games of 1928 Celebrated at Amsterdam*. Amsterdam: J.H. de Bussy, Ltd. Printers & Publishers, 1928.

Pound, R. W. "The Future of the Olympic Movement: Promised Land or Train Wreck?'(Opening Address)." *Pathways: Critiques and Discourse in Olympic Research. Ninth International Symposium for Olympic Research*, 1–19. Accessed October 22, 2012. http://www.la84foundation. org/SportsLibrary/ISOR/isor2008d.pdf

Robertson, C., and S. Lyall. "For Pentathletes, All Business on the First Date." August 11, 2012. http://www.nytimes.com/2012/08/11/sports/olympics/in-olympic-pentathlon-riding-horses-theyve-only-just-met.html?pagewanted=1#undefined

Savre, F., J. Saint-Martin, and T. Terret. "An Odyssey Fulfilled: The Entry of Mountain Biking into the Olympic Games." *Olympika* XVIII (2009): 121–136.

Schwier, J. "Doing the Right Things." *Sportwissenschaft* 13, no. 2 (1998): 7–13.

Spivak, M. "Éducation physique, sport et nationalisme en France du second empire au front populaire: un aspect original de la défense nationale." Thèse pour le doctorat d'Etat. Université Paris 1983.

Tauber, P. *Vom Schützengraben auf den grünen Rasen: Der Erste Weltkrieg und die Entwicklung des Sports in Deutschland*. Berlin, Münster: Lit, 2008.

Union Internationale de Pentathlon Moderne (UIPM). "History." *Official Homepage of the Union Internationale de Pentathlon Moderne (UIPM)*. Accessed October 14, 2012. http://www. pentathlon.org/inside-uipm/history

Union Internationale de Pentathlon Moderne (UIPM). "Modern Pentathlon." *Facebook*. Accessed October 12, 2012. https://www.facebook.com/home.php#!/modpen?fref=ts

Union Internationale de Pentathlon Moderne (UIPM). "Modern Pentathlon @UIPM_HQ." *Twitter*. Accessed October 12, 2012. https://twitter.com/UIPM_HQ

Union Internationale de Pentathlon Moderne (UIPM). "Official Modern Pentathlon Channel." *YouTube*. Accessed October 14, 2012. http://www.youtube.com/user/uipmchannel?feature=sub_widget_1

Union Internationale de Pentathlon Moderne (UIPM). "Rules for Combined Event Running and Shooting." *Official Homepage of the Union Internationale de Pentathlon Moderne (UIPM)*. January 2012, 99–127. http://www.pentathlon.org/images/Rules/ii%205%20combined%20event%2017%201%202012final.pdf

Union Internationale de Pentathlon Moderne (UIPM). *2nd Day Congress Summary*. October 20, 2012. http://www.pentathlon.org/results/competition-results/results/pentathlon/776-uipm-congress?k2item=1971

Union Internationale de Pentathlon Moderne (UIPM). *UIPM 2012 Media Statistics* (forwarded by Karen Myers, UIPM Headquarters, on February 13, 2013).

Union Internationale de Pentathlon Moderne (UIPM). *2011 Modern Pentathlon Media Key Facts* (forwarded by Karen Myers, UIPM Headquarters, on February 13, 2013).

Verband für Modernen Fünfkampf NRW. "IQ-Shooting kündigt Vertrag mit der UIPM." *Hintergründe zur Kündigung des Vertrags mit der UIPM*. Accessed June 16, 2012. http://www.fuenf-nrw.de/newsdet.php?newsid=85

Waquet, A. "Le football des Poilus: analyse de la diffusion du football dans l'armée française au cours de la Grande Guerre." *Stadion* 36 (2010): 33–53.

Welch, P. "Admission to the Programme: A Privilege Earned, Not Given." *Olympic Review*, no. 273 (1990): 332–337.

Wells, A. "Olympics 2020: IOC Removes Wrestling from Olympic Program." *Bleacher Report* (February 12, 2013). Available at: http://bleacherreport.com/articles/1526010-olympics-2020-iocremoves-wrestling-from-olympic-program

London is Just Around the Corner: Belgium, Britain and Sport

Pascal Delheye, Stijn Knuts and Thomas Ameye

Department of Kinesiology, KU Leuven, Tervuursevest 101, bus 1500, Leuven, Belgium

Answering the legitimate call for a more transnational approach to the history of sport in Europe, we seize upon the 2012 Olympic Games as an opportunity to look back on Belgo-British contacts in sport since the Middle Ages. Contextualising this history within the wider Belgo-British political, economic and cultural contacts is, indeed, much more revealing than recounting a superficial story about the three medals the Belgian Olympic delegation actually obtained in London. We illustrate that transnational flows and contacts – crucial to the shaping and diffusion of sport – are not always reflected at the level of the Olympic Games. The cases of cycle racing and soccer demonstrate the divergent adoption and adaptation processes of specific sporting disciplines in Belgium and Britain. At the end of the paper, we also reflect on David Cameron's competitive sport policy in primary education, and raise the question whether the dissipation of public funds for elite sport – to the detriment of 'Sport for All' – is still defendable in times of government budgetary scarcity.

Introduction

In 2007, *Eurostar*, the high-speed railway service connecting Brussels with London through the Channel Tunnel, launched a marketing campaign in Belgium with the catchphrase 'London is just around the corner', stressing that it only takes 1 h and 51 min to reach London from Brussels. Similarly, in 2012, one of Flanders' biggest sports associations dedicated a special section of its periodical to the forthcoming Olympics in London and suggested a visit to the Games, 'especially because the British capital is practically located in our back yard'.[1] Because of this proximity, the Belgian Olympic and Interfederal Committee as well as the Belgian Government made great efforts to be visible in the British capital during the Olympics. The so-called Belgium House, the country's sportive embassy, was located in the beautiful Temple area of central London, and attracted a multitude of visitors. There, Belgium presented its tourist attractions by means of a 'virtual cycling tour' through its provinces. Tourists could discover Belgium by indulging in its 'national passion', cycle racing.[2]

It is not surprising, then, that in the weeks and months prior to the Games, the Belgian media speculated specifically about the forthcoming clash between the strong British cycling team, including the newborn *Tour de France* heroes Bradley Wiggins, Christopher

Froome and, of course, Mark Cavendish, and the strong Belgian team, including Tom Boonen and Philippe Gilbert, who together won more than half of all the UCI World Tour Classic Cycle Races in 2011 and 2012. The fact that the men's road race was scheduled on the first day of the Olympic competition gave extra weight to this event. The combination of London's proximity and the fact that people could watch the event without buying a ticket resulted in a mass of Belgian cycling aficionados – including two of the authors of this paper – crossing the Channel for one day and attending the Games for the first time.

More important than the enormous disappointment among Belgian (and British) supporters after Alexander Vinokourov 'received' the gold medal is the question of whether this proximity of Britain to Belgium also engendered historical contacts, especially with regard to sport. The fact that England is called the cradle of modern sport makes this question even more interesting. Was Belgian sport merely a copy of the British example, or did sport in Belgium go its own way after its introduction into the country? The case of cycle racing certainly suggests the latter. Cycle racing is Belgium's most popular sport – even according to *The Telegraph*[3] – and the one in which it has been most successful in terms of Olympic results (see Table 1). In contrast, British enthusiasm for this sport seemed to be rather limited until the success of 'Team GB' and Bradley Wiggins' victory in the *Tour de France* just before the start of the London Olympics. Is it a coincidence that Wiggins was born in Ghent, Belgium, as the son of a professional cyclist active in the city's track racing circuit?[4]

The clear difference in the cultural impact of one sport in these two countries lays bare the need for more insight into the sporting interactions or 'transnational' flows between Belgium and Britain. Establishing the dynamics and turning points in this shared history and contextualising them within the broader political, cultural and economic context will

Table 1. Belgium's best Olympic sports in terms of medals.

Sport	Gold	Silver	Bronze	Total
Cycling	6	8	11	25
Archery	10	6	3	19
Fencing	5	3	5	13
Equestrian sports	4	2	6	12
Track and field	3	7	2	12
Judo	2	1	8	11
Sailing	2	4	3	9
Shooting	2	4	3	9
Rowing	0	6	2	8
Water Polo	0	4	2	6
Weightlifting	1	2	1	4
Swimming	1	1	2	4
Boxing	1	1	2	4
Wrestling	0	3	1	4
Tennis	1	0	1	2
Soccer	1	0	1	2
Figure skating	1	0	1	2
Bobsleigh	0	1	1	2
Gymnastics	0	1	1	2
Hockey	0	0	1	1
Tug of war	0	0	1	1
Speed skating	0	0	1	1
Total	40	54	59	153

help to better understand adoption and adaptation processes with regard to sport. The sources available for such an undertaking consist of the existing literature on the sporting histories of Belgium and Great Britain, supplemented with some original research. There is surely a body of work available for both nations, although there still remain a lot of historiographical gaps to be filled, especially when it comes to the history of their interactions. While the interest in British sports history has expanded considerably over recent decades, the scope and size of such historical study of sport in Belgium is still rather limited.[5] In Britain, however, the country's sporting relations with a small continental nation such as Belgium have never been the explicit focus of a study. It is, therefore, the aim of this paper to bring together many isolated snippets of information on this topic, and to come to a first overview of the history of the sporting interactions between the two countries. In the final section, this overview will be used to reflect on the Belgo-British interactions and interdependencies in light of the Olympic Games, especially the three London Olympiads of 1908, 1948 and 2012. Such a long-term history of transnational contacts is, we feel, much more interesting and revealing than the superficial story of the three 'meagre' medals the Belgian Olympic delegation actually obtained in London. Hence, our paper is also a kind of answer to the recent and legitimate request for a more transnational approach in the history of sport.[6]

Export of Traditional Games During the Middle Ages

The majority of the territories that would subsequently make up Great Britain and Belgium were part of the common political, economic and cultural sphere of the Roman Empire as early as the first century AD. Following the collapse of Roman rule, the connections shaped by this Empire continued all through the Middle Ages and into early modernity. The political forces of both the southern Low Countries and the British Isles were initial and integral parts of the network of dynastic power relations, and the conflicts arising from them, which characterised Europe during these centuries. Alliances as well as hostilities between both were common. A sizeable part of the 1066 army of William the Conqueror, for instance, consisted of Flemings, while the fact that the Duchies of Flanders and Brabant were ruled consecutively by the French and both the Spanish and Austrian Habsburgs – all enemies of the English monarchy at one point – between the ninth and the eighteenth centuries ensured a regular presence of English or British military forces on what would become Belgian soil. Conflicts as far apart as the Hundred Years' War and the Spanish Succession War were at least partially fought out by English troops in the southern Low Countries.[7]

Second, these political and military interactions were, certainly until the sixteenth century, strongly related to the intense trade between both regions. For both England and the southern Low Countries, this trade relationship was crucial to their respective economies. As early as the eleventh century, London was 'one of the mercantile capitals of Flanders': a sizeable community of Flemish merchants resided there and was occupied with importing English wool into Flanders and exporting Flemish cloth to the British Isles. Indeed, Flemish cloth manufacturers strongly depended on English wool for their prosperity. Initiatives such as the thirteenth century Flemish Hanze of London, led by merchants from Bruges, were meant to guarantee its import.[8] This economic relationship only intensified during the fifteenth and sixteenth centuries, as the Low Countries became one of the continent's commercial powerhouses. Until its sacking by Spanish troops in 1585, Antwerp was the commercial and cultural capital of western Europe, and as such attracted a lot of attention from English traders. Thomas Gresham, for instance, was strongly inspired by the Antwerp Stock Market in building the London Stock Exchange in 1565.[9]

Simultaneously, the Reformation and the subsequent repression of the Protestant minorities in the southern Low Countries by the Spanish caused many of the region's inhabitants to flee to the northern Low Countries or across the Channel to England, where they were safe from religious persecution.[10] It was this flow of people who ensured that English society of the period was thoroughly influenced by ideas and practices from this region in fields like the sciences and the arts.[11] Indeed, this 'cultural bridge' established between the British Isles and the Low Countries also seems to have engendered significant changes in the games played by the inhabitants of Albion.[12] In the early 1980s, German historian Heiner Gillmeister proposed a theory on the medieval and early modern origins of ball games in which he argued that modern 'British' sports such as golf, cricket or tennis were descendants of games played during the Middle Ages in the Low Countries. These were imported into Britain during the sixteenth and seventeenth centuries by Flemish migrants. Gillmeister finds evidence for this in, for instance, the names of specific games, which show strong etymological similarities with the Dutch names of similar games played in the Low Countries.[13] Although Gillmeister's theory has been subject to debate ever since, other scholars do agree with him on points such as the Flemish ancestry of cricket.[14] As a consequence of their cultural and economic interaction with the British Isles, the southern Low Countries crucially influenced games that would later be perceived as 'essentially British'.

Import of Modern Sport During the Industrial Revolution

The word 'sport' was literally introduced in the Low Countries in 1648, when it first appeared in Henry Hexham's 'Nederdutch and English' dictionary.[15] The term's introduction seemed to foreshadow Great Britain's dominance in its sportive interactions with the southern Low Countries, then still under Austrian rule, from the late eighteenth century onwards. In 1773 Spa, a small town near Liège, hosted the first modern horse races on the European continent. The sizeable British tourist contingent in this 'spa' – the English word is in itself indicative of the role the town played in forming the spa culture – was instrumental in organising the exhibition of this new variant of traditional horse racing, which was developed in Britain from the 1750s onwards. In the following decades, other cities with a notable British presence such as Brussels (1779) or the coastal town of Ostend (1830) also saw the introduction of modern horse racing through initiatives of such expatriates.[16]

The role British nationals played in introducing modern horse racing into the southern Low Countries heralded an ever-larger influence of British sporting culture in the region, especially from the nineteenth century onwards. Again, this dynamic was strongly connected to the interactions between both regions in other domains. Politically, Britain played an important role in the establishment of the Belgian state itself. After the successful insurrection of the southern Low Countries in 1830 against the northern-dominated United Kingdom of the Netherlands, established after the Congress of Vienna (1815), Britain proved to be a cautious ally of the new state and helped to secure its existence. The 1839 Treaty of London, which officially recognised Belgium as a sovereign state, was strongly shaped by British interests.[17] The first Belgian king, Leopold I of Saxe-Coburg and Gotha, had even been married to a British princess and was a British citizen before becoming King of the Belgians in 1831. Even after taking his place on the Belgian throne, he maintained close relations with British royalty.[18]

Economically, Britain's status as an industrial pioneer, imperial power and 'workshop of the world' made it a powerful influence in terms of emulation for many European states.[19] Of all these, Belgium effectively was one of the first to successfully establish itself as an industrial nation by the 1850s.[20] This rapid industrialisation was strongly influenced by British practices and ideas. Early Belgian industrialists such as the Ghent-based linen producer Lieven Bauwens or the Scottish-born Walloon industrial pioneers William and John Cockerill could only become successful through the import or copying of British machinery and production modes.[21] The introduction of free trade in Belgium, in its turn, was inspired by Richard Cobden's campaign against the British Corn Laws during the 1840s, and ensured that important trade relations were established between both nations.[22]

The second half of the century would prove a particularly crucial period for the establishment and spread of British sporting culture. From the 1850s onwards, a number of sports with pre-modern roots that had undergone a process of codification and rationalisation in the previous decades became clearly nested in British culture. Soccer and rugby became essential parts of the curricula of the English public schools, and were subsequently taken by the old boys of public schools to Oxford and Cambridge. Meanwhile, outside the educational sector, sports clubs were being established by members of the British upper and middle classes who had enjoyed a sport-filled education at public school and/or university. To these British sportsmen, their games were initially an effective mode of distinguishing themselves from the working classes and forging new bonds with the aristocracy. With the weight it gave to 'disinterestedness' and 'fair play', the ideology of amateurism became a potent contributor to the function of modern British sport as a mode of social distinction.[23]

Almost simultaneously with their becoming institutionalised in Great Britain, the country's growing global influence engendered the spread of these modern sports outside its borders.[24] As one of the first thoroughly industrialised continental nations, geographically close to the British Isles and characterised by important ties to British trade and industry, Belgium was exposed to this new sporting culture from an early time. One of the crucial catalysts of this process of cultural transfer was the sizeable British expatriate colonies in the main Belgian cities (Brussels, Antwerp, Liège and Ghent), where they were active as representatives of British trade and industry or – in the case of Ostend or Spa – spent their leisure time. They began playing the games of their home country in public in these cities, and thus (unintentionally) exposing Belgians to these new leisure practices.[25]

Rowing had already been introduced into Belgium during the 1840s, and cricket and hockey were played in Brussels and Antwerp by British expatriates as early as the 1860s.[26] In Brussels, the so-called Pelouse des Anglais in the Bois de la Cambre urban park functioned as a cricket pitch, whereas in Antwerp, British inhabitants were responsible for the founding of a cricket club in 1892.[27] Indeed, many of these early sports clubs were almost exclusively British affairs. The first Belgian lawn-tennis clubs, founded in the 1880s in Courtrai, Liège and Brussels, contained none or very few native Belgians, while early golf associations such as the *Bruges Golf and Sport Club* (1889) reflected their predominantly British makeup in their names.[28] As the early sport periodical *La Belgique Sportive* reported in 1887, 'sports are by their nature and etymology English'. The language these 'sportsmen' used was the French of the country's social elites rigged with English expressions, as reflected in 'club' names such as the *Boating Club des Etudiants de Louvain* (1879).[29] Although Belgians increasingly practiced the sports imported from Britain themselves, their clubs and activities still very much reflected the influence of the British model.

The influence of the British model was manifestly present with regard to 'football' (soccer).[30] Several clergymen who taught in elite Catholic schools were staunch supporters of the British educational sport model. It seems that the anglophile priest and poet Guido Gezelle already played football in 1849 at the minor seminary of Roeselare, which housed a large colony of English pupils at the time.[31] Also figures such as the Benedictine monk Gérard van Caloen or the canon Francis Dessain, who had themselves studied or taught at Catholic colleges in England, acquired a taste for what they saw as the educational qualities of sport, and began to promote them on their return from England.[32] The presence of British pupils in Belgian schools combined with the support of some anglophile Belgian educators was surely a catalyst for the diffusion of soccer. After what Roland Renson has called 'an incubation period' of a couple of decades, the import of soccer manifested itself at the club level.[33] Clubs such as the *Brugsche Football Club* (1891) or the *Football Club Liègeois* (1892) were all in some way linked to local colleges or their former students.[34] British expatriates continued to play a crucial role in this early institutionalisation process. In 1882, a number of British traders active in the harbour of Antwerp had already founded the *Antwerp Football Club* (AFC) as the first official soccer club on the Belgian soil.[35]

As already suggested by their education, the majority of the members of these clubs were upper or middle class, the sons of traders, people from the professions or aristocrats. British sports such as soccer or tennis effectively remained socially very exclusive until the beginning of the First World War.[36] In many cases these elitist sporting men did not limit themselves to one sport discipline. The *Athletic and Running Club de Bruxelles* (1896), for instance, competed in athletics and soccer. Vice versa, many of the soccer clubs founded during the 1890s actually offered multiple sports to its members. Thus, the *Union Belge des Sociétés de Sports Athlétiques* – founded in 1895 – represented a wide diversity of sports before it became the *Union Royale Belge des Sociétés de Football-Association* (URBSFA), i.e. Belgium's national soccer association, in 1912.[37]

Forever Under Albion's Yoke?

Despite its fundamental importance to Belgium's sporting life, however, British sporting culture did not have a monopoly on the institutionalisation of modern sport in Belgium. In a number of sports, the impact of ideas and practices from across the Channel was effectively paralleled by those coming from other directions. In horse racing, for instance, the British pioneering role of the eighteenth century was to a large extent taken over by racers and organisers from France after Belgian independence in 1830.[38] In rowing and yachting, the British expatriates who influenced early rowing competitions in 1850s Antwerp were quickly rivalled by Dutch clubs from Amsterdam or Rotterdam, which had an even longer boating tradition than the British.[39] Belgium was, indeed, a 'meeting place' of sportive influences from different countries.[40] Although these influences often had a British 'flavour', native Belgians added their own accents and shapes to the 'British' sports they then imported.[41]

Moreover, some groups in Belgian society were distrusting of the growing role that foreign superpower Great Britain played in shaping the leisure of the Belgian population. Until the beginning of the First World War, gymnasts regarded sports such as soccer as physically damaging and pedagogically ineffective, as opposed to the 'rational' gymnastics they practiced.[42] Flemish nationalists criticised modern sport as an 'English disease', which diluted the Flemish language through the use of English in clubs and associations.[43] British sportive influences were, therefore, not all-encompassing or universally accepted. This criticism was not only limited to groups outside the sphere of active sport participants: dissatisfaction with certain aspects of British sporting culture was also becoming widespread within the growing number of sport clubs and national associations.

Most notably, the strict British definition of amateurism, which often determined who could compete in any given sport against British nationals, vexed Belgian sportsmen. In rowing for instance, the controversial Henley Rules introduced at the Henley Regatta in 1879 excluded not only everyone who had ever rowed for money from competing as an amateur, but also all those who made a living out of any kind of manual labour. This 'labour bar' was later also adopted by the Amateur Rowing Association (1882), the British national governing body for rowing. Henceforth, if foreigners wanted to row against a British team they were obliged to follow the same strict rules.[44] However, the Belgian rowing association, the *Fédération Belge des Sociétésdes d'Aviron* (1887), refused to adopt this labour bar – although it did exclude professionals from participating in races. Together with those from France and Italy, Belgian rowers consolidated this opposition to Henley amateurism in founding the *Fédération Internationale Sociétés d'Aviron* (FISA) in 1892, in which British rowers were not represented.[45]

The case of cycle racing is probably the best illustration of the complexities of the Belgo–British relationship in the field of sport. After the short-lived and mainly French-inspired success of this sport in Belgium in the late 1860s, the crisis engendered in France by the Franco-Prussian war of 1870–1871 brought Belgian – as well as French – cycling practically to a standstill for most of the decade. When the sport reluctantly reappeared in the country during the late 1870s and early 1880s, it was especially British cycling and the high-wheeled Ordinary bicycle produced there that inspired the growing number of Belgian racers[46] and the early Belgian cycling press featured a lot of news on British racing events.[47] Simultaneously, a number of urban cycling clubs were formed which were thoroughly inspired by British examples or had Englishmen on their organising committees.[48] The *Antwerp Bicycle Club* (1882), for instance, was founded by a number of upper class youths who based their rules on the statutes of the British St. Charles' Bicycle Club, while the English student John-Alban Randolph was co-founder of the Ghent-based *Vlaamsche Wielrijderskring* in 1885.[49] The British cycle industry was closely followed by Belgians and on the occasion of the annual Stanley Show in London, a large exhibition of British cycle producers, Belgian cycling periodicals published special issues or large feature articles until well into the 1890s.[50] Of course, to cycle racers, competing in Britain was clearly prestigious. Indeed, the Antwerp-based racer Emile de Beukelaer's status as one of the country's most successful cyclists of the 1880s was partly due to his victory in one of the period's many unofficial world championships in London in 1887.[51]

Here as well, however, the question of amateurism created tensions. Although the *Fédération Vélocipédique Belge* (FVB, 1883), the country's first national governing body for cycling, attempted to come to a succinct definition of amateurism from its foundation onwards, Belgian cyclists remained very lenient in the matter when compared with their Dutch or German counterparts. In 1886, Belgian 'amateurs' were even allowed to earn money in races by the FVB, as compensation for their travel costs.[52] A year earlier, the FVB had criticised 'perfidious Albion' and its *National Cyclists' Union* (NCU), which had threatened to bar Belgian racers from competing against its members if the former were known to have won cash prizes for racing.[53] Such claims to authority of the NCU over Belgian racing were seldom received well and in 1887, they even caused a rift in the FVB. When the NCU was asked by the English expatriates' *Cureghem Cricket Club* to organise a cycle race in Brussels on the occasion of Queen Victoria's Jubilee, the FVB banned its members from competing. Only a Belgian association, it stated, could organise races on Belgian soil. A number of Belgian riders rejected its authority however. They resigned from the association and founded a rival governing body.[54]

With the establishment of a new, unified cycling association in 1889, the *Ligue Vélocipédique Belge* (LVB), and the introduction of a stricter amateur classification, which completely banned professional racing practices, Belgian cyclists now seemed to follow the British lead, but as the 1890s progressed and cycle racing became ever more popular, the continuing opposition of the NCU to professional racing again vexed Belgian cyclists. They increasingly looked towards France, where professionalism – commercially interesting for both racers and cycle manufacturers – was wholly accepted.[55] In September 1893, a number of clubs and racers resigned from the LVB and founded the *Union Vélocipédique Libre* (UVL). Together with the Brussels cycling track, they organised the first Belgian cycle races for professionals.[56] Confronted with a large number of secessions, the LVB was forced to accept professionalism. Although internal disagreements played a considerable role in this conflict, the UVL and their supporters defended their actions by scorning the 'hypocrisy' of *British* amateurism in particular, and the ways in which the British cycling unions tried to impose their rules and habits on other countries.[57]

As the decade continued, this fight against 'perfidious Albion' was also picked up by the Belgian representatives on the *International Cycling Association* (ICA, 1892), the first international governing body for bicycle racing. The ICA was dominated by British associations, who remained in favour of upholding amateurism. Belgium came into regular conflict with the ICA and in both 1895 and 1896 it threatened to secede.[58] Indeed, in 1900 Belgium, together with representatives from France, Italy and a number of other nations effectively did so and founded the *Union Cycliste Internationale* (UCI), with former racer Emile de Beukelaer as its first president. Commenting on the whole series of events, former LVB president Raoul Claes proudly stated that 'l'omnipotence d'Albion' had finally been breached. Just like in the ongoing Boer War, he stated, the united 'little ones' had beaten the powerful British forces.[59]

The above examples show how the popularity of 'British' sports in Belgian society increased around 1900 and became incorporated into national, specifically Belgian, contexts and discourses. Sport was increasingly represented as part of a nation's specific identity, as a way in which it could increase its presence and status on the world stage through international competition and contacts.[60] This 'internationalism', with its continuing tensions between cosmopolitanism and national ambitions, certainly struck a chord in Belgium. Despite the international economic crisis of the 1870s, Belgian trade and industry continued to expand and Belgian companies were increasingly influential on the world stage.[61] By 1900, the country's industrial production was topped only by Great Britain.[62] The ideology of 'expansionism', which saw international competition in trade, industry and imperialism as a sure path to national prosperity, had influential adherents among the Belgian political and economic elites and was especially stimulated by King Leopold II.[63] Sport and its rapidly developing networks of international competition fitted perfectly into his expansionist discourse.

Around 1900, national conceptions of sport increasingly determined Belgium's position in these competitions. Soccer, for instance, became increasingly 'nationalised', as new clubs were founded in which British expatriates were no longer dominant and which reflected the political (Catholics vs. Liberals) and linguistic (French vs. Dutch speakers) tensions in the Belgian society.[64] In 1904, the first national soccer team exclusively made up of Belgian nationals was formed. Appreciation for British sporting achievements remained of course: when a Belgian selection played the English national team in 1912, even the expansionist periodical *L'Expansion Belge* praised the English soccer 'tradition'.[65] Likewise, the British model of education through sport remained popular with educators, and even in governmental circles.[66]

Moreover, figures such as Cyrille Van Overbergh, Director-General of Higher Education, Sciences and Arts, especially saw British sport and the values it taught (fair play, character formation) as a way of successfully improving *Belgian* international prestige by training strong young men.[67] Although admiring of British sporting culture, they especially hoped that Belgium itself would benefit from following the British model. In this sense, too large an influence of the ideas of other nations could lead to conflict, as the examples of rowing and cycling illustrate. This made Britain's relationship with Belgian sport especially prone to conflicts: although the 'motherland' of sport, Britain should not be allowed to wholly determine Belgium's sporting future.

This was, again, linked to broader Belgo–British relations and the question of the Belgium monarch's Congo Colony played a significant role here. After decades of unsuccessful attempts to gain a colony for Belgium, including an attempt to buy existing colonies from Great Britain, King Leopold II had acquired the Congo Free State as his private possession in 1885. He did this by strategically manoeuvring between the imperial interests of the European Great Powers, including Britain.[68] With the increasing demand for rubber in the bicycle and automobile industries from the 1890s onwards, Leopold's Colony proved very lucrative.[69] Around 1903, however, the repression and abuse of the local Congo population was challenged by Roger Casement and E.D. Morel, two British activists who founded the *Congo Reform Association* in 1904 and began an international protest campaign against Leopold II's bloody rule in the region.[70]

Campaigns such as this engendered a growing anti-British mood in Belgium. Influenced by Leopold II's propaganda, the majority of Belgians perceived Morel and Casement's activities as moral hypocrisy, an attempt by British tradesmen to acquire a new colony.[71] Morel's continuing criticism of the treatment of the local population, even after the Belgian state had acquired Congo from the King in 1908, ensured these sentiments persisted. In 1908, *L'Expansion Belge* mockingly advised the British to look into the abuse happening in their own overseas possessions, before criticising those of others. Only a few pages back in the same issue, the Racing Club de Bruxelles was praised for having defeated skilled English soccer teams in recent years with a squad consisting solely of Belgians.[72] Sporting contacts between the two nations seemed to reflect Belgian assertiveness towards British interests in imperial matters.

Countries of War and Sport?

The outbreak of the First World War engendered a new episode of intense interactions between Britain and Belgium. When the German armies ignored Belgium's official neutrality and invaded the country in order to attack France from the north, Britain and Belgium became military allies. Indeed, this violation of the internationally recognised Belgian neutrality, and especially the numerous atrocities committed by German troops against Belgian civilians in the process, ensured the country a central place in the British imagination. The 'Rape of Belgium' became a crucial topos in British war propaganda, as stories of rape, murder and destruction, such as the sacking of the Leuven university library in 1914, allowed the British to claim that one of its reasons for going to war was to protect 'brave little Belgium' from German barbarism.[73] The many British troops and campaigns in the small Belgian sector of the frontline, moreover, would make 'Flanders fields' a lasting icon of the horrors of trench warfare in the British collective memory.[74]

From these intense political and military contacts, there followed a resurgence in the number of occasions on which Belgium and Britain cooperated, especially – and not unsurprisingly – in the field of military sport. This was most notably the case in soccer. In 1917 the *Front Wanderers*, a Belgian military soccer team, toured Britain and played a number of matches against civilian clubs such as Chelsea and Aston Villa for charity. The proceeds went to *British Gifts for Belgian Soldiers*, an organisation which provided Belgium's military with sporting equipment. Indeed, it seemed these military sporting contacts stimulated the further popularisation of soccer in Belgium, where it would become one of the most popular spectator sports in the interwar period. In August 1918, the Belgian committee for military sport ordered every company to organise football matches and many ordinary soldiers thus acquired a taste for the game, which they took with them into civilian life.[75] After the Armistice, these Belgo–British military soccer contacts were institutionalised by the founding of the Kentish Cup in 1919. This was an annual tournament between British, Belgian and French army teams and was first conceptualised by the British general Reginald John Kentish and the Belgian F.A. König on their meeting in Brussels.[76]

However, these harmonious sporting events would prove to be far from general during the interwar decades, even in military sports. Unlike Belgium, for instance, Britain was not officially represented at the Inter-Allied Games, a military sport tournament between the Allied forces that took place in Paris during the summer of 1919.[77] Although the reasons for this absence remain largely unknown, it was indicative of the reluctance on the part of British sporting officials to involve themselves in competitions with Europe's continental states in the interwar period, especially in the field of soccer. Again, the amateurism ideology proved to be a point of division. In 1921, the *Football Association* (FA) forbade its member clubs to play any more games against continental teams, including Belgian teams, as recent games, according to the British, had not conformed to the FA's strict definition of amateurism. Despite attempts by the *Fédération Internationale de Football Association* (FIFA) – and especially the strong Belgian element in its senior positions – to solve the matter by organising a summit in Brussels, the FA withdrew from the international association.[78] The new World War of 1940–1945, however, once again proved a catalyst for Belgo–British sporting contact. This was – again – especially the case in soccer. In 1941, the large number of Belgian refugees in England, both civilian and military, had already engendered the founding of a soccer association of expatriates, the *Belgian Football Association in Great Britain*. Clubs of refugees or soldiers were thus given the chance to play against each other or, in the Inter-Allied Football Competition organised from 1943 onwards, against British teams. A number of top Belgian players were even recruited by civilian clubs such as Queens Park Rangers for the duration of the war.[79] Also interesting to note is that some British military physical training methods – as a result of the war – were adopted in the Belgian army.[80]

The aftermath of the Second World War witnessed the rapid decline of Britain's status as a world power, with notable effects on the country's international positioning. Together with Belgium, the British resolutely associated itself with the Western, American-dominated anti-Communist bloc, which began to take shape after the war and in sporting terms was institutionalised around the Olympics. Only a few months prior to the London Games of 1948, both countries became members of the Western European Union, a cooperative union between those western European nations interested in organising a common defence against the Communist threat. In 1949, both countries were also founding members of NATO.[81] In the matter of European integration, however, both followed a markedly different path. Belgium was one of the founding members of the first

European institutions, which it saw as a sure way of guaranteeing its own political and economic interests in post-war Europe.[82] Britain on the other hand, expressed far more scepticism towards the European project, which it saw as a possible limitation of its own independence. The British only became members of the European Union (EU) in 1973. Belgium's capital Brussels, as the official seat of the EU, has become a popular target for British politicians wanting to criticise what they see as the bureaucratic nature of 'Europe' and its attempts at limiting Britain's sovereignty. Indeed, as a recent scholarly volume states, the British have been mostly 'on the sidelines' in the European integration project.[83] Consequently, Belgian politicians who have significant roles in European politics risk the disdain of British Euro-sceptics, as the Belgian EU President Herman 'Rumpy Pumpy' Van Rompuy has experienced.[84]

Although Belgo–British relations in the field of European politics have been – and are – problematic where European integration is concerned, in the field of sport both became undeniably members of an integrated European sport space during the post-war decades. This is aptly illustrated by the many contacts between Belgian and British soccer clubs in the UEFA's European tournaments over the course of these post-war decades. Equally however, this sporting interaction did not come without tensions. The Heysel drama of 1985, in which the aggressive behaviour of Liverpool supporters caused the trampling of 39 Juventus fans in Brussels' Heysel stadium prior to an UEFA-cup final, is especially important in this respect. In Britain, this soccer disaster on foreign soil was yet another episode in the sprawling soccer crisis of the 1980s. In Belgium, however, the drama became a potent 'place of memory'.[85] Indeed, the incident gave Belgian sport fans and policy-makers a first-hand experience of Britain's much publicised soccer hooligans. The cultural image of British sport created by this experience was diametrically opposed to the exemplary status of British sporting culture around 1900. Further incidents, such as the misbehaviour of English supporters in Brussels and Charleroi during the European Soccer Championships of 2000 seemed to consolidate the image in the Belgian public imagination of English fans as drunken, dangerous and disorderly.[86]

Nevertheless, British sporting culture continues to fascinate many Belgians. The fact that there are perhaps more Belgian fan clubs of English soccer teams than from any other foreign country, including teams not in the top echelon such as Portsmouth FC, or even First Division outfits such as Millwall FC, indicates that British sporting culture – at least in soccer – still holds a special status among many Belgians because of its long tradition and 'special' atmosphere.[87] Furthermore, some Belgian football players are 'big' in the Premier League: Marouane Fellaini (Everton), Thomas Vermaelen (Arsenal), Eden Hazard (Chelsea), Romelu Lukaku (Chelsea/West Bromwich Albion), Moussa Dembélé (Fulham and Tottenham Hotspur), Christian Benteke (Aston Villa) Simon Mignolet (Sunderland), Jan Vertonghen (Tottenham Hotspur), etc. Because of their good performances in the first months of 2013, a Belgian newspaper even asserted that Belgian soccer players are a better Belgian export product than beer and chocolates and are – in comparison with other foreign players – 'the best import product of the Premier League'.[88]

The most important Belgian soccer player is, of course, Vincent Kompany, team captain of Manchester City. In 2012, after his team won the Premier League Championship, he was elected player of the year in the 'best domestic football competition in the world'.[89] More important is the fact that he is probably the most influential 'Belgian' in Belgium. After he scored with a pro-Belgium 'tweet' attacking the most important Flemish nationalist, Bart De Wever, some journalists believe that Kompany's voice – given extra weight by the possibility of the Belgian national team qualifying for the Football World Cup in Brazil – could be decisive in keeping the country together after the crucial elections of June 8, 2014. In any event, 'Vince the Prince' was crowned by the influential news magazine *Knack* as Belgium's 2012 Person of the Year.[90]

And the Olympics?

This subtitle could be read as a statement. The Olympics are not so important in the context of the whole of the Belgo–British sporting relationships during the past two centuries. Is this true? The answer is, of course, ambivalent. In Olympic terms, Britain and Belgium are heading two 'international' rankings: London is the only city that has held the Games three times; Belgium is the only country that has supplied two chairmen for the IOC. However, these records are, at least in part, the result of contingencies. Belgium, in the era of Jacques Rogge, is not at all a great sports nation and is much less prominent at the head of international sports federations than before 1950.[91] Thus, Rogge has certainly not been elected president of the IOC 'because of' his Belgian nationality. England (Great Britain), to be sure, is the cradle of modern sport and still one of the big sports nations today, but London could claim the 2012 Games only after some diplomatic blunders by the then French president, Jacques Chirac, who was so certain that Paris could cash in on its role as favourite that he suffered from a kind of *hubris*.[92]

With regard to the Belgian delegations to the London Games of 1908, 1948 and 2012, mostly 'national' conclusions – on the Belgian side of the continuum – can be drawn. The 1908 Games are interesting because they were the first official Games to which the Belgian Olympic Committee could send a delegation. Indeed, the Belgian Olympic Committee (BOC) was founded on the occasion of the 1906 Intercalated Games in Athens. Leading up to these Games, the organising committee had asked Captain Clément Lefebure, commander of the military *Ecole Normale de Gymnastique et d'Escrime* in Brussels, to ensure Belgian participation.[93] Hence, it is quite remarkable that the BOC was founded by Lefebure, *nota bene* the most ardent proponent of Swedish Gymnastics in Belgium, and not by Henry de Baillet-Latour, the official IOC member for Belgium. The reason is astonishing – certainly with the title of this paper in mind. In February 1906, Baillet-Latour happened to be in England and had ordered his concierge to forward only important documents to him.[94] The latter judged an envelope from the *Ecole Normale de Gymnastique et d'Escrime*, including a letter from Lefebure, to be 'inutile'.[95] In this way, Baillet-Latour only got to read the letter in which he was asked to become a member of the planned committee on March 15, 1906, even though it had been written on February 11, 1906. Lefebure did not wait for Baillet-Latour's response and called together an inaugural meeting in the Ravenstein Hotel in Brussels on February 18, 1906. It was Lefebure's proposal to assign the presidency to Edouard de Laveleye, President of the *UBSSA*, while he himself would take up the position of secretary general.[96]

Nonetheless, Baillet-Latour was supposed to become the President of the Belgian Olympic Committee, as Pierre de Coubertin had written in a letter to Lefebure in which he ventilated his discontent with the situation. Coubertin accused Lefebure of deliberately ignoring the regular procedures appertaining to the setting up of a national Olympic committee. Lefebure countered by saying he had not done anything out of the ordinary and stated that he was not pleased with the tone that Coubertin used in his letters.[97] Eventually, Baillet-Latour became a member of the Belgian Olympic Committee on March 18, 1906.[98]

During the preparatory period, the Belgian Olympic Committee was augmented with committee members from the Belgian sports federations whose sports were on the programme in London, unlike the situation during the Intercalated Games in Athens. An important obstacle, however, was the search for funding. In contrast to the Athens organisational committee for the Intercalated Games of 1906, the London committee placed no funds at the disposal of the participating countries and the BOC finally succeeded in prying 7500 BEF from the government.[99] As many as 88 Belgian participants were officially registered for the 1908 Games, but some of them did not compete.[100] Of the 22 participating countries, Belgium won one gold, five silver and two bronze medals and placed tenth in the final ranking. The host country, Great Britain, took the crown in the medal standings, after a number of rivalries between British and American athletes.[101] The second part of the telegram of BOC Chairman Edouard de Laveleye, which was read by Pierre de Coubertin during the farewell banquet, thus did not correspond completely with reality: 'All congratulations for splendid organisation and fair play of Games.'[102]

A large delegation also travelled to London for the 1948 Games, in part because of the support of the *Union Royale Belge des Sociétés de Football-Association*, and the campaigns of BOC President Rodolphe William Seeldrayers (who would become President of FIFA in 1954).[103] Apparently, the Belgian delegation was also supported 'in natura'.[104] Indeed, the London organising committee had asked participating countries to bring as much food as possible with them to London because of the post-war scarcities, as the Olympiad became known as 'The Austerity Games'.[105] The Belgian delegation manifested itself primarily in cycling (gold, silver and bronze) and athletics (gold and bronze) on a total of seven medals.[106] The Belgian middle-distance runner Gaston Reiff won the 5000 m, which was run in the pouring rain, against the Czech star Emil Zatopek. The Belgian parachutist lieutenant Etienne Gailly – who, during the war, had been part of the Belgian Brigade stationed in England and ran cross-country races for a local club – played a star role in a marathon drama. He reached Wembley Stadium first as the seemingly obvious winner but collapsed and, totally exhausted with only one lap to go on the cinder track, had to let two other athletes pass him and finally came in third.[107] Seeldrayers concluded in his report on Belgian participation in the 1948 Games by stating that in the future the BOC would have to devote more attention to the general physical condition of the athletes and would have to play much more a coordinating role, particularly for those sports federations with deficient leadership. He also commented on the need for the training of officials and the need either to develop or attract trainers of international calibre if the country wanted to count at international level. Seeldrayers was also concerned about the uninvited involvement of the government in elite sport events.[108]

As such, these concluding remarks are interesting in terms of placing the 2012 Games in perspective. Although the Belgian politicians (from both federal and regional governments) almost stumbled over each other in the Belgium House in London, the medal harvest was poor. The bronze medal of Walloon judoka Charline Van Snick on the first day of competition confirmed Belgium's good international results in judo (see also Table 1) and raised the hopes of the other 113 athletes in the second biggest Belgian Olympic delegation in history. However, Belgium's disappointment after the cycling road race was symptomatic of the whole Olympiad. With a total of one silver medal and two bronze medals, the size of the Belgian delegation was certainly not reflected in its medal-harvest. Ironically, the highest Belgian medal was won by Lionel Cox, an amateur athlete from Seraing who works full-time as a labour inspector in the Brussels Capital Region. In the light of the amateur ideals of Pierre de Coubertin, this was, of course, a great personal achievement, but it was also seen as a kind of reprimand of the 'professional' elite sport structures in Belgium. Certainly for the Flemish government, the results were disappointing, as they only obtained one 'Flemish' medal, the bronze plaque of Evi Van Acker in sailing (i.e. the former Olympic sport discipline of Jacques Rogge).

Concluding reflections

While the 2012 Olympics was very successful for the British organisers, this was certainly not the case for the Belgian delegation. As a consequence, and as has been the case in recent decades following Olympic failures, the two perennial discussions in Belgium/ Flanders again reared their heads: (1) Should more money go to elite sport to the detriment of 'Sport for All'? (2) In the available budget for elite sport, should choices be made as regards the financing of specific disciplines? It remains to be seen whether the possible measures will lead to a bigger medal harvest in Rio de Janeiro. The primary question is, however, whether financial investments in the quest for a greater medal harvest could really be seen as 'good governance' from a broader social perspective. Is the dissipation of funds for elite sport – to the detriment of Sport for All – defendable in times of government budgetary scarcity? Is elite sport really more than *panem et circenses* then? In that way, the policy recommendations of British Prime Minister David Cameron following the success of the British athletes during the London Games are remarkable (and criticised in educational circles):

> I want to use the example of competitive sport at the Olympics to lead a revival of competitive sport in primary schools. We need to end the 'all must have prizes' culture and get children playing and enjoying competitive sports from a young age, linking them up with sports clubs so they can pursue their dreams. That's why the new national curriculum in the autumn will include a requirement for primary schools to provide competitive sport.[109]

All in all, after reading this paper, it has to be clear that transnational flows and contacts are not always reflected at the level of the Olympic Games and *vice versa*, that the Olympic Games tells us more about national (sport) policies than about the shaping of these sports in transnational dynamics. The fact that bronze-medal winner Evi Van Acker was elected Belgium's 2012 Sports Woman of the Year certainly illustrates the appreciation for Olympic medals among Belgian journalists, but it also highlights the relatively low international level of Belgium's elite success with regard to Olympic sport. On the other hand, the fact that cycle racer Tom Boonen was elected Belgium's 2012 Sports Man of the Year, with world champion Philippe Gilbert as his runner-up, illustrates the continuing existence of favourite 'national' sport disciplines, especially in Eddy Merckx' country. That bicycle racing is not yet a global sport – although it *is* growing globally – is no criterion for Belgian sport rankings.[110]

Notes on Contributors

Pascal Delheye studied physical education, sport management and history at the Universities of Leuven and Lyon. In 2001, he obtained a PhD fellowship of the Research Foundation – Flanders (FWO). His doctoral research, for which he won the Young Investigators Award of the European College of Sport Science in 2003, focused on the history of physical education and its origin as an academic discipline. After post-doctoral research at the Universities of Leuven and Berkeley, he became professor of sport history at KU Leuven in 2008.

Stijn Knuts studied cultural history at the University of Leuven, where he also obtained an additional master-title in comparative global history. He is currently working on a doctoral dissertation on the history of cycling and bicycle racing in Belgium between 1860 and 1940. His earlier publications focus on processes of local, regional and (sub)national identity formation through bicycle racing in early twentieth-century Belgium.

Thomas Ameye studied physical education and sport management at the Universities of Leuven and Lyon. He is preparing a doctoral dissertation on the rise, evolution, institutionalisation and legitimisation of Olympism in Belgium. In 2006, he was laureate of the Postgraduate Research Grant Programme of the IOC's Olympic Studies Centre, and, in 2010, was awarded the Ian Buchanan

Memorial Scholarship of the International Society of Olympic Historians. In May 2013, he became Director of the National Cycling Museum, Roeselare, Belgium.

Notes

1. "Dossier. Londen, 2012." (*Sporta Magazine*, March, 2012, 4, 5).
2. *New London*, 13.
3. "Belgium," (*The Telegraph Online*, March 13, 2012).
4. *Humo*, July 10, 2012.
5. Johnes, "Britain;" Stokvis, "Belgium and the Netherlands;" Delheye and Renson, "Belgique" for some review articles.
6. See, f.i., Tomlinson and Young, "Towards a New History of European Sport."
7. Murray, *Vlaanderen*, 27; Gevaert, *Slagveld van Europa*; Blom and Lamberts, *Geschiedenis*, 57.
8. Brooke and Keir, *London*, 179 and 268–9; Blom and Lamberts, *Geschiedenis*, 32–4 and 81.
9. Murray, *Vlaanderen*, 183–5; Marnef, "Gresham and Antwerp."
10. Some sixteenth-century London neighbourhoods were almost exclusively inhabited by Low Countries refugees (see Murray, *Vlaanderen*, 27 and 31–6).
11. See, f.i., Murray, *Vlaanderen*, 149–50 and passim; Hefford, "Flemish Tapestry."
12. On this image see Murray, *Vlaanderen*, 27.
13. Gillmeister, "The Flemish Ancestry," 54–74.
14. Terry, "The Seventeenth Century Game of Cricket."
15. Found by Jan Luitzen in Hexham, *Het groot woorden-boeck: gestelt in 't Nederduytsch, ende in 't Engelsch*. Thanks to Nicoline van der Sijs et al. a digital version of this dictionary became available in 2010. In the framework of his PhD research, Jan Luitzen will further analyse the introduction of sport terminology in the Netherlands, using his digital library containing thousands of sports books and dictionaries.
16. Van der Beken, "Inleiding tot de beschrijvende historiek," 20–6, 86–91, 139, 143–6; Guttmann, *Sports*, 70–1. On coastal and spa tourism in Belgium see Gobyn, *Te kust en te kuur*, 28–9, 293–6.
17. Coolsaet, *België en zijn buitenlandse politiek*, 21–72; Witte, "De Constructie," 29–235.
18. Coolsaet, *België en zijn buitenlandse politiek*, 35–9, 41–2, 60; Deneckere, *Leopold I*.
19. Bagini, "Great Britain," 1004–6.
20. Witte, "De Constructie," 45–6 and 163–71; Gubin and Nandrin, "Het liberale en burgerlijke België," 372–77; *Algemene Geschiedenis*, 57–8 and 128–39.
21. Coppejans-Desmedt, "Bauwens, Lieven."
22. Gubin and Nandrin, "Het liberale en burgerlijke België," 377; Coolsaet, *België en zijn buitenlandse politiek*, 161; Boeren, "De handelsbetrekkingen," 122–8.
23. Holt, *Sport and the British*, 74–116; Mangan, *Athleticism*; Lowerson, *Sport and the English Middle Classes*, 1–28.
24. There is a considerable body of literature on the cultural transfer of British sport to the European continent, see f.i. Eisenbergh, *English Sports*; Idem, "Towards a New History;" Heraiz and Sanchez, "The British Influence."
25. For an international comparison with regard to the role of these expatriates see, f.i., Eisenberg, "The rise," 383–4; Lanfranchi and Taylor, *Moving with the Ball*, 33.
26. Delheye and Renson, "Belgique," 121.
27. Ameloot, "Ontstaan en ontwikkeling," 23–5; Stynen, "Proeftuinen," 426; Den Hollander, "Sport in 't Stad," 251, 258 and 302–3.
28. Ameloot, "Ontstaan en ontwikkeling," 52–64 and 79–80; Den Hollander, "Sport in 't Stad," 305–306; Gobyn, *Te kust en te kuur*, 134.
29. *La Belgique Sportive*, 1/1 (1887): 8, quoted in Den Hollander, "Sport in 't Stad," 170; Ameloot, "Ontstaan en ontwikkeling," 70–1; Lanfranchi and Taylor, *Moving with the Ball*, 20–5; Deleu, *Honderd jaar*, 7–8.
30. Neirynck, "De scholen;" Renson, "Corpus Alienum," 99–102; Schalembier, "Historiek," 71–9 and 101; Vanysacker, *Van FC Brugeois tot Club Brugge KV*, 39.
31. Delheye, "Struggling for Gymnastics;" Strobbe, *200 jaar dichters, denkers en durvers*.
32. Vangrunderbeek, Soors and Delheye, *Omnes currunt*, 27; Renson, "Corpus alienum," 101–3.
33. Renson, "Corpus alienum."

34. Renson, "Corpus alienum," 103; Schalembier, "Historiek," 100–18.
35. Den Hollander, "Sport in 't Stad," 257–60; Schalembier, "Historiek," 91–4 and 113–4. With regard to the (more recent) history of soccer clubs in Belgium, see also Duke and Renson, "From Factions to Fusions." Their paper was the result of an excellent Belgo–British cooperation.
36. Ameloot, "Ontstaan en ontwikkeling," 100; Schalembier, "Historiek," 103–4.
37. Den Hollander, "Sport in 't Stad," 251 and 268–76; Schalembier, "Historiek," 119–55. On the UBSSA see also Boin, *Livre d'or*.
38. These French protagonists had themselves already been thoroughly influenced by British practices. See, f.i., Van der Beken, "Inleiding tot de beschrijvende historiek," 31–2 and 40–50.
39. Den Hollander, "Sport in 't Stad," 91–162 and 180–2.
40. Tolleneer, "The Dual Meaning," 95. With regard to gymnastics there was, of course, a huge influence from Germany and Sweden. See, f.i., Delheye, "Struggling for Gymnastics;" Delheye, "Happel in Antwerp."
41. For recent revisionist literature in which the primordial role of Great Britain in shaping European sport is questioned see, f.i., Dietschy, "French Sport," 509–13; Tomlinson and Young, "Towards a New History", 499–503.
42. Delheye, "Struggling for Gymnastics in Belgium."
43. Tolleneer, "The Attitude," 217–22; Renson, "Corpus alienum," 105–6.
44. Guttmann, *Sports*, 94–6.
45. *Idem*, 96–7; Den Hollander, "Sport in 't Stad," 164–74. Only in 1947 did a British rowing association become a member of the FISA.
46. Knuts, Delheye and Vanysacker, "Wentelende wielen," 18–9. Paradoxically, the British were first introduced to cycling by the French in the late 1860s as well (see Ritchie, *Quest for Speed*, 23–39 and 153)
47. *Vélo Revue*, 1/1 (1893): 1–2.
48. See also Knuts and Delheye, "Cycling in the City."
49. De Laet, *125 jaar*, 6–7; Le Vélo [Organe officiel du Vlaamsche Wielrijderskring], 1/1 (1886): 1–2 and 8.
50. *Le Vélo*, 1/4 (1886); *Le Cycliste Belge Illustré*, 2/62 (1891): 8.
51. *Antwerp Bicycle Club. Organe Particulier du Club*, February (1922): 1.
52. *Le Véloce*, 2/361 and 2/364 (1894); 3/10 (1895).
53. *Idem*, 2/356 and 2/361 (1894).
54. Lauters, *Les débuts*, 70–88.
55. *Idem*, 93 and Ritchie, *Quest for Speed*, 254–87.
56. Lauters, *Les débuts*, 142–5; *Organe de l'Union Vélocipédique Libre*, 1/1 (1893): 1–2.
57. *Organe de l'UVL*, 2/19 (1894): 1–2 and 2/22 (1894): 1–2.
58. Ritchie, *Quest for Speed*, 260 and 295–8; Mattheus, "De interne," 182–90.
59. *Revue Vélocipédique Belge*, 13/13 (1900): 194–5.
60. Eisenberg, "The rise," 376–7, 393–4 and 398; Keys, *Globalizing Sport*, 1–4.
61. See also Ameye, Gils and Delheye, "Daredevils and Early Birds."
62. Deneckere, *1900*, 10, 17 and 20–3; Gubin and Nandrin, "Het liberale en burgerlijke België," 372–77.
63. Dumoulin, "Het ontluiken," 729; Coolsaet, *België en zijn buitenlandse politiek*, 171–81; Delheye, "Struggling for Gymnastics."
64. Lanfranchi and Taylor, *Moving with the Ball*, 31–5; Den Hollander, "Sport in 't Stad," 261–2; Schalembier, "Historiek," 98–9 and 110–2.
65. Schalembier, "Historiek," 171–80; *L'Expansion Belge*, 5/5 (1912): 297.
66. *Honderd jaar*, 10; Renson, "Corpus alienum," 119–20. See, f.i., *Le Sportsman*, 25–6 November 1905: 33.
67. Delheye, "Struggling for Gymnastics."
68. Coolsaet, *België en zijn buitenlandse politiek*, 144–5 and Stengers, *Congo*, 45–86 and 87–98.
69. Delheye, "Struggling for Gymnastics."
70. Coolsaet, *België en zijn buitenlandse politiek*, 153–4. For the historical debate on these abuses, see, f.i., Hochschild, *King Leopold's Ghost* and Stengers, *Congo*, 307–8.
71. Stengers, *Congo*.

72. *L'Expansion Belge*, 2/3 (1909): 140–5 and 157.
73. Horne and Kramer, *German Atrocities*; De Schaepdrijver, *De Groote Oorlog*; Gullace, "The Blood of Our Sons," 17–33; Steen, "Poor Little Belgium;" Derez, "The Oxford of Belgium," 111–38.
74. Winter, "Battlefield," 164–76.
75. Boin, *Livre d'or*, 268 and 273–275. See also Fraiponts and Willocx, *Kroniek*, III, 13–5.
76. Boin, *Livre d'or*, 270–2.
77. Terret, *Les Jeux Interalliés de 1919*, 99–101.
78. Fraiponts and Willocx, *Kroniek*, III, 106; Boin, *Livre d'or*, 110 and Lanfranchi and Taylor, *Moving with the Ball*, 37–48. Between 1909 and 1921, Edouard de Laveleye was FIFA's vice-president. In 1924 his compatriot Joseph d'Oultremont was elected to this post, which he fulfilled until 1927.
79. Boin, *Livre d'or*, 277–84.
80. Vanmeerbeek, "Plus de sueur, moins de sang."
81. *Politieke geschiedenis van België*, 391–400; Blom and Lamberts, *Geschiedenis*, 298–99.
82. Coolsaet, *België en zijn buitenlandse politiek*, 557–63; Dujardin and Dumoulin, "Maakt eendracht nog altijd macht?", 1499–505.
83. Gowland, Turner and Wright, *Britain and European Integration*, 1–3.
84. *De Tijd*, February 25, 2010: 10; *The Daily Mail Online*, April 17, 2012 (http://www.dailymail.co.uk/debate/article-1254085/QUENTIN-LETTS-Mr-Rumpy-Pumpy-gets-little-grumpy.html).
85. Schaevers, "Brussel;" Sibaja, "Hooliganism," 114.
86. *De Morgen*, June 17, 2000: 3; *Het Belang van Limburg*, June 17, 2000: 1 and 32; *Het Belang van Limburg*, June 19, 2000: 2.
87. A total of 12 Belgian fan clubs for English teams were found. These included West Ham United (two clubs), Tottenham Hotspur, Chelsea (The Mighty Blues), Aston Villa, Millwall, Manchester United and City, Arsenal, Liverpool, Southampton and Portsmouth. See also http://www.voetbalbelgie.be/nl/article.php?id=4859 (April 17, 2012).
88. *Sportwereld* (*Het Nieuwsblad*), March 12, 2013: 1 and 6–7.
89. http://bleacherreport.com/articles/1306268-10-reasons-the-premier-league-is-the-best-in-the-world (with a prominent picture of Vincent Kompany).
90. *Knack* 42/50 (December 12–18, 2012).
91. Because of limited space available for this paper, we do not look at the Paralympics here – in which Belgian athletes and administrators, however, were very active. See, for instance, De Meyer, *People in Motion*.
92. See, f.i., http://en.wikipedia.org/wiki/Bids_for_the_2012_Summer_Olympics.
93. This appeared from the letters he wrote to – among others – Pierre de Coubertin and Cyrille Van Overbergh and from letters from the organising committee to Pierre de Coubertin (Lausanne: OSC IOC: Notice 0101993: Correspondence à Pierre de Coubertin 1906–1907; Brussels: State Archives: T038, 504). A letter from Clément Lefebure to Lars Mauritz Törngren, at that time director of the Central Gymnastics Institute in Stockholm, revealed that the Greek organising committee also addressed Nicolaas-Jan Cupérus in this regard, i.e. the leader of German Gymnastics (*Turnen*) in Belgium and Europe. However, Cupérus refused to cooperate with Lefebure (because the latter was the most ardent propagator of Swedish Gymnastics in Belgium). See Delheye, "Struggling for Gymnastics;" Idem, "Struggling for Gymnastics in Belgium;" Stockholm: National Archives: Lars Mauritz Törngren Arkiv: 8XLI, 2238.
94. Letter from Henry de Baillet-Latour to Pierre de Coubertin, March 17, 1906 (Lausanne: OSC IOC: Notice 0101993).
95. Idem.
96. Procès verbal de la séance du 18 février 1906 (Brussels: State Archives: T038, 504).
97. Lausanne: OSC IOC: Notice 0101993: Correspondence à Pierre de Coubertin 1906–1907.
98. Letter from Clément Lefebure to Pierre de Coubertin, March 19, 1906 (Lausanne: OSC IOC: Notice 0101993). Henry de Baillet-Latour did not become president until 1923; 2 years later he was also elected IOC president.
99. Together with the 500 BEF from Ernest Solvay, who also donated to the Games in Athens, one arrived at a total budget of 8000 BEF, *La Vie Sportive* (*LVS*), June 9, 1908 and July 9, 1908.
100. Cook, *The Fourth Olympiad*.

101. *LVS*, July 9, 1908; Constable, *The IV Olympiad*; Renson, *Enflammé*, 39–40.
102. Cook, *The Fourth Olympiad*, 791; Renson, *Enflammé*, 39–40.
103. Seeldrayers, *Jeux Olympiques*.
104. Renson, *Enflammé*, 101–2.
105. Daniels, *The XIV Olympiad*; Renson, *Enflammé*.
106. Also a silver medal in boxing and a bronze medal in fencing.
107. Hampton, *The Austerity Olympics*, 204–5; Renson, *Enflammé*.
108. Seeldrayers, *Jeux Olympiques*; Renson, *Enflammé*.
109. See http://www.number10.gov.uk/news/competitive-sport-for-children-at-the-heart-of-olym pics-legacy (August 11, 2012). See also *The Guardian*, August 12, 2012.
110. The transnational history of cycling and bicycle racing will be further explored and analysed in the doctoral research of Stijn Knuts.

References

Ameye, Thomas, Bieke Gils, and Pascal Delheye. "Daredevils and Early Birds: Belgian Pioneers in Automobile Racing and Aerial Sports During the Belle Époque." *International Journal of the History of Sport* 28, no. 2 (2011): 205–239.

Algemene geschiedenis der Nederlanden: vol. 10 Nieuwste Tijd. Haarlem: Fibula-Van Dishoeck, 1981.

Ameloot, Anne. "Ontstaan en ontwikkeling van de tennissport in België: bijdrage tot het archief van de moderne sport (MOSAR)." Unpub, Master's Diss., KU Leuven 1984.

Bagini, Eugenio. "Great Britain." In *Europe – 1789 to 1914 – Encyclopaedia of the Age of Industry and Empire*, edited by John Merriman, and Jay Winter, Vol. 2, 999–1014. New York: Thomson Gale, 2006.

"Belgium." *The Telegraph Online*, March 13, 2012. (http://www.telegraph.co.uk/sport/olympics/ countries/8662622/Belgium-London-2012-Olympics.html, last consulted June 13, 2012).

Blom, Hans, and Emiel Lamberts. *Geschiedenis van de Nederlanden*. Baarn: HB Uitgevers, 2004.

Boeren, Rita. "De Handelsbetrekkingen tussen België en Groot-Brittannië." Unpub. Master's Diss., KU Leuven 1983.

Boin, Victor, ed. *Livre d'or jubilaire de l'U.R.B.S.F.A., 1895–1945: histoire du football en Belgique et au Congo Belge*. Brussels: Leclercq & De Haas, 1950.

Brooke, Christopher, and Gillian Keir. *London, 800–1216: The Shaping of a City*. Berkeley, Los Angeles: University of California Press, 1975.

Constable, George. *The IV Olympiad: London 1908, The International YMCA (The Olympic Century 5)*. Los Angeles, CA: World Sport Research & Publications, 1999.

Coolsaet, Rik. *België en zijn buitenlandse politiek. 1830–2000*. Leuven: Van Halewyck, 2001.

Cook, TheodoreAndrea. *The Fourth Olympiad: Being the Official Report of the Olympic Games of 1908*. London: The British Olympic Association, 1909.

Coppejans-Desmedt, Hilde. "Bauwens, Lieven." *Nationaal biografisch woordenboek, I*, 98–107. Brussels: Palcis der Academiën, 1964.

Daniels, George. *The XIV Olympiad: London 1948, Oslo 1952 (The Olympic Century 12)*. Los Angeles, CA: World Sport Research & Publications, 1999.

De Laet, Willy. *125 jaar Royal Antwerp Bicycle Club*. Antwerp: RABC, 2007.

Delheye, Pascal. "Happel in Antwerp (1857–1916) and Euler in Brussels (1860–1882): Two Different Faces of German Turnen in Belgium." In *Südwestdeutsche Turner in der Emigration*, edited by Annette Hofmann, and Michael Krüger, 27–50. Schorndorf: Hofmann, 2004.

Delheye, Pascal, and Roland Renson. "Belgique." In *Histoire du Sport en Europe*, edited by James Riordan, Arnd Krüger, and Thierry Terret, 113–145. Paris: L'Harmattan, 2004.

Delheye, Pascal. "Struggling for Gymnastics. The Scientisation and Institutionalisation of Physical Education in Belgium (1830–1914)." Unpub. PhD Diss., KU Leuven 2005.

Delheye, Pascal. "Struggling for Gymnastics in Belgium: The Rhetorics of the Battle of the Systems (1860–1914)." *Stadion: International Journal of the History of Sport* 32 (2006): 57–81.

De Meyer, Marcel. *People in Motion: 50 Jaar-Ans-Years Belgian Paralympic Committee*. Roeselare: Roularta, 2010.

Den Hollander, Marijke. "'Sport in 't Stad: sociaal-historische analyse van de sport in Antwerpen 1830–1914." Unpub. PhD Diss., KU Leuven 2002.

Deneckere, Gita. *1900: België op het breukvlak van twee eeuwen*. Tielt: Lannoo, 2006.

Deneckere, Gita. *Leopold I, de eerste koning van Europa 1790–1865*. Amsterdam: Bezige Bij, 2011.

Derez, Mark. "'The Oxford of Belgium'. Een kwestie van beeldvorming." In *Aan onze helden en martelaren... Beelden van de brand van Leuven (augustus 1914)*, edited by Marika Ceunen, and Piet Veldeman, 111–138. Leuven: Peeters, 2004.

De Schaepdrijver, Sophie. *De Groote Oorlog: het koninkrijk België tijdens de Eerste wereldoorlog*. Amsterdam: Atlas, 1999.

Dietschy, Paul. "French Sport: Caught between Universalism and Exceptionalism." *European Review* 19, no. 4 (2011): 509–525.

Dujardin, Vincent, and Michel Dumoulin. "Maakt eendracht nog altijd macht?" *Nieuwe geschiedenis van Belgie III: 1950-heden*, edited by Vincent Dujardin, et al., 1353–1533. Tielt: Lannoo, 2006.

Duke, Vic, and Roland Renson. "From Factions to Fusions: The Rise and Fall of Two-Club Rivalries in Belgian Football." *International Review for the Sociology of Sport* 28, no. 1 61–77.

Eisenberg, Christiane. "The Rise of Internationalism in Sport." In *The Mechanics of Internationalism: Culture, Society and Politics from the 1840s to the First World War*, edited by M. H. Geyer, and J. Paulmann, 375–403. Oxford: Oxford University Press, 2001.

Eisenberg, Christiane. "Towards a New History of European Sport?" *European Review* 19, no. 4 (2011): 617–622.

Eisenberg, Christiane. *"English Sports" und Deutsche Bürger: Eine Gesellschaftsgeschichte 1800–1939*. Paderborn: Schöningh, 1999.

Fraiponts, Jean, and Dirk Willocx. *Kroniek van het Belgisch voetbal. Deel 3: Olympiërs en Mannekens. 1914–1925*. Antwerpen: Assoc, 2005.

Gevaert, Marc. *Slagveld van Europa: duizend jaar oorlog in de Zuidelijke Nederlanden*. Roeselare: Roularta, 2007.

Gillmeister, Heiner. "The Flemish Ancestry of Early English Ball Evidence." In *Sport History: Olympic Scientific Congress, University of Oregon, Eugene/Oregon, July 19–26, 1984*, edited by Norbert Muller, and JoachimK. Ruhl, 54–74. Niedernhausen: Schors, 1985.

Gobyn, Ronny, ed. *Te kust en te kuur: badplaatsen en kuuroorden in België 16de-20ste eeuw*. Brussels: ASLK, 1987.

Gowland, David, Arthur Turner, and Alex Wright. *Britain and European Integration Since 1945: On the Sidelines*. London: Routledge, 2010.

Gubin, Eliane, and Jean-Pierre Nandrin. "Het liberale en burgerlijke België: 1846–1878." In *Nieuwe geschiedenis van Belgie I: 1830–1905*, edited by Els Witte, Jean-Pierre Nandrin, Eliane Gubin, and Gita Deneckere, 239–440. Tielt: Lannoo, 2006.

Gullace, Nicoletta. *"The Blood of Our Sons": Men, Women and the Renegotiation of British Citizenship During the Great War*. New York: Palgrave MacMillan, 2002.

Guttmann, Allen. *Sports: The First Five Millennia*. Amherst: University of Massachusetts Press, 2005.

Hampton, Janie. *The Austerity Olympics: When the Games Came to London in 1948*. London: Aurum, 2008.

Hefford, Wendy. "Flemish Tapestry Weavers in England: 1550–1775." In *Flemish Tapestry Weavers Abroad: Emigration and the Founding of Manufactories in Europe*, edited by Guy Delmarcel, 43–62. Leuven: Leuven University Press, 2002.

Herraiz, Antonio Rivero, and Garcia R. Sanchez. "The British Influence in the Birth of Spanish Sport." *International Journal of the History of Sport* 28, no. 13 (2011): 1788–1809.

Hochschild, Adam. *King Leopold's Ghost: A Story of Greed, Terror, and Heroism in Colonial Africa*. Boston: Houghton Mifflin, 1998.

Holt, Richard. *Sport and the British: A Modern History*. Oxford: Clarendon, 1989.

Deleu, Gilbert, ed. *Honderd jaar universitaire sport te Leuven: historisch overzicht en catalogus*. Leuven: KU Leuven, 1981.

Horne, John, and Alan Kramer. *German Atrocities, 1914: A History of Denial*. Yale: Yale University Press, 2001.

Johnes, Martin. "Britain." In *Routledge Companion to Sports History*, edited by S. W. Pope, and John Nauright, 444–460. London: Routledge, 2010.

Keys, Barbara. *Globalizing Sport: National Rivalry and International Community in the 1930s*. Harvard: Harvard University Press, 2006.

Knuts, Stijn, and Pascal Delheye. "Cycling in the City? Belgian Cyclists Conquering Urban Spaces, 1860–1900." *International Journal of the History of Sport* 29, no. 14 (2012): 1942–1962.

Knuts, Stijn, Pascal Delheye, and Dries Vanysacker. "Wentelende wielen: anderhalve eeuw fietsen en wielrennen in Vlaanderen." In *Vlaanderen fietst! Sociaalwetenschappelijk onderzoek naar de fietssportmarkt*, edited by Teroen Schccrdei, Wim Lagae, and Filip Boen, 15–70. Ghent: Academia Press, 2011.

Lanfranchi, Pierre, and Matthew Taylor. *Moving with the Ball: The Migration of Professional Footballers*. Oxford: Berg, 2001.

Lauters, Francis. *Les débuts du cyclisme en Belgique*. Brussels: Office de Publicité, 1936.

Lowerson, John. *Sport and the English Middle Classes 1870–1914*. Manchester: Manchester University Press, 1993.

Mangan, James A. *Athleticism in the Victorian and Edwardian Public School: The Emergence and Consolidation of an Educational Ideology*. Cambridge: Cambridge University Press, 1981.

Marnef, Guido. "Gresham and Antwerp." Lecture at Gresham College, London, June 19, 2008 (available online at http://www.gresham.ac.uk/lectures-and-events/gresham-and-antwerp).

Mattheus, Ruben. "De interne geschiedenis van de Koninklijke Belgische Wielrijdersbond, de Union Cycliste Internationale en haar Belgische voorzitters (1882–1922)." Unpub. Master's Diss., KU Leuven 2005.

Murray, John J. *Vlaanderen en Engeland: de invloed van de Lage Landen op Engeland ten tijde van de Tudors en de Stuarts*. Antwerp: Mercatorfonds, 1985.

Neirynck, Robert. "De scholen der Jozefieten, Xaverianen en Benediktijnen en de ontwikkeling van de voetbalsport in België (1863–1895)." Unpub. Master's Diss., KU Leuven 1985.

New London. "Promotional folder, Spring " 2012.

Renson, Roland. "Corpus alienum: naschoolse sport in het katholiek onderwijs." In *Voor lichaam & geest: katholieken, lichamelijke opvoeding en sport in de 19de en 20ste eeuw*, edited by Marc D'Hoker, Roland Renson, and Jan Tolleneer, 99–121. Leuven: Universitaire Pers Leuven, 1994.

Renson, Roland. *Enflammée par l'Olympisme. cent ans de Comité Olympique et Interfédéral Belge, 1906–2006*. Roeselare: Roularta, 2006.

Ritchie, Andrew. *Quest for Speed: A History of Early Bicycle Racing, 1868–1903*. El Cerrito: Ritchie, 2011.

Schaevers, Mark. "Brussel: het Heizelstadion. Een voetbalwedstrijd in 1985." *België: een parcours van herinnering. 2*, edited by G. Buelens, J. Tollebeek, S. De Schaepdrijver, et al., 287–297. Amsterdam: Bakker, 2008.

Schalembier, Bruno. "Historiek van het voetbal in België tot de Eerste Wereldoorlog." Unpub. Master's Diss., Ghent University 1998.

Seeldrayers, RodolpheWilliam. *Jeux Olympiques de Londres: rapport de Mr. RW Seeldrayers, Président du CNEP-COB (Rapport officiel)*, 1948.

Sibaja, Rwany. "Hooliganism, British Isles." In *Sports Around the World*, Vol. 1, edited by John Nauright, and Charles Parrish, 113–115. Santa Barbara, CA: ABC-CLIO, 2012.

Steen, Karolien. "'Poor little Belgium': België in de Britse propaganda uit de Eerste Wereldoorlog." Unpub. Master's Diss., Ghent University 2000.

Stengers, Jean. *Congo. Mythes et réalités*. Brussels: Racine, 2007.

Stokvis, Ruud. "Belgium and the Netherlands." In *Routledge Companion to Sports History*, edited by S. W. Pope, and John Nauright, 350–359. London: Routledge, 2010.

Strobbe, Johan. *200 jaar dichters, denkers en durvers. Een biografie van een college: het Klein Seminarie van Roeselare*. Roeselare: Lannoo & Klein Seminarie Roeselare, 2006.

Stynen, Andreas. "Proeftuinen van burgerlijkheid: stadsnatuur in negentiende-eeuws Belgie." Unpub. PhD diss., KU Leuven 2010.

Terret, Thierry. *Les Jeux Interalliés de 1919: sport, guerre et relations internationales*. Paris: L'Harmattan, 2002.

Terry, David. "The Seventeenth Century Game of Cricket: A Reconstruction of the Game." *The Sports Historian* 20, no. 1 (2000): 33–43.

Tolleneer, Jan. "The Attitude of the Belgian Catholic Gymnasts to Modern Sports (1895–1914)." In *De Belgische Katholieke Turnbond, 1892–1992*. Unpub. PhD Diss. edited by Jan Tolleneer, 217–227. KU Leuven, 1992.

Tolleneer, Jan. "The Dual Meaning of "Fatherland" and Catholic Gymnasts in Belgium, 1892–1914." *International Journal of the History of Sport* 12, no. 2 (1995): 94–107.

Tomlinson, Alan, and Christopher Young. "Towards a New History of European Sport." *European Review* 19, no. 4 (2011): 487–507.

Van der Beken, Marc. "Inleiding tot de beschrijvende historiek van de moderne paardenrennen in ons land." 1986. Unpub. Master's Diss., KU Leuven.

Vangrunderbeek, Hans, Roel Soors, and Pascal Delheye. *Omnes currunt, sed unus accipit bravium: van aartsbisschoppelijk sportverbond tot koninklijke Vlaamse voetbalbond 1907–2007*. Leuven: Acco, 2008.

Vanmeerbeek, Roger. "Plus de sueur, moins de sang? Entraînement physique et sport militaire en Belgique 1945–1995." Unpub. PhD Diss., KU Leuven 2012.

Vanysacker, Dries. *Van FC Brugeois tot Club Brugge KV (1891–2010): de maatschappelijke inbedding van een Brugse, Vlaamse, Belgische en Europese voetbalploeg*. Brugge: Van de Wiele, 2010.

Winter, Caroline. "Battlefield Visitor Motivations: Explorations in the Great War Town of Ieper, Belgium." *International Journal of Tourism Research* 13 (2011): 164–176.

Witte, Els, Craeybeckx, Jan, and Meynen, Alain, eds. *Politieke geschiedenis van België: van 1830 tot heden*. 6th ed. Antwerp: Standaard, 1997.

Witte, Els. "De Constructie van België." In *Nieuwe geschiedenis van Belgie. I. 1830–1905*, edited by Els Witte, Jean-Pierre Nandrin, Eliane Gubin, and Gita Deneckere, 29–235. Tielt: Lannoo, 2006.

Monarchy, Socialism and Modern Capitalism: Hungary's Participation in Three London Olympic Games

Nikoletta Onyestyák

Semmelweis University, Budapest, Hungary

Olympic sport is a double-edged sword. It has the potential to bring nations together and to transmit values, but it can also demonstrate international political tensions and conflicting national structural characteristics. As part of the International Olympic Movement from the very beginning, Hungary is one of the few nations to have taken part in the (Summer) Olympic Games in London for the third time. The Olympic presence of Hungary has been almost continuous in spite of the significant transformations of its state ideology, sport structures and political background. In 1908, within the framework of the Austro-Hungarian Monarchy, the Hungarian Kingdom endeavoured to demonstrate its autonomy and courage with its memorable Olympic successes in London. A People's Republic was being formed in Hungary at the time of the second London Olympic Games in 1948. The socialist ideology and the self-display of socialist–communist ambitions characterised the preparation and the participation of the Hungarian athletes. Hungary is celebrating the year of its third London Games with a democratic system in the background, built up from 1989, and a new Constitution adopted in 2011. Furthermore, the Hungarian Sport Act was renewed in 2012, due to which the Hungarian Olympic Committee has gained increased power, which might provide new ways of solving the financial problems within Hungarian elite sport.

Introduction

The creation of the Modern Olympic Movement not only provided a significant opportunity for outstanding athletes of various nations to demonstrate their strength and preparedness in different sports in a peaceful framework of sportsmanship, but the international Olympic arena also produced new types of struggles, including competition at an international level for medals and for national honour, competition for positions in international sporting bodies, primarily in the International Olympic Committee (IOC), and even the fight for the right to host the Olympic Games.

London, in 2012, has become the first city to host the games for the third time, but if we analyse the circumstances surrounding these three occasions, we can see that London had to overcome major difficulties. Its debut in 1908 was a decision made suddenly after the withdrawal of Rome due to the eruption of Vesuvius; Rome having only two years to prepare for the competitions. The second hosting also happened in a challenging time after the destructions of the Second World War, when all nations were focusing on their recovery after losses endured during the six years of the war. The selection of the host city for 2012 was celebrated in Singapore in 2005. At long last there were no natural catastrophes and no extensive destructive wars that put obstacles in London's way, and finally that city has had seven years to prepare to host the 30th Summer Olympic Games.

Not only has the host city had to cope with different internal and international difficulties, within specific political, ideological and structural frameworks, but many participating countries have also had to do so. In the beginning of the twentieth century, the organisation, structuring and financing of sport in Central and Eastern Europe were still in its infancy, and the creation of the International Olympic Movement gave a significant impetus to the development of competitive sport. Until after the First World War, Hungary was a monarchy with a common Austrian–Hungarian monarch, an emperor in Austria and a king in Hungary. Having its own parliament and government, most political matters were decided within the country but there were some matters in which Hungary had to conciliate with Austria, and autonomous Hungarian actions were restricted. After the Second World War, the introduction of a socialist ideology and political structure created new targets. With a focus on sport, the main aim was to reach outstanding results at international level and to display the excellence of the socialist regime. The new system changed the role of sport in society along with the position of its athletes. Finally, after the 1989–1990 regime changes, sport had to maintain its high-level performance within the framework of a free market, characterised by the cutbacks of state financial resources. Sport has had to cope with the challenges of the market, economic competition and other social and global threats.

Unfortunately, sport could never totally separate itself from politics, its ideological expectations and its structural foundation. Its financial decisions and its diplomatic casting deeply influenced the preparation, participation and results of Hungarian athletes in the great international events. The main aim of this paper is to present the political and ideological background in Hungary during the time of three different London Olympic Games, and to highlight those personal and organisational differences, which strongly influenced the performance of Hungarian Olympic athletes.

The research is principally based on document analyses. Official documents of the respective ministries, political parties, sport governing bodies and minutes and correspondence of the Hungarian Olympic Committee (HOC) were studied, and Hungarian references concerning the London Games' final reports were evaluated. Important researchers reflected on topics related to the Hungarian Olympic Movement and successes, so this work also used different books, articles and publications. In describing the current situation, the statements are based on the revised version of the 2004 Hungarian Sport Act[1] and the statutes of the reorganised HOC.[2]

London 1908

During the nineteenth century, national consciousness increased within the multi-national Austrian Empire, and some years after the Hungarian revolution for independence of 1848–1849, the Austro-Hungarian Compromise of 1867 was made, which inaugurated the dual structure of the Austro-Hungarian Empire. There were only three common Imperial and Royal Ministries: the Foreign Ministry, the Ministry of the War and the Ministry of Finance. All other state functions were handled separately by each of the two states. Consequently, sport was a national matter, but in some cases the liberty of the sportsmen was restricted due to imperial considerations.

Hungary's Olympic participation, along with that of Britain, began with the very first modern games. The HOC was formed in 1895, being the sixth national Olympic committee to be created. Ferenc Kemény, who was also a founding member of the IOC, played an important role in the introduction of Olympism and its values into Hungary.

The background for modern sport was being consolidated at the end of the nineteenth century in Hungary on the basis of the influence of two main European sporting schools. Hungarian sport organisations followed either the traditions of the English athletic movement, which was basically the fields of individual and competitive sport, or the German Turnen system, which favoured the public and pedagogical aspects of sport, using gymnastics as a focus. Clubs and institutions were created within both systems, but the comprehensive governing bodies of sport were divided due to the strong tensions between athletes and gymnasts.[3] The HOC turned out to be an important battlefield for the opposing ambitions of the gymnasts and athletes. During this early history of the sporting institution process in Hungary, the political leadership regarded sport as a possible field for its national endeavours; consequently, the HOC followed the official sporting and political aims of the state. Its presidents were selected from the main sports clubs/organisations of the time, but they were at the same time political actors. At the turn of the twentieth century, they generally came from wealthy aristocratic families. Albert Berzeviczy, the first president of the HOC, was also president of the Hungarian Parliament and later held the position of Minister of Religion and Public Education. The second president of the HOC, Count Imre Széchenyi, was an important politician regarding agricultural matters at the time. His successor, Count Sándor Teleki, was a colonel in the Hungarian army. Géza Andrássy, who was elected to lead the HOC a few months before the first London Olympics of 1908, was at the same time a deputy in the parliament.

The main Hungarian sport organisation, following the system of the English athletic movement, was the Hungarian Athletic Club (MAC). Founded in 1875, athletics also appeared at the federation level in 1897. The German Turnen system was followed by the National Gymnastics Club (NTE), the first sports club in Hungary, which was founded in 1867, and the federation responsible for its creation was the Hungarian Federation of Body Training Clubs (MTESz), created in 1885. The gymnastics–athletics conflict gave a special atmosphere to Hungarian sporting life at the turn of the century, supported by a much-reported argument in the related press. Newspapers entitled *Gymnastic Case*, and later, *National Sport*, supported the ideology of the NTE, and *Sporting World* was connected to the MAC.[4]

The ideological rivalry of the two main sporting clubs and their respective federations also influenced the activities of the HOC and began a continuing struggle within that organisation for positions on its board of directors, which only lessened in the second decade of the century. Ferenc Kemény was the first secretary general of the HOC and was also a member of the IOC. As an influential personality within the NTE, he soon became an important target for MAC pursuit. In spite of his commitment to the Olympic Movement, and as a result of the hostile actions of the MAC leaders, he finally decided to resign from his IOC and HOC positions in April 1907.[5] Consequently, he could not visit the London Olympic Games officially, and both his crucial positions related to the Olympic Movement had to be filled as the fourth Olympic Games was approaching.

Until his resignation, Mr Kemény had been considered the key individual between the IOC and the HOC. He was a good friend of Baron De Coubertin, and they were in continuous correspondence with each other. On the November 18, 1906, Coubertin informed Ferenc Kemény, in a confidential letter, about the obstacles of organising the 1908 games in Rome and the endeavours of the Greeks to break up the IOC.

The correspondence reveals that they discussed the possibility of choosing London as a new host city, and they agreed that 'these Olympic Games would be gorgeous if they could be held on the banks of the Thames'.[6] Although the official IOC decision had not yet been made, Mr Kemény and Pierre De Coubertin had already begun to prepare their respective organisations for the celebration of the Olympic Games in London.

Soon, when the final venue of the 1908 games had been nominated, correspondence concerning the preparation with the English organisers began. Kemény forwarded the main information to the Hungarian Ministry of Religion and Public Education, responsible, inter alia, for sporting matters, and sketched the main duties that were to be carried out in Hungary, writing:

> I would respectfully like to make your Excellency aware that I have received a letter from Lord Desbrough, the President of the British Olympic Association, in which he refers to the fact that the 1908 Olympic Games would be held in London. He requests me to officially take the necessary actions in order to create the formation of the Hungarian Olympic Committee. [...] On this basis I presume to ask your Excellency to take further measures and to separate 10,000 crowns from next year's budget for Hungary's participation in the 1908 London Olympic Games.[7]

The HOC was, at the outset, an organisation that functioned only periodically. After considering the requirements necessary for Olympic preparations, the Minister of Religion and Public Education, Count Albert Apponyi, declared that the HOC should function on a continuous basis in the future. Nevertheless, at the time of Lord Desborough's invitation, Minister Apponyi's role was only to 'proceed towards congregating an Olympic assembly with the cooperation of the partner associations' until the December 15 of the year before the Olympic Games, according to a decree from 1904.[8] Consequently, he sent a letter concerning this matter to the presidents of the following sport federations: the Hungarian Athletics Federation, the Hungarian Federation of the Rowing Associations, the Hungarian Cycling Federation, the Hungarian Football Federation, the Hungarian Federation of the Body Training Clubs and the Hungarian Fencing Federation. At the same time, he was asked by Ferenc Kemény to nominate the official delegate to the Olympic Games on behalf of the Ministry of Religion and Public Education, which traditionally had been Ferenc Kemény himself.[9] This request was absolutely logical because from the beginning of modern Olympic history, as an IOC member and the HOC Secretary General, he was always appointed the Hungarian representative.

With the approach of the congregation of the HOC, the struggle within the organisations escalated. Yet, in March 1907, Mr Kemény was asked by the editor of the prominent sports newspaper *Sporting-World* to write an editorial about the necessity of an overall Olympic assembly, with the participation of all sports federations. However, in spite of this request, the sports periodical reported two weeks later that there was 'a violent and harsh struggle among the sport federations within the framework of the Olympic Committee for the leadership of the Olympic organisation'.[10] The article touched upon the unacceptable actions of the MAC concerning the preparations for the Olympic Assembly. The president of the Athletics Federation, István Bárczy, ignored that organisation's duty to cooperate and conciliate with the gymnasts' organisations, and peremptorily sent out invitations to the Olympic Assembly, intentionally not inviting Mr Kemény. The Secretary General of the MAC, Szilárd Stankovits, contacted the Minister Count Apponyi by letter after having observed that the other federations were disappointed about the excessive ambitions of the Athletics Federation. These federations also objected to the hostile activity of the MAC towards Ferenc Kemény.

The Athletics Federation lobbied the Ministry hoping to reach their main aim of redrafting the 1904 decree on the Olympic Assembly. They listed three important and convincing reasons supporting the need for revision. First of all, the MAC leaders pointed out that the Olympic Games were traditionally a significant athletic competition, which would even be more like that in England, the home of modern athletics; subsequently, they considered it desirable to have members of the Athletics Federation in a majority on the HOC. The actual decree did not support any inequity of representation of the different sports in the HOC.

Second, the Federation stressed that a considerable tension had recently developed within Hungarian sport that might serve as an obstacle to cooperation amongst the federations, and which would deter the work of the HOC. They thought that having a majority representation of athletics within the HOC could help resolve this misunderstanding and eliminate this structural obstacle.

Third, the current decree offered an exaggerated degree of authority to the Hungarian members of the IOC, at the time being led by Ferenc Kemény. This situation, in their opinion, disabled the work of the Committee. The MAC representatives stated that Ferenc Kemény was completely unpopular within sporting society, and consequently, they considered him inconvenient and undeserving of being a representative of Hungarian sport abroad.[11]

On the April 4, 1907, a year before the inauguration of the first London Games, Ferenc Kemény sent a staggering letter to the Hungarian Olympic Preparatory Commission, apologising for his absence from the Assembly (he was invited by five federations, not including the Athletics Federation) and asking them to accept his resignation from both the HOC and IOC. He wrote:

> When I see that the London Olympiad and my international membership are being used by the Hungarian Athletics Federation to capitalize on their quest for power, and they want to sell me for their own aims as a cheap instrument and use me as a weapon in this struggle — being a person outside the federations — my only duty can be to make an effort towards the reparation of the peace. My last and strongest tool regarding that is my departure and resignation from my IOC membership, a duty I have fulfilled since the foundation of the organization.[12]

After Mr Kemény's resignation, six federations began preparatory work for the Olympic Games by reorganising the HOC on the basis of its renewed statutes and listing the tasks of the committee regarding the forthcoming Olympic Games. The organisational and institutional background of the Hungarian Olympic athletes seemed to be settled, and even Ferenc Kemény regarded this peaceful cooperation as personal recompense. He wrote:

> I see that my intention paid off and my forecast was fulfilled, inasmuch as with the cost of my sport-harakiri; the Olympic peace is settled, which hopefully will be the base for the development of a general Hungarian sport peace. I wish, with all my heart a long life to it![13]

Kemény's place on the IOC still had to be filled, so the Hungarian Olympic Assembly proposed Gyula Muzsa as his successor. Minister Apponyi decided to delegate Mr Muzsa to represent Hungary at the IOC Hague Congress in May 1907, with the task of officially informing the assembly about Kemény's withdrawal and to ask them to proceed on the basis of the Olympic Statutes concerning the fulfilment of Hungarian membership. Géza Andrássy, president of the MAC, was elected IOC member in 1907, and Gyula Muzsa also became an IOC member in 1909. Since then, Hungary has had two members in the IOC.

The background of the 1908 London Olympic Games was not only significant because of the institutional struggle. It was first in London, in 1908, that the teams paraded behind their national flags in the Olympic Games' opening ceremony, which also brought forth nationalist intentions. The participation of the nations of the Austro-Hungarian Empire was an interesting and disputed question. Austria, Bohemia and Hungary paraded separately in 1908, representing different nations, as the whole idea of the opening parade was a new initiative. Four years later in the Stockholm Games, Bohemia was required to march together with the Austrians. Hungary was able to maintain its separateness, using its own nameplate to introduce its athletes, but the position of the Hungarian team was immediately after the Austrian team; the Hungarians did not proceed in alphabetical order.

It was not only the team parade that created a conflict within the Monarchy, as the participation of those athletes serving in the common army was also restricted. A special verdict forbade their participation in the national team; they were forbidden to compete in international events as Hungarians until 1908. Just before the London Games, this restriction was relieved for individual athletes, but Hungarian fencers, who were also soldiers of the Monarchy, were still not allowed to participate in the team events. In spite of these restrictions, Hungarian dominance in the sabre events commenced in the first London Olympic Games.

Twenty-one sports, representing 109 events, were contested in the first London Games, with participating athletes representing 22 National Olympic Committees. Hungarian participation consisted of 63 male athletes in the delegation to London, while this number had been only four at the previous games in Saint Louis. Results in track and field, wrestling and swimming were outstanding, and international public opinion increased, especially due to the fencers' performance.

The fencing matches were held during the 'main' portion of the Olympics. The events were contested outside of the stadium at a nearby site described as 'the fencing ground of the Franco-British Exposition'. There were four events, épée and sabre, for both individuals and teams. The French reigned in the two épée events, sweeping the individual medals and the team gold by beating the team of Great Britain, which had the youngest (Ralph Chalmers) and oldest (Cecil Haig) competitors in the sport. Hungarians dominated the sabre, winning the team finals against Italy 11:5. In the individual finals, there were five Hungarian fencers among the six finalists: Jenő Fuchs (first), Béla Zulawszky (second), Jenő Szántay (fourth), Péter Tóth (fifth) and Lajos Werkner (sixth).

Fuchs' individual victory began the Hungarian winning streak in this event. From 1908 until 1964, a Hungarian fencer always won the sabre gold medal at the Olympics, with the exception of 1920 when Hungary was not invited after the First World War. Hungarians also won all of the world championships in individual sabre from 1923 through 1937 and, after the Second World War, between 1951 and 1955.

Fuchs was of Jewish origin, and the Jews had been barred from bearing arms in the nineteenth century. He did not belong to any fencing club or win any national tournament, but went to the Olympics after placing third in the qualifying competition for the 1908 Olympics. Fuchs was also a top-ranked rower and bobsledder in Hungary.

It is worth mentioning that Ferenc Kemény, the earlier HOC president, visited some of the events of the 1908 London Games incognito, but did not seek out his old Olympic friends as he wanted to avoid even the semblance of intervention in Olympic questions related to the Hungarian team. He received letters from his former Olympic colleagues, R. Tait McKenzie, a professor from Philadelphia, who had desired to have the chance to meet with him in London, and from Coubertin as well, who in his letter of the September 22, 1908, explained:

I learned about your visit to London through Baron Laveyele, and I am awfully sorry that you did not permit me to shake hands with you. Our old colleagues would have also been happy to have seen you again. It is a pity that you did not inform us in advance.[14]

The great assembly of the HOC celebrated its closing session on the December 19, 1908, accepted the Olympic Report, which was to be forwarded to the Minister of Culture, and, having completed its tasks, concluded its business until its reorganisation before the forthcoming Olympic Games of 1912.

London 1948

After the immense devastation of the Second World War, the British again undertook a challenging task, the organisation of the Olympics. Not only did the organisers had difficulties to face, but the post-war international political system created a touchy situation in most of the Eastern European countries including Hungary. Political chaos dominated in Hungary, which led to the party-state dictatorship of Mátyás Rákosi, starting in 1948.

The first post-war democratic parliamentary elections were held on the November 4, 1945. The Soviet Union was occupying the country, and the Hungarian Communist Party availed itself of the occupiers' support. Despite the sweeping victory of the Independent Smallholders Party, a coalitional government was to be formed under Soviet pressure, with the participation of the three left-wing parties (the Social Democrats, the Communists and the Peasants). Gradually their power was whittled away by the use of communist 'salami tactics'. This was a method employed by the Communists to weaken the unity of their adversaries and to set aside and eradicate them. The 1947 elections had already been won by the Communists due to the obvious manipulation of votes, and after the 1948 enforced fusion of the Social Democrats with the Communists, a totalitarian dictatorship began.

Previously, in the coalition era, all parties attempted to use sport for their own interests. A few days after the siege of Budapest, at the end of February 1945, the Temporary Government in Debrecen recognised the establishment of the National Sport Committee, and prominent personalities of sport such as Imre Németh (later Olympic champion in hammer throw), Antal Zempléni and Károly Pataky (sport journalists) began to meet regularly to support the resuscitation of sporting life. Ferenc Mező[15] presented a successful lecture on 'The past and present of the Olympic Games'.[16] All their efforts were extremely important, as the war had resulted in important losses for Hungarian sport. Many athletes, swimmers, water polo players, fencers and football players were killed during the war, on the battlefield, or by the fascists. István Tóth and Antal Vágó, members of the Hungarian football team, were executed by the fascists, as were canoeists Kamill Balatoni, Miklós Kövér, Károly Nagymajtényi and János Veszely. Géza Kertész, football trainer, and Béla Ipoly died on the battlefield.[17]

Among Hungarian elite athletes, many trainers and sport directors of the twentieth century were of Jewish origin, and many of them were executed by fascist soldiers. The president of the sport club MTK, Alfréd Brüll, and two Olympic winners in fencing, János Garay (1928) and Oszkár Gerde (1908, 1912), perished in death camps,[18] and another Olympic winner in fencing, Attila Petschauer (1928, 1932), died in a forced labour battalion. He was one of the heroes in the Oscar-award winning film, director István Szabó's masterpiece, *Sunshine*. Fellow fencer, Endre Kabos, also Olympic champion (1932, 1936), died in November 1944 on Budapest's Margaret Bridge when it was blown up. Ferenc Kemény also lost his life in November 1944. The circumstances of his death were not clarified. He was said to have committed suicide together with his wife in order to escape the atrocities of the war, but this has never been officially confirmed.

Sporting activity and competition was not completely suspended in the first years of the war, but the destruction of the previous two years emptied the competition fields. The Hungarian football team played its last international match on November 7, 1943, and the athletes had to wait in deprivation until August 19, 1945, to play again. The opponent was Austria. Hungarian elite fencers could not participate in world championships from 1937 until 1951. After the war wound down, the fencers who had not been killed were gathered together to continue their training in the troublesome post-war situation.[19]

The fate of Károly Takács, Olympic champion in shooting in 1948 and 1952, was also strongly affected by the war. By 1936, he was a world-class pistol shooter, but was denied a place in the Hungarian shooting team for the 1936 Summer Olympics on the grounds that he was a sergeant, and only commissioned officers were allowed to compete. This prohibition was lifted in Hungary after the Berlin Games, but he also became a master sergeant in 1942. During army training in 1938, his right hand was badly injured when a faulty grenade exploded. Takács was determined to continue his shooting career and switched to shooting with his left hand. He won the Hungarian national pistol shooting championship in the spring of 1939, and was a member of the Hungarian team that won the 1939 ISSF World Shooting Championships. In 1945, he was imprisoned by the Americans, but as soon as he was allowed to go home he started to train again. Takács surprised the world by winning the gold medal at the 1948 Summer Olympics in London at the age of 38, which also meant a promotion for him in his military career. First he was awarded the rank of major, and in 1954 became a lieutenant colonel. He won a second gold medal at the 1952 Summer Olympics in Helsinki and also took part in the 1956 Summer Olympics in Melbourne, where he finished eighth.[20]

After the war, the first national sports organisation was established in February 1945. It was the National Sport Committee, which consisted of 15 members at its inception. Later, it increased in number and power, and the national parliament also ratified its functioning. The bylaws of the new sport administrative body listed the main operative functions: the reactivation of the federations; the assessment of the stage of Hungarian sport and the reorganisation of its main institutions. As a political task, the Committee had to make a list of all those sport-related people who were German-friendly or related to the fascist party.[21] The new political orientation also appeared in the Hungarian press: a new newspaper on sport was launched, which did not hide its open political propaganda activity. In the first issue of *Népsport*, the editor expressed:

> The youth of the workers and the peasants, two important historical classes, are behind us, and we support this youth with fair, straight work. [...] We will deal with the politics, and we will work with all our strength to remove even the last traces of the Nazi-spirit destruction from Hungarian sport. The sport organ of the reactionists [Nemzeti Sport] has become mute forever.[22]

On November 23, 1945, the sport division of the Ministry of Religion and Public Education delivered a report on Hungarian sports life that mirrored the newspaper's tone. The report expressed that:

> ... where the soldiers of the Red Army have already flown the flag of liberty, the flames of life have started to flicker. [...] The work of the Federations will be reorganized democratically; the new officials will be monitored to ensure that they had no role in the creation and management of the fascist-spirit of sport over the past years.[23]

Concerning the organisation of sport, the activities of the different parties' sport departments increased, and on the basis of their membership they created new clubs. The so-called 'Friendship' Sport Club was of the 'Social Democrats'; the 'Kinizsi' Sport Club belonged to the Independent Smallholders. After the arrival of the first IOC invitation to the 1948 Olympic Games, the Hungarian parties, responding to the IOC requests on January 7, 1947, convened an important sport congress, during which they entered into discussion, on the one hand, regarding sport leadership in Hungary, and on the other, the reorganisation of the HOC. The parties circuitously discussed the future position of the new HOC, whether it was to be autonomous or overseen. Although the Communists supported the subordination of the Olympic body under the National Sport Committee, those members at the meeting agreed upon the creation of a separate committee, to be under the control of the Main Sport Council. The new HOC was formed on February 16, 1947, for a definite time period of four years. Holding the key posts were communist Alajos Jámbor (president), Sándor Barcs (co-president) from the Independent Smallholders and Jenő Verebes (Secretary General).

As part of the preparations for the first post-war Olympic Games, another new newspaper called *Sporting Life* was launched on the first day of 1947. Ferenc Mező expressed in its editorial that *Sporting Life* 'would be the trombone of the Olympic spirit, which was willing to join together the different nations and its people'.[24]

The composition of the IOC was somewhat problematic after the Second World War as some of the earlier members had died or disappeared. Hungary had no active member in the IOC for a while; its two earlier members could not complete their tasks as Gyula Muzsa died in 1946 and Miklós Horthy junior was imprisoned by the Gestapo – the latter remained abroad after his release. Consequently, before the second London Games, there was another lapse of Hungarian presence on the IOC. Nevertheless, Hungary's intention to continue its participation in the Olympic Movement was undiminished, and on February 17, 1947, Ferenc Mező was invited to represent the IOC in Hungary. He was a member of the Social Democratic Party, and at the same time the leader of the Physical Education Office of the Ministry of Religion and Public Education. He played an important role in the reorganisation of the Hungarian sport administration after the Second World War, and afterwards continued his work in the International Olympic Movement.[25] In contrast with the first half of the twentieth century, after the Second World War, Hungary had only one IOC member until 2000, when Tamás Aján was elected as the second Hungarian on the Committee.

The Hungarian Communist Party recognised quite quickly that sport could be a strategic exhibition field for political ideologies. In November 1947, the party was the first to develop its sport programme in 29 points 'in order to solve all the questions related to Hungarian Sport', which was published in 1947 in the November 23 issue of *Népsport*. The programme emphasised the need for the organisation of mass sport, the development of quality sport, the importance of sport education, the protection of athletes' health, the strengthening of the sport institutions and the support of international sporting relations with democratic countries. However, a few months later, in March 1948, the Hungarian National Independence Front, composed of the five main parties (Communists, Social Democrats, Peasants, Smallholders and National Democrats), also formulated its own common sports programme, in which they expressed that one of the most important tasks was to raise money and to guarantee the financial conditions concerning the London Games. On the other hand, they were saying that mass sporting activity needed to be established and consolidated quickly in Hungary.[26] The Front did not function for very long as it was soon devastated by the Communist salami tactics.

When the IOC Olympic invitation arrived in 1947, sport in Hungary was already being overseen by the Hungarian Communist Party. There were two opposing opinions within the party; some members believed that the participation of any communist country would be harmful, whereas others believed that Hungary should demonstrate the superiority of the peoples' democracy in the Olympic Games. The party prescribed severe regulations for both sports leaders and athletes in order to safeguard them from harmful capitalist ideology. Hungarian athletes could finally go to London.

In the spring of 1948, the National Sport Office was created and authorised to govern international relations in sport. Consequently, the autonomous HOC was put under its total control, which in practice meant the nationalisation of the Olympic institution. The centralisation of Hungarian sport organisations was exceptionally intense as important international sporting events were to be held in 1948. Hungarian athletes could only participate in events held in western countries with the permission of the state security service, which built up an expanded monitoring system. The security service consisted of communist agents, gathered from all walks of life, and consequently, athletes were also installed into it as secret agents. When competing abroad, athletes had to be accompanied by agents of the Party, the Federations and the National Sport Office, and later, its successor organisations. Sometimes, if travel by an individual considered by the security services as 'dangerous' was seen as crucial (for the sake of the results), unreliable athletes were allowed to travel out of the country if the leaders of the Sport Office and HOC, Gusztáv Sebes or Gyula Hegyi, could vouch personally for the behaviour of those athletes.

Sport became a tool increasingly used to express the superiority of the 'socialist political system', and its Stalinist principles, to disseminate its ideology and to a stark contrast to capitalism, thus emphasising the advantages of socialism. The requirement of outstanding international sporting results required the use of large sums of money to support elite sport and to create adequate institutions and facilities for sport. The Hungarian Communist Party clearly expressed its expectations towards the Olympics: 'The success of Hungarian athletes in the London Games would increase our reputation, reinforce the faith in the Hungarian restoration, and would reinforce the acknowledgement of our sport-power'.[27]

The National Sport Office considered Hungarian performance at the 1948 Olympics extremely important as it was the first summer games in which Hungary participated as a developing socialist country, so special support was given for its preparation. On May 4, 1948, less than three months before the opening ceremony, the Sport Office authorised the building of a collective Olympic training camp. The location of the venue was also selected by the party and sports leaders at the time, who were searching for a place with similar climate parameters to London, as they were anxious about the humid weather in England. Tata, a lakeside town, seemed to be adequate, and on May 30, 1948, building operations started there, and within one month, a roofed sports hall, a boat house, a gym, a track and field court, a horse stable and dressing rooms with showers were built, and a college was converted into a modern hotel.

At first, 11 of the 13 sports federations opposed the idea of collective training, arguing that it was harmful to take the athletes out of their habitual environment and family milieu. They further argued that the free time of the athletes could not be reasonably used, and the lack of modern facilities impeded the athletes' professional work.[28] Nevertheless, successes in the London Olympics seemed to justify the use of the camp. The track and field stadium in Tata was built to the same specifications as Wembley Stadium, which might be important considering that Imre Németh, after his preparations in Tata, was able to break the world record in the hammer throw in London. The further development of the camp continued after London until its official opening as a complex training venue in 1951. It continues to be used to prepare Hungarian Olympic athletes to this day.

According to recollections of Olympic athletes, the main attraction of the place was the abundant catering, which allowed the athletes to reserve food for their family members who lived in impoverished conditions. Gyula Bóbis, London gold medallist in wrestling, declared:

> I have competed for 24 years, [. . .] and my main problem was that I could never eat suitably. I am grateful to my current leaders, because this is not a problem any more. I am grateful for the Tata training camp, where I could reach my best shape ever, reaching 107 kilos.[29]

Female fencers remembered:

> To be together all the time, the military-like order and the discipline seemed to be strange, but soon we realized the many advantages to the camp. [. . .] Athletes from all sports were together there, watching each other's trainings, challenges, and we soon became a community. Consequently, a united, determined Hungarian team could travel to London.[30]

These memories reveal another important characteristic of the socialist era. Being a top athlete signified a distinctive status, security, provisioning, a chance to travel abroad and a chance to import western goods illegally. During their preparation period, the income of many Olympic athletes increased, their apartment problems were solved and they were given financial support if they required it.[31]

The groundwork of the National Stadium also started just before the 1948 London Games, so important construction projects were attached to elite sport. Nevertheless, the HOC had to cope with all its duties related to the preparations and participation in the 1948 winter and summer games with the lack of a secure financial footing. In the budget calculations, the minimum requirement for the winter games was 300,000 forints, while for the summer games more than 2,500,000 forints were required. Eventually, the central support funded the participation of 129 Hungarian athletes.

Hungary's performance in the first post-war games completely measured up to the expectations of the communists with its 28 Olympic medals (10 gold, 5 silver and 13 bronze), finishing in fourth place in the unofficial ranking of the participating nations. The 1948 Olympic Games can be considered a successful starting point for the following decades of outstanding Hungarian performance in gymnastics.

The gymnastics competitions in London were to be held in the Empire Stadium, but torrential rain on the weekend of August 7–9 rendered it unfit for the events, and the whole competition was therefore moved to Empress Hall, Earl's Court. The official report of the 1948 Games emphasises that gymnastics had been maintained at the high level seen in the Olympic Games before the war, and it also points out that the physique of the men's teams coming from the devastated areas of Europe was marvellous. Hungary won a silver medal in the women's team all-around and a bronze in the men's team all-around, as well as another two bronze medals, and a silver and gold individual medal.

The long war period was reflected in the average age of the teams; for instance, the age of the Hungarian team was over 30. The most successful competitor, Ferenc Pataki, had previously expected to participate in the Olympics in 1940, but due to the war he could only be there in 1948, winning a gold medal with his marvellous floor exercise, beating his team-mate János Mogyorósi-Klencs, who finished second. They both won a bronze medal, achieving the same points in the vault, and another bronze in the team all-around.

Pataki represented the changes in sport related to the post-war political transition. He started his sporting career at the 7th district Levente Club, whose framework resulted from the 1921 Law on Physical Education adopted by the right wing, German-friendly government of the time. The main objective of the Levente Movement was to ensure physical activity for all men under the age of 21, including them in a sport-frame military training. This law tried to solve the problem resultant from the 1920 peace treaty, which limited the permitted number of soldiers in Hungary. After the war, one of the first steps taken by the Soviet-friendly Hungarian government was the abolition of the Levente Movement, so Ferenc Pataki had to enter the socialist style Workers' Training Club, which was monitored by the Hungarian Socialist Workers Party, and later from 1950 he was a gymnast at the Red Meteor Club.

After the end of the London games, the returning Olympic team was received by János Kádár,[32] Minister of Home Affairs, and at a ceremonial reception he greeted the athletes with the following:

> All of you, our dear athletes, should be aware that our glorious performance in the Olympic Games was due to the sacrifice of the Hungarian working people. In the international field of sport it is well known, that the new democratic leading forces allowed this great development of Hungarian sporting life. You were worthy representatives of the Hungarian working people, who have successfully risen from a deep gulch. Our nation is working and building. Be the leading flag-carriers of the big building work in your field, in sport![33]

London 2012

As a consequence of the 1989–1990 political and economic transformations, the earlier, so-called socialist sport model collapsed in Eastern Europe, and restructuring was carried out in several organisations. Curiously, relevant changes at the top or the middle managerial levels were not attached to the restructuring, and consequently, a modernised sport model could not be founded.

The external and internal political, economic, and social changes posed permanent challenges in the countries concerned and the sports sphere seemed to be unable to give truly successful and adequate answers to many of them.[34]

Hungarian sport is widely believed to be a loser within the 1989–1990 political and economic transitions. People inside and outside sporting circles argued that sport had been de-valued and the state had withdrawn from it, but as Földesiné believes, this general interpretation and the explanation for the failure has proved to be mistaken.[35] It is true that elite sport was in an outstanding position during state socialism, having been provided with all the financial means possible even under the worst economic circumstances. Nevertheless, social inequalities were present even within elite sport due to the Olympic centralism, and other fields of sports were left in an unfavourable position.[36]

After the 1989–1990 transformation, the consecutive governments in power have changed their approach to sport, and continuous structural and legal alterations have been carried out. Within 20 years, three sport acts and several amendments to them were issued and the highest sport authority's organisation was restructured eight times followed by the nomination of nine new national sport presidents, ministers, ministers of state and under-secretaries.[37]

After long debate, a National Sport Strategy was accepted by the Hungarian Parliament in 2007, with two main aims: the maintenance of the high status of Hungarian elite sport and the promotion of participation in sport. It seems to be a little unrealistic to try to fulfil both aims, especially the first one, while the lack of financial guarantees makes this even more complicated.[38]

More than 20 years after the political and economic transition in Hungary, sport seems to be exposed more than ever to the influence of the tendencies of the market. Those sports which – in spite of the Hungarian sporting traditions and international successes – are not regarded as good fields for business are struggling in a challenging situation, dependent on the support from government and public and private foundations. In this new capitalist era,

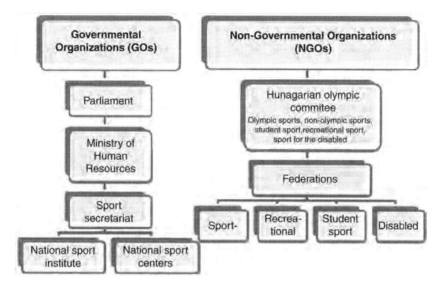

Figure 1.   The structure of Hungarian Sport governing bodies in 2012.

the separation of governmental and non-governmental sectors has become a reality; a clear border can be drawn between the public and civil organisations.[39] This also means that non-governmental civil organisations have recovered their autonomy, and sports clubs, federations and civil directive bodies have begun to function on their own. There is no continuous political interference in their decisions, no political control over their activities and no special political expectations from them (see Figure 1).

State activity in sport is confined to legal regulation, primarily to the current Sport Law[40] in which the legal, institutional, financial and infrastructural foundations of sport are defined. After the numerous variations surrounding the sport institutional system since the political and economic transformation, the actual system gives an especially reinforced power to the HOC, commissioning it as the main governing organisation of the non-governmental sector of sport. The governance of all fields of sport, including elite sport, mass sport, student sport, competitive and non competitive sport and sport for the disabled, is featured within the HOC, being operated by autonomous departments. The HOC is now the only official administrative channel between the state and the civil sport sector, being responsible for all fields of sport and the management and distribution of state financial support. It actually has different sport departments focusing on all fields of sport, but this does not overshadow its traditional tasks related to the Olympic Games. Consequently, the HOC defined its main goals for the 2012 London Olympic Games as follows:

(1)   in spite of the unfavourable changes in sport financing, finishing among the first 20 in the competition of the participating countries regarding the medal contest and the non-official point contest;

(2)   obtaining the right to participate in 20–22 sports, and in the most competitive events possible, proving the versatility of Hungarian sport culture and the diversity of our Olympic traditions and ambitions;

(3)   athletes, who qualified for the Olympic Games, should display their best performance in the competitions;

(4) athletes of the Hungarian team should compete according to the principles of fair play, and without doping;

(5) upon the completion of the Games, a review of the results can show if the goals were entirely met. Furthermore, the larger question of how the Olympic Committee will be able to function in the future regarding all of its sport-related tasks and challenges can begin to be addressed.

Olympic Hosting – Hungary, Great Britain

The year 2012 marked London's third time of hosting the Olympic Games; the city had already proved its aptitude, from an organisation perspective, in two previous historic periods, and in addition, Great Britain has proved to be an outstanding performer in the field of sport. Hungary is the only IOC member to place in the top 10 countries in the unofficial Summer Olympic Games' ranking which has not yet hosted an Olympic competition.

When the modern Olympic Movement was launched with the foundation of the IOC in 1894, and seeing the financial problems related to Athens' ability to organise the first Olympics, Hungary offered to replace the Greek city in case of its withdrawal, but finally the Greek crown prince took up the question. Hungary endeavoured to gain the privilege of hosting the Games in 1920, and an unofficial poll concerning this question was held at the 1914 IOC Congress. The strong support of Budapest was unambiguous, but the losing nations of the First World War were penalised by the sporting world and were not even able to participate in the 1920 Olympics. Budapest competed for the hosting of the 1936 games as well, but lost to Berlin, and its bid for 1944 was swept away by the war. After the commanding Hungarian results in the Helsinki Games in 1952, Budapest tried again to make a potential bid, but to offer international attention and glorification to a communist dictatorship by giving it the right to organise the Summer Games was not an option for the IOC.

In the last few decades, the interest of nations, athletes and markets towards the Olympic Games has increased immensely, and consequently, the Olympics has become a mega event that only powerful and economically potent nations are able to host. With the launching of the series of Youth Olympic Games, a new opportunity was created for smaller and weaker countries with big sporting ambitions.

Conclusions

The Olympic Games have, over time, become irreversibly intertwined with politics. This is evident in the use of the games as a political tool by some of the host cities, governments of the participating countries, political pressure groups and even terrorists. In many cases, the political events surrounding the games have overshadowed the sporting achievements of the games themselves, or at least historians cannot only commemorate the sporting performances of the earlier generations for what they are, but must report on the political, economic and ideological framework of the sport movement. This means that the games have effectively become more of a publicity and media tool than an environment for sporting competitiveness, especially in the era of the Cold War when political structures had to be supported through sport.

The celebration of the Summer Olympic Games in London happened in three totally different time periods of the modern Olympic Movement (Figure 2). The first occasion was in the years of dénouement, when London had to correct the mistakes committed in the first three games. Hungary participated for a fourth time in the first London Games, and its main challenge was to cope with the conflicting conception about its national

	London 1908	London 1948	London 2012
State structure	Austro-hungarian monarchy	II.Hungarian republic	III.Hungarian republic
Main state sport institution	Ministry of religion and public education	National sport office under the ministry of religion and public education	Sport secretariat under the ministry of human resources
HOC function	Direction of the olympicissues in hungary	Direction of the olympicissues in hungary	Direction of all sport questions, as a non-governmental,public organization
HOC president	Count géza andrássy	Alajos jámbor Gusztáv sebes	Zsolt Borkai
Hungarian IOC members	Count géza andrássy	Ferenc mező	Pál schmitt Tamás aján
Number of hungarian Athletes	63	128	157
Medals won (G/S/B)	3/4/2	10/5/13	8/4/5
Hungary's non-official ranking	7.	4.	9.

Figure 2.   Comparison of the three London Olympic Games.

framework within the Austro-Hungarian Empire and with the fact that Hungary had not yet created a separate state sports body. Therefore, Hungarian sport depended on existing clubs, patronising aristocrats, and the Ministry of Religion and Public Education for financial and infrastructural support. Lobbying activity and international recognition of the president of the HOC were crucial aspects concerning the advocacy of sport and elite sport. The struggle between the two main sport clubs and federations, the athletes and the gymnasts infected Hungarian sport and led to the renouncement of a talented and internationally accepted sport diplomat, Ferenc Kemény.

The era of the second London Olympics was totally unfavourable for Hungary as the newly introduced socialist regime was commencing its 40-year reign and sport became a strategic field for the politicians. Consequently, plans were created to increase the level of Hungarian elite sport, which required extensive financial support from the state. Being a top athlete indicated a special status, and politicians tended to explain the superiority of the socialist system by using outstanding sporting results.

In 2012, the legal regulation of sport in Hungary has provided an official and structured framework to attract capital from the market in addition to governmental support of sport, and the increased role of the HOC verifies the commitment of the government towards sport.

Notes on Contributor

Nikoletta Onyestyák, PhD, Assistant professor in Semmelweis University Budapest, Department of Sport Management and Recreation. PhD in Sport Sciences in Hungarian Sport History. Member of the International Society for the History of Physical Education and Sport.

Notes

1. 2004. évi I. törvény a sportról, http://www.mob.hu/downloadmanager/details/id/64/
2. http://www.mob.hu/images/MOB/20120226_MOB_Alapszabaly.pdf
3. Szabó, *A torna atlétika háború nagy vesztese.*
4. Szikora, *A magyar egyetemi és főiskolai sport története 1918-ig. DOC IV. évfolyam 1. szám,* 5–30.
5. Szikora, *A Nemzetközi Olimpiai Bizottság első magyar tagja.*
6. Coubertin's letter to Ferenc Kemény on November 8, 1906. Mező Ferenc Gyűjtemény K-82/19.
7. Letter of Mr Kemény to the Minister of Religion and Public Education on February 6, 1907. MOL – VKM – K592 – 1923 – 14 – 48013/13230/1907/389.
8. Letter of the Minister of Religion and Public Education to the sport association on March 9, 1907. MOL – VKM – K592 – 1923 – 14 – 48013/13229/1907.
9. Letter from Ferenc Kemény to count Apponyi on February 7, 1907. MOL – VKM – K592 – 1923 – 14 – 48013/13229/1907.
10. Sport-Világ 1907. XVI/13.
11. MAC letter to Minister Apponyi on March 30, 1907. MOL – VKM – K592 – 1923 – 14 – 48013/32378/1907.
12. Kemény's letter to the Hungarian Olympic Preparatory Commission on April 4, 1907. MOL – VKM – K592 – 1923 – 14 – 48013/37933/1907.
13. Letter of Ferenc Kemény to Román Malecki, Editor of Sport-Világ, April 14, 1907. Sportvilág XVI./16. 133.1.
14. Collection of Ferenc Mező, K-83-24.
15. Dr Ferenc Mező is one of the most important figures in Hungarian sport historiography. His interest in sport was first piqued with the Athens Olympic Games. He is considered to be the most important collector and researcher of them even today. As a classical philologist, he primarily researched the history of antique Greek Olympic Games and the Hungarian reception of classical antique authors. He participated in the literature section of the 1928 Olympic Games artistic contest with his work entitled "The History of the Olympic Games". According to the jury, this book was unique worldwide in its thoroughness and the author was honoured with the gold medal.
16. Collection of Ferenc Mező, K-67-13.
17. Vida, *Sportpolitikai irányelvekés határozatok a magyar sporttörténelemben.*
18. Szabó, *Reason of World-Wide Success, Kézirat.*
19. Elek and Elek, *Így vívtunk mi.*
20. Takács, *Takács Károly Katonai és Sportpályafutása,* 385–94.
21. Credentials, February 20, 1945. Documents of the Ministry of Religion and Public Education. 1039/1945.
22. Népsport I/1. April 24, 1945. Editorial.
23. Summary report for the Ministry of Religion and Public Education. November 23, 1945. NSB iratok 1946–178.
24. *Sporting Life,* 1947. I./1.
25. Szabó, *A szellem világbajnoka. ME-DOC IV. évfolyam 1. Szám,* 79–83.
26. Documents of the National Sport Committee, March 1, 1948. Vegyes iratok, 18, csomó.
27. Kutassi, *A Magyar Kommunista Párt Sportpolitikája,* 150.
28. Váradi, Mihály – Marton, László, *A Tatai Edzőtábor szerepe a magyar sport életében.*

29. Szalay, *A magyar sport 40 éve (1945–1985)*.
30. Elek and Elek, *Így vívtunk mi*, 77.
31. Papp, *A félévszázados Tatai Edzőtábor történetének*.
32. After the 1956 Hungarian revolution, János Kádár became the emblematic figure of the Hungarian regime for three decades, holding the position of the first secretary of the Hungarian Socialist Working Party.
33. Speech of János Kádár at the reception of the 1948 Olympic athletes, August 19, 1948, Népsport.
34. Földesiné, *Interaction of Sport and Society*.
35. Földesiné, *What Does Hungarian Sport Expect from Society Rightly or Wrongly? Hungarian Sport Science Booklets V. MSTT*, 49–64.
36. Földesiné, *Transformation of Sport in Eastern Europe*, 5–21.
37. Földesiné, *Class or Mass*, 147–56.
38. Földesiné, *What Does Hungarian Sport Expect from Society Rightly or Wrongly?*, 49–64.
39. Földesiné, *Post Transformational Trends*, 137–46.
40. Hungarian Law on Sport: 2004. I. tv., with amendments of 2011. CLXXII. tv, http://net.jogtar. hu/jr/gen/hjegy_doc.cgi?docid=A0400001.TV

References

Elek, I., and M. Elek. *Így Vívtunk Mi. Sport*. Budapest, 1968.

Földesiné, S. G. "The Transformation of Sport in Eastern Europe: The Hungarian Case." *Journal of Comparative Physical Education and Sport* XV, no. 1 (1993): 5–21.

Földesiné, S. G. "Post-Transformational Trends in Hungarian Sport (1995–2004)," *Physical Culture and Sport Studies and Research* XLVI (2009): 137–46.

Földesiné, S. G. "Class or Mass: (Sport for All) Policy at a Crossroads." *Physical Culture and Sport Studies and Research* XLVI (2009): 147–56.

Földesiné, S. G. *The Interaction of Sport and Society in the V4 Countries*. Budapest: Hungarian Sport Science Booklets V. MSTT, 2011.

Földesiné, S. G. *What Does Hungarian Sport Expect from Society Rightly or Wrongly? Hungarian Sport Science Booklets V. MSTT* 49–64.

Kolléga, T. I. *Magyarország a XX. Században*, Vol. 3. Szekszárd: Babits Kiadó, 2000.

Kutassi, L. *A Magyar Kommunista Párt Sportpolitikája (1944–1948)*. Budapest: Kossuth, 1987.

Papp, I. *A Félévszázados Tatai Edzőtábor történetének és fejlődésének legfontosabb állomásai*. Budapest: Szakdolgozat, Tf, 1998.

Szabó, L. *The Reason of World-Wide Success of Hungarian Jewish Sportsmen*. Kézirat, 2009.

Szabó, L. *A szellem világbajnoka. ME-DOC IV. évfolyam 1. szám*, 2011. http://www.medok.ro/ME. dok-2011-1.pdf

Szabó, L. *A Torna Atlétika Háború Nagy Vesztese. Kemény Ferenc és Kora*. Budapest: Semmelweis Egyetem TSK, 2011.

Szalay, P., ed. *A magyar sport 40 éve (1945–1985)*. Budapest: Sportpropaganda, 1985.

Szikora, K. *A magyar egyetemi és főiskolai sport története 1918-ig. ME-DOC IV. évfolyam 1. szám*, 2011. http://www.medok.ro/ME.dok-2011-1.pdf

Szikora, K. *Nemzetközi Olimpiai Bizottság Első Magyar Tagja. Kemény Ferenc és Kora*. Budapest: Semmelweis Egyetem TSK, 2011.

Takács, F. "Takács Károly katonai és sportpályafutása." *Hadtörténelmi közlemények* 125, no. 2 (2012): 385–94.

Váradi, Mihály – Marton, László. *A Tatai Edzőtábor Szerepe a Magyar Sport Életében*. Tata: Tatai Edzőtábor, 1982.

Vida, B. *Sportpolitikai Irányelvekés Határozatok a Magyar Sporttörténelemben 1944–1948 Között*. Budapest. Szakdolgozat, TF, 2002.

From Best to Worst? Romania and Its Nostalgia for Olympic Successes

Simona Petracovschi[a] and Thierry Terret[b]

[a]Faculty of Physical Education and Sport, West University of Timisoara, Timisoa, Romania; [b]Center for Research and Innovation in Sport (CRIS), Université Lyon, Lyon, France

While the Los Angeles Olympic Games in 1984 constituted Romania's best performance ever, 2012 London Olympic Games were characterised by the worst performance in its history. During the time between these two events, the country went from being a communist regime to a liberal government. This transition invites consideration of the transformation Romania's sports policy underwent and its repositioning with regard to the Olympic Movement, both before and after the 1989 turning point. Analysis suggests that, in failing to professionalise Romanian sport, the Romanian Olympic and Sports Committee (COSR) was tempted to readopt a model of state-financed sport, with the aim of reinstating the nation to its former position among the world's sporting elite.

1. Introduction

After the 1984 Olympic Games in Los Angeles, where Romania received a total of 53 medals on account of the boycott by Eastern Bloc countries,[1] the performance of the national team remained constant, winning between a minimum of 18 medals, as in Barcelona in 1992, and a maximum of 25, as in Sydney in 2000. Taking these results into account, French economists Andreff and Andreff forecast, on the basis of economic theories, the number of medals each nation would win in the future and, consequently, its ranking on the international scene. They thus forecast that Romania would obtain between 19 and 23 medals during the Beijing Olympic Games in 2008. This figure proved, in fact, to be far from reality since the country received only eight medals.[2] The mediocre results obtained there led Romanian officials to declare in the press[3] that the best result the Romanian Delegation could hope to achieve in London in 2012 would be eight Olympic medals. The final result slightly exceeded this forecast given that the delegation returned home from the Games with nine medals and 27th place in the unofficial country rankings, but the country was very far from the world elite it had belonged to a few years earlier.

The recent plummeting of Romania's position in world sport was obviously linked to the political turning point of 1989 and the end of the Cold War, but this offers no direct explanation as to how Romania succeeded in maintaining its rank among the great sporting nations at the four Olympiads following the fall of communism, before beginning its descent down the international hierarchy in 2008. In this respect, moreover, the London Olympic Games were a clear indicator of this recent trend, since it was there that Romania obtained the lowest number of victories in its Olympic history for half a century. It would in fact appear that the country benefited, for a while, from the sports system surviving from the communist period, particularly in the case of gymnastics and rowing, before the leaders of the Romanian Olympic and Sports Committee belatedly understood the limits of this legacy and attempted to introduce new strategies. Changes in policy direction and difficulties in giving up nostalgia for a system that was politically outdated, but sportingly victorious, became clear from the study of documents in the International Olympic Committee (IOC) archives and Romania's national archives, and that of Romanian sports newspapers archived in the Central University Library of Timisoara or available online. Using these sources, a particular effort will be made to characterise first Romanian policy for high-level sport prior to the fall of communism, then the role of national federations which continued to defend the idea of state control after 1989, although the position of the Romanian Olympic Committee (ROC) was to professionalise Olympic sports.[4] Finally, it will be shown how failure of Romanian policy led to nostalgia for past successes, which paradoxically revived the temptation to adopt a model of state-financed sport.

2.   Organisation of Sport and the Olympic Movement in Communist Romania

The sports policy of Romania under Nicolae Ceausescu presented singular characteristics, which included the rationalisation of investment in high-level sport in favour of individual sports, leading to consistent international results in the 1970s.

Indeed, the communist Romanian state, ruled by Nicolae Ceausescu with an iron hand since the mid-1960s,[5] quickly understood, in the shadow of the USSR, the role that international sports organisations could play in the Cold War and major competitions. The Romanian President, trapped in the strong cult of his own personality and permanent self-staging,[6] was perfectly aware of the ability of sport to convey propagandist messages, not only to his own people and Western nations, but also to the Soviet Big Brother. Towards the end of his dictatorship, moreover, he did not hesitate to fly the flag for speeches on world peace and Olympic sport, which were intended to promote each country's right to independence, including within the Communist Bloc.[7]

Under his authority, physical education and sport were decreed as being activities 'of national interest',[8] and a central state body, the National Council of Physical Education and Sports (CNEFS), was set up in 1967,[9] in keeping with the continuity of former organisations: Organisation for Popular Sport (from 1946 to 1949), Committee for Physical Culture and Sport (from 1949 to 1957) and Union for Physical Culture and Sport (from 1957 to 1967).[10] In the 1970s, the fundamental aim of the CNEFS was to accomplish the general objectives set out by the 'Romanian Communist Party programme for the construction of a multilaterally developed socialist society and Romania's progress towards communism', to which some more sport-specific objectives were added at the Romanian Communist Party (PCR) Congresses for the periods 1976–1980 and 1981–1990. Its action concerned as much mass sport as high-level sport. From an ideological point of view, mass sport was designed to promote the communist doctrine in the population, and performance sport to serve as propaganda through international competitions. Political authorities thus declared:

> By their scope and the interest they reveal in all countries of the world, the Olympic Games have become a social phenomenon which, in a way, engages the prestige of the participating countries. This situation requires a number of complex measures which will lead to both

improvement of the masses in the main sporting disciplines and continuous performance improvement vis-à-vis present requirements, in line with our country's prestige which never ceases to increase at the international level.[11]

In view of such grand objectives, CNEFS policy in the 1970s included several programmes for the building of facilities, and grants to clubs and Olympic or other federations (worker, school, university, etc.). Sports infrastructure was thus considerably upgraded, with significant impact on the development of sport for all, now becoming a national cause. Just like in all the countries of the Eastern Bloc, the Soviet 'GTO' programme (Goiov k trudu i oborone – Ready for Labour and Defence) was introduced into the Romanian sports system[12] and took on a national aspect with Ceausescu when the *Spartakiades* were transformed into *Daciadas*[13], considered to be the 'real Olympiads of Romanian sport'.[14]

The institutional set-up of the state relied on a small number of people, in order to ensure control and autocratic management of funds supplied by the state. In 1974, Army General Marin Dragnea was thus appointed at the head of the CNEFS, while already President of the ROC. In a similar way, ex-Olympic champion Lia Manoliu was Vice President of the CNEFS and ROC.[15] As for the ROC, its role was to maintain contact with the IOC to defend and represent Romania's position and, beyond that, to lean on the Olympic Movement in favour of communist ideology. Moreover, in the 1980s, J.A. Samaranch, appointed as IOC President, called upon Romanian Alexandru Siperco to become one of the Committee's vice presidents. In this position, Siperco contributed to making the IOC 'custodian of the Olympic concept and leader of the Olympic Movement'.[16] In particular, he focused his efforts on taking the institution from the role of patronage of the Olympic Games to that of effective and permanent management of the Olympic Movement, by setting up continuous liaison with international federations and National Olympic Committees (NOCs), and ensuring that national and international federations respectively recognised the authority of the NOCs and IOC.[17] Last but not the least, Siperco was notably the author of a report concerning the famous Rule 26 on amateurism, in which he promoted the idea of an amateur sportsman in line with the communist model, i.e. completely supported by the state, quite unlike the liberal model that favoured private backing.[18]

In the 1970s, the state directed its financial aid towards elite sport, targeting both world and European levels. Behind the state slogan 'The Romanian flag must be hoisted up the highest mast', the victorious participation of Romanian sportsmen and women in the international arena was perceived as being the best possible propaganda for the country. For this reason, international-level sports facilities were required, which explains why the sports budget was always negotiated between the Ministry of Foreign Trade and the State Planning Committee, before being submitted to the Central Committee of the Romanian Communist Party for the final decision. Furthermore, in the case of surplus money in other ministries, the former was automatically reallocated to sport, as was the case in 1976, for example, when part of the Ministry of Culture's budget was transferred to the CNEFS.[19]

A further important aspect of the sports policy of Ceausescu and the PCR was the rationalisation of its medal-winning strategy for men and women, in terms of the effort invested. Collective sports thus appeared to be unprofitable compared to individual sports, and in particular gymnastics, since investing in a sports team may result, at best, in only one medal, while an individual sportsman bringing home only one medal would also do so with much lower financial investment and identical international prestige.[20] In spite of the high performances achieved by Romania in handball where it became world champion four times between 1961 and 1974, while also picking up a bronze medal at the Olympic Games in 1972 and 1980, as well as a silver one in 1976, collective sports were gradually shown less interest by the PCR and, as a result, received less financial aid from the state. As it happened, it was possible to defend Romanian interests by means of other strategies, more institutional than financial. And so, after the 1967 IOC Congress in Tehran, Anghel Alexe, President of the ROC,[21] requested a change be made to Article 35 of the Olympic Games' General Rules, relating to the number of representatives per country and per event, suggesting that the number of athletes in individual events be limited to two per country, on the grounds that it could boost the number of nations participating in the Olympic Games.[22] The ROC likewise requested, once again, at the Munich Congress in 1971 that the number of events in which the same competitor may compete be restricted, so as to increase the chances of other nations.[23] And so it came as no surprise that, when the IOC suggested reducing the number of teams competing in the final Olympic collective sports tournament from 16 to 8, the ROC clearly opposed the proposal which would have decreased the qualification chances of its teams. At the 1969 IOC Congress in Dubrovnik, the ROC thus reaffirmed that such a decrease 'was not advisable since it may lead to less interest among the public for collective games in general and on certain continents in particular'.[24]

The rationalisation policy applied to the participation of Romanian athletes in international competitions was used on a permanent basis by Ceausescu, including, moreover, in fields other than sport, to obtain maximum results while reducing financial losses. This cost-cutting strategy explains why it was not unusual for Romania to send incomplete teams to international competitions, for example without the necessary support staff. It was the same strategy that explained why Romania increased, in vain, the number of requests for the modification of Article 38 of IOC rules and regulations, so that:

> the Summer and Winter Games Organising Committees take care of costs for the umpires, timekeepers and judges of each Olympic discipline. In this way, costs for the NOCs would be reduced, enabling them to focus efforts more on sports delegations and less on officials.[25]

The strategy was seen to be fruitful. In the period from 1964 to 1980, Romania won between two and six gold medals in the Olympics, for a total of 12 to 27 podium places. Its position in the country rankings increased constantly, going progressively from 14th place in 1964 to 7th place in 1980, a significant performance for a country that had roughly 21 million inhabitants throughout the decade of the 1970s. Nadia Comaneci's gymnastic achievements gave the country exceptional renown.[26] Romania's sporting peak was just around the corner. And the country reached it in Los Angeles in 1984.

3.   The Los Angeles Olympic Games: Peak of Romanian Sport

The reasons why Romania decided not to take up Moscow's call for boycott, thus becoming one of the rare communist nations to travel to the Los Angeles Olympic Games in 1984, have already been studied.[27] Investigations converge towards the idea that the country was attempting to escape from the control of the USSR at a time when the Soviet Bloc was beginning to weaken. Yet, objective reduction of the competition does not, however, suffice to explain why the Los Angeles Games were, for Romania, the most victorious of its Olympic history. It is thus necessary to identify exactly what, in Ceausescu's sports policy, was potentially capable of favouring these results and, more especially, how belief in the government's responsibility for this success was able to develop.

From this point of view, it can be first observed that the Romanian state's sports policy in 1984 was in perfect continuation of that of the years preceding the Games. The same logic for economy and optimisation may be found in it. And so, the cost of the national team's participation in Los Angeles, reaching a total of $120,000, was not covered by the

Romanian budget, but rather financed in equal measure by Olympic Solidarity and the Los Angeles Olympic Organizing Committee (LAOOC).[28] Furthermore, while the Romanian Delegation could have been larger due to the number of places remaining from the non-participation of competitors from other communist nations, the decision was made to restrict the number of athletes and to base selection on merit and medal-winning potential. This decision aimed to show that the sports policy adopted was intended to serve the state, the nation and by extension, the Romanian people, but in no way the individual.[29]

In the same way, when the Romanian team returned on home ground crowned with 53 medals, the wins were presented by the country's political authorities and its mainly state-controlled press as being the result of the policy adopted by the PCR and Ceausescu. Official discourses notably interpreted the number of medals as being the consequence of the position adopted nine years earlier, in 1975, during a national conference where Ceausescu had encouraged the development of clubs and sports organisations with a view to preparing athletes to meet international requirements. Arguments were also based on the diversity of the sports where Romania had proved to be at its advantage. Among the 53 medals obtained in Los Angeles, the 20 victories were in fact won in 12 different disciplines, with the concerned athletes belonging to 31 different clubs and sports associations, located in 17 different provinces, in addition to the capital Bucharest. By recalling these figures and showing that they were contributing to the democratisation of excellence in comparison with the Moscow Games four years earlier,[30] official propaganda was in fact building a specific conviction, that of state action driving the whole of the Romanian population towards progress and world recognition. Indeed, by emphasising the fact that 70% of the Romanian medal winners had been born or had grown up in a rural environment, and that medal distribution was fairly well balanced in terms of sex (28 for women and 25 for men) and teams (59 women for 68 men),[31] official statistics set benchmarks in collective representations. The year 1984 benefited, in addition, from a particular position in the Romanian calendar, since it was precisely 40 years since the Romanian army had taken the offensive against Nazi Germany. The majestic celebration of this anniversary on August 23, 1984, namely a few days after the Closing Ceremony of the Los Angeles Games, was obviously given symbolic value through the association of the two events. It was, indeed, during this show and nowhere else that the Romanian athletes were celebrated. Here, they were able to parade around the stadium as a sign of their recognition, alongside other personalities with services rendered to the PCR or its Leader.[32]

Last but not the least, the propaganda arsenal benefited from the aid of the IOC itself. Indeed, 1984 was also the year when Nadia Comaneci, Romania's champion with the most titles, decided to end her sporting career. On May 6, 1984, IOC President Juan Antonio Samaranch travelled to Bucharest to award her the Olympic Order.[33] In his declaration, he highlighted her contribution, and that of the whole of Romania's national team, to the creation of modern gymnastics. By valorising Romania's role in the Olympic Movement, he helped strengthen the positive image that Ceausescu had always endeavoured to give his own political action.

In reality, the year 1984 corresponded to a decrease in financial aid from the state for sport. The President of the ROC since 1974, General Marin Dragnea, was dismissed a few months prior to the Los Angeles Olympic Games,[34] on the grounds that he was not a member of the PCR Central Committee and that he could not become one since his dossier was not in order.[35] This represented a marked change in Ceausescu's policy, by reducing direct financial support for sport and asking sports clubs to finance themselves in the same way as other areas of social life.[36] The new ROC President, Haralambie Alexa (1984–1987), scrupulously followed the new instructions.

At the same time, Ceausescu succeeded in linking his name to the boycott refusal, receiving, in exchange, albeit not the goodwill of the Olympic authorities, at least their comprehension. Samaranch thus returned to Romania, in 1988, to offer Ceausescu the Olympic Order as a token of gratitude for his commitment to promoting Olympic ideals and, more generally, his action in favour of pacifism and sport.[37] It was, in fact, true that when Samaranch was appointed at the head of the IOC in 1981, the ROC sent him a letter in which it encouraged the Olympic Movement to follow the Call for Disarmament and Peace launched by the Democratic Front and Socialist Unity parties in Romania, a 'national representative body grouping all political and social forces of the country, including the sports movement'.[38] Moreover, the same year, Ceausescu awarded the Tudor Vladimirescu Order to Samaranch, on the occasion of the World University Games held in Bucharest.[39] It came as no great surprise that Ceausescu then sustained and even strengthened his pacifist message, endeavouring to use placatory discourse to counterbalance symbolically the extremism of a dictatorship on its last legs.

The Seoul Olympic Games in 1988 were the last Games in which communist Romania took part, finishing in eighth place in the unofficial country rankings. The collapse of communist Europe in 1989 left Romanian sport deprived of material aid from the state, but with a centralised structure that was well defined and fundamentally true to Coubertin's pyramid principle,[40] on which the model found in the USSR and its satellite nations was based.[41] Just as in many other sectors of social life,[42] Romania then had to rebuild a system opposed ideologically to the years of communism, without the necessary financial and human means to rethink the one bequeathed by the Ceausescu period. A challenge that proved all the more difficult to take up since previous propaganda had succeeded in implanting the idea of a performing and democratic sports policy that was recognised by international sporting authorities.

4. Romanian Olympic Sport After 1989: Somewhere Between Legacy and the Need for Change

From the setting up of the ROC in 1914 until 1940, the position of president was always held by a member of the aristocracy, with the last President (1930–1940), being King Carol II of Romania. Between 1948 and 1989, only members of the PCR held the position. Then, from 1990 onwards, it was the turn of former Romanian high-level sportsmen and women to be appointed president, including athlete Lia Manoliu from 1990 to 1998, tennis player Ion Tiriac from 1998 to 2004 and rugbyman Octavian Morariu since 2004. Against a background of political regime renewal, these men and women from the milieu and elected by their peers initially seemed inclined to turn their backs on a sports policy that had been entirely subjected to political authorities for half a century. In reality, however, choosing these people did not represent a complete and immediate break from the former system.

In 1989, the new ROC President, Lia Manoliu, was indeed not just an Olympic discus champion who had taken part in six Olympic Games, she had also been Vice President of the CNEFS and ROC between 1972 and 1989. Under her presidency, Romanian athletes won 18 and 20 medals, respectively, at the Olympic Games of Barcelona and Atlanta, finishing 14th in the country rankings, considerably lower results than those of the Seoul Games, the last before the collapse of the Eastern Bloc, where the Romanian Delegation had been awarded 24 medals.[43] Following the liberalisation of the regime, the ROC was able to offer Romanian champions prizes in the form of money or goods (cars, apartments, land, etc.), although the financial cost of such prizes constituted a major obstacle.

New questions were raised among sports leaders, as to where the money should come from. Under what conditions may the state hand over material rewards to athletes who had represented a country characterised by 'poverty and primitive capitalism'?[44] The solutions put forward by Lia Manoliu failed to live up to aspirations, with the 'Olympic Stamp Law' and the launching of a collaborative venture with the Autonomous Agency for Sports Lottery.[45] As indicated by James Riordan, in its transition period on the way towards capitalism, Romania may be characterised as having been hit by 'post Marxistkleptocracy'.[46]

In 1998, however, the deaths of Lia Manoliu and Alexandru Siperco, Romania's member of the IOC, thrust Ion Tiriac into the presidency of the ROC. The ex-tennis player was, at the time, a wealthy businessman, having succeeded in increasing the value of the money won on the tennis courts through profitable investments. His appointment at the head of the Romanian Olympic movement was expected, for many, to represent the trigger point they were waiting for and the means required to attract capital. Yet, while some were of the belief that Tiriac would invest his money in sport, the intention of the ROC President was quite different: on the contrary, as a businessman, he intended sport to generate the necessary capital itself, by setting up a system aimed at attracting sponsors, similar to the one implemented in Italy by the Italian National Olympic Committee. Aware of the fact that the communist legacy was coming to an end, he wished to establish a new vision of the relationship between sport and public authorities.

This set-up worked for the Sydney Olympic Games in 2000, where the 16 Romanian medal winners were rewarded, for the very first time, by ROC sponsor Ford, in the form of car donations. Two years later, and although Tiriac had remained far from any political involvement, he pushed for the drafting of a new law on physical education and sport, which would take into account, for the first time, the issue of social protection for high-level athletes.[47] In 2007, the Romanian state likewise decided to award high sums of money to athletes ranking in the first six places at the Olympic Games, ranging from €35,000 for the winners to €7000 for those in sixth place.[48] At the London Games, the amounts were doubled, with the main sponsor of the Romanian Olympic and Sports Committee also awarding cars to the medal winners. It should be noted, in addition, that high-level athletes continued to benefit from a specific financing plan for university training, which granted access to universities of sports sciences without having to pay anything. Finally, Tiriac succeeded in convincing the government of Adrian Nastase, member of the Social Democratic Party (SDP), to launch a project for the construction of 410 sports halls, thanks to an external loan of 165 million euros. Resulting from the relationship between the ROC President and the Prime Minister, the project was not, however, coupled with a parallel project for social reform:[49] between 2000 and 2004, the 410 sports halls were built on political instruction, with beneficiaries being those towns where the SDP was in power, while the percentage of people practising sport remained low throughout Romania and barely reached 19% of the working population.[50]

In 2003, Romania made known its wish to join the European Community three years later and began undertakings to reorganise and simplify the governmental organigram. The Ministry of Youth and Sport, set up in 1990,[51] was completely transformed, with sport becoming the responsibility of a new and more independent body: the National Sports Agency. With only 8 medal winners and 17th position in the country rankings, the return from the Beijing Games in 2008, coupled with the upcoming presidential elections, led to a demand for the reinstatement of a dedicated ministry. However, the Prime Minister at the time, Calin Popescu Tariceanu (National Liberal Party) took a clear stance on the matter when he explained that sport no longer represented the only means for social and material ascension as it had done in the time of communism, and that henceforth the new generation had 'other possibilities'.[52] For him, there was no doubt whatsoever that the sporting results of the 1980s were no longer achievable, but he believed that there were other areas where the country may stand out. As for Tiriac, he was not far from thinking along the same lines: the return of the Romanians among the international elite would no longer be possible without state contribution. Such discourse represented a break from the general convictions of the Romanians themselves and the hope they sustained of experiencing once more the successes of the 1980s in stadiums and gymnasiums. Romania's President, Traian Basescu (since 2004), did not hesitate, moreover, to contradict his Prime Minister[53] and ordered the reorganisation of the new Ministry for Youth and Sport in December 2008, just after the presidential elections. A little more than two years later, in January 2011, sport moved into the fold of a grand new Ministry of Education, Research, Youth and Sport, as part of a special agency, the National Authority of Sport and Youth (ANSJ).

5. London 2012: Responsibilities and Fatalism

Pre-1989 relations between the ROC and CNEFS had clearly not posed a problem, since political power and sporting power were in the same hands. With the end of the communist regime, however, the country found itself having to become accustomed to a new type of management and division of responsibilities, although it failed to find a satisfactory balance. Sports federations remained, in reality, under state control through the ANSJ, in an organisation bequeathed by the Ceausescu period. As for the COSR, it was a non-governmental organisation that Ion Tiriac had turned into a relay for private financing, and which his successor Octavian Morariu, elected in 2004, likewise wished to maintain in this direction. Admittedly, Octavian Morariu had been President of the National Authority for Sport in 2003 and 2004, thus renewing the traditions of communist Romania when the presidency of both the CNEFS and the ROC was attributed to one and the same person, but he strove to pursue the policy driven by Tiriac. He succeeded, in particular, in changing the ROC into the COSR, taking his inspiration from the French model.[54] His ambition was to lead a policy aimed at redefining responsibilities, by placing national federations under his control and no longer under state control. With the COSR being responsible for performance sport, public authorities would therefore maintain their responsibilities for sport for all, placed under the control of the Ministry of Administration and Interior, and for school and university sport, administered by the Ministry for Education, Research and Youth, while the whole was coordinated by the central apparatus, yet decentralised at the level of departmental councils.[55]

The COSR's wish to recover part of the ANSJ's responsibilities was not understood for merely ideological and political reasons, but also for financial ones. Legislation on sport as defined from 2002 onwards proved to be badly articulated with the Fiscal Code. Income from the Olympic Stamp remained low and the place of sponsors restricted, due to the lack of fiscal deduction possibilities. In addition, the Romanian Lottery, whose statutes stipulated that a financial contribution be made to sport, did not always fulfil its obligations. As for the industry of gambling and bookmaking, it also failed to swell the sports budget. In fact, in the Olympic year 2012, the COSR received only 30% of the budget initially requested from the government, in the form of 9 million RONs (2 million euros) worth of direct subsidies and 22 million RONs (4.9 million euros) resulting from taxes on the sales of alcohol and the national lottery. In addition, this reduced subsidy was itself lower than that given by the state to a federation like the Romanian Wrestling Federation for instance.[56] Under such conditions, the COSR requested the transfer of all sports federations to its own organisations, including the Institute for Sports Medecine, the Institute for Research on Sports Issues and the three mountain sports centres dedicated to the physical training of the country's national teams. The federations were, however, reluctant to accept the request, accusing the COSR of wanting to privatise sport with money from the state without having been able to modify legislation on sponsors.[57] Consequently, the COSR was sent back to its main mission since 1989: relations with the IOC and Romania's participation in the Olympic Games. As it happened, the London Games in 2012 served to reveal a fragile situation where the need for change found itself fighting against nostalgia for past successes.

The budget forecast for 2012 was limited to 31 million RONs (6.9 million euros), a figure that was lower than both that of Athens in 2004 (39 million RONs, i.e. 8.7 million euros) and of Beijing in 2008 (53 million RONs, i.e. 11.8 million euros). Romania therefore sent a smaller delegation to London, with 105 athletes, and 4 substitutes, participating in 15 different disciplines. They were accompanied by 60 trainers and officials. The final results of this situation were two gold (Sandra Izbasa and Cătălina Ponor in gymnastics, Alin Moldoveanu in shooting), five silver (Alina Dumitru and Corina Căprioriu in judo, Roxana Cocos in weightlifting and the men's sabre team) and two bronze medals (women's gymnastics team and Răzvan Martin in weightlifting). While the Olympic champions were generally the subject of laudatory discourses in the national press with regard to the material conditions and low resources available for their training, the mediocre performance of the national team was, on the other hand, largely attributed to the COSR which took offence, even publicly.[58] Reaction from the press was, in fact, equal to the hopes placed in the Romanian Delegation, as confirmed by analysis of the two main specialist newspapers before and after the Games: the *ProSport* and *Gazeta Sporturilor*.[59]

Prior to the start of the events, both daily newspapers focused on two points concerning the COSR, implicitly criticising its budget choices and the distance it maintained vis-à-vis the political authorities. Journalists reminded readers that the COSR was expected to make a profit of 1.7 million dollars from the London Olympic Games, thanks to the contributions made by two programmes (TOP and Olympic Solidarity), and in spite of the cost of Romania House with its rent of 250,000 dollars. Admittedly a positive result, but from which came the implicit conclusion that directing more investment towards the athletes would have made it possible to reinforce the Romanian Delegation, more particularly so when it was emphasised that the COSR had inaugurated a new head office (including a Romanian Olympic Museum) the previous year with a cost of 5 million euros. This latent criticism was, however, not visible in the generalist press where, on the contrary, the COSR was presented as being a model for the national economy. The *Jurnalul National* newspaper, for example, compared the economic and sports results of the country, noting that Romania had succeeded in keeping its place among the 'G-20' of sport, whereas its economic results placed it in a more distant 50th place in the world.[60] The article also mentioned the fact that the COSR had built its development plan for a period of at least four years – duration of an Olympic cycle – whereas many public institutions had not yet got this far.

Furthermore, although Romania House was inaugurated in the presence of Prime Minister Victor Ponta,[61] COSR President, Octavian Morariu, had said, the day before, that he hoped no political leader would come to comment on the sports results of the Romanian Delegation, thus displaying his independence from the political world.[62] Athletes themselves adopted a similar position during an event that was also reported in the press. On 29 July, a national referendum was organised in Romania to decide if the country's President, Traian Basescu, suspended at the time, should be permanently dismissed.[63] The polling station set up in London for the Romanian athletes triggered a media clash when judoka Alina Dumitru, gold medallist in Beijing and silver medallist in London, declared that she would not vote on the grounds that the political situation was of no interest to her, recalling, at the same time, that in Beijing, the President of Romania had called her to congratulate her while in London, nobody had yet contacted her.[64]

The general suspicion with regard to the COSR increased following the performance and results of the Romanian team in the Olympic events. Faced with reality, hopes that had been sustained for a while turned into fatalism, expressed notably in the sports where Romania still harboured illusions, in particular gymnastics, rowing and fencing. In London, the supremacy was enjoyed by the Romanian school of gymnastics since Nadia Comaneci was, for example, mentioned nostalgically by journalists who felt that it had even favoured Romanian gymnast Catalina Ponor when her direct competitor, Italian Vanessa Ferrari, demanded in vain that she be awarded the same mark.[65] Rowing was also a sport where Romania had shone in the past with Elisabeta Lipa, who was declared best sportswoman of the twentieth century by the International Rowing Federation, having participated consecutively in six Olympic Games, with five Olympic golds, two silver and one bronze. Having become President of the Romanian Rowing Federation, the champion could do little more than observe her team's complete and utter failure to win any medals whatsoever in London. The team of 8 athletes, including the coxswain, had not missed an Olympic podium for 32 years, yet returned home to Romania empty-handed, having failed to develop a winning spirit.[66] In the case of fencing, journalists regretted the fact that the Romanians' expertise in this field had led nations to take inspiration from their training methods and go so far as to train in Romania. The team from South Korea, for example, who had come many a time to the national centre in Izvorani, was said to have benefited from the experience of the Romanian fencers, before taking their place, and knocking out Romania's women fencers in the semi-final.[67]

In these examples, journalists' fatalism was marked with nostalgia. Recalling missed medals enabled boundaries to be defined between a victorious past and a present which was much less so. Regrets were all the more greater in that, for many, the influence of the country was still dependent upon its sporting performances, with sport remaining a model to be followed by the Romanian society.[68] At the end of the London Games, Prime Minister Victor Ponta declared, moreover, that sport continued to constitute Romania's best ambassador, and added, with a rare note of optimism, that, thanks to athletes and men of science, the country remained highly regarded abroad.[69]

6. Conclusion: Romania, Olympic Games and *Ostalgia*

With the implementation of a liberal regime, Romania embarked upon its path towards the professionalisation of high-level sport. Yet, the poor sporting results in London in 2012, heralded by those in Beijing four years earlier, showed that turning the country's back on its legacy of communist structures was not successful, until supporting the system through private financing was conceivable. Resistance from Romanian federations to the COSR's attempt to control them, and their wish to limit its role to relationships with the IOC, thus confirmed to what extent the post-Cold War transition period was conducive to the emergence of lasting nostalgia for the old regime.

Admittedly, the phenomenon of nostalgia in sport is not specific to post-socialist nations.[70] It did, however, take on forms here that were particularly prominent, and of which Maria Todovora has highlighted two distinct aspects.[71] The author in fact opposes 'restorationist nostalgia', which aims to restore the past, and 'restorative nostalgia', which has more curative objectives. In the second version, nostalgia does not correspond to a real desire to relive the experience of the past, but rather to the need to refer to an imagined and henceforth inaccessible past in order to restructure the present time.[72] As confirmed by Canadian comparative literature specialist Linda Hutcheon:

> It is the very pastness of the past, its inaccessibility, that likely account for a large part of nostalgia's power [...]. This is rarely the past as actually experienced, of course; it is the past as imagined, as idealized through memory and desire. In this sense, however, nostalgia is less about the past than about the present.[73]

In the case of post-socialist nations, the feeling has been called *Ostalgia* by several specialists in political sciences and cultural history.[74] Sociologist Dominik Bartmanski has, for example, clearly shown that it corresponds to the construction of 'mnemonic bridges', making it possible to ensure the imaginary continuity of a certain community feeling.[75] The way in which *Ostalgia* manifests itself in many cultural, political and social fields in Romania, also reflects a sort of 'metaphorical desire for cryogenics'.[76] Popular songs, for example, gave people the feeling that 'Ceausescu Hasn't Died'.[77] These momentary nostalgic revivals, however, materialised a lesser degree of regret for the old regime than a way of ensuring a more acceptable transition towards an uncertain future.

In Romania, the Olympic decline contributed all the more to disseminating *Ostalgia*, in that falling sports results were accompanied by the country's inability to regain the influence Romanians felt they had enjoyed within Olympic authorities through the personality of Alexandru Siperco.[78] Since the death of Siperco, who had enjoyed unprecedented longevity in office within the IOC, Romania had struggled to come together behind a new personality. Ion Tiriac submitted an application on two occasions and, on both the occasions, was rejected. Nadia Comaneci also made known, in vain, her wish to join the Olympic institution in 2004, on the grounds that she was living in the United States and not in Romania.[79] Current COSR President Octavian Morariu is, however, developing a more laborious strategy: following his election in 2009 as member of the Executive Committee of the Association of European Olympic Committees (EOC) and Vice President of the EOC Commission responsible for relations with the European Union, the moral authority and influence over Romanian and international sport conferred by these roles place him in a more favourable position than his predecessors with regard to the IOC. Yet his application, submitted in 2010, remained pending at the time of the London Games, incidentally reviving nostalgia for a time gone by.[80]

Notes on Contributors

Simona Petracovschi completed her PhD at the Henri Poincaré University of Nancy, France, in 2005. She now works as a lecturer in Sport Sociology at the Faculty of Physical Education and Sport in the West University of Timisoara, Romania.

Thierry Terret is Professor of Sports History, former Director of the *Centre de Recherche et d'Innovation sur le Sport* at the University of Lyon, France, and Rector of La Réunion Island. His main research focuses on gender, politics and transculturalism.

Notes

1. Romania was one of the rare allies of the USSR to not follow the call for boycott of the Los Angeles Olympic Games, launched by Moscow.
2. Andreff and Andreff, "Economic Prediction of Sport Performances."
3. http://www.goldmansachs.com/our-thinking/topics/global-economic-outlook/olympics-and-economics-.pdf (accessed November 2, 2012).
4. Riordan, "Sports After the Cold War."
5. Tismaneanu, *Stalinism for All Seasons*.

6. Trond, *Nationalism and Communism in Romania*.
7. "The Political Concept and Actions of President Nicolae Ceausescu: The Noble Mission of Sport in the Struggle for Peace" (*Sportul*, no. 11 846, January 25, 1988).
8. According to Article 2 of Law 29 in 1967, concerning the development of physical education and sport, published in *Buletinul Oficial*, no. 114, December 29, 1967.
9. Defined as a 'central specialised citizen-oriented organ' under state control for the development of physical education and sport (Postolache, *Din istoria mişcării sportive muncitoreşti şi de mase*, 257).
10. Postolache, *Din istoria mişcării sportive muncitoreşti şi de mase*.
11. Arhivele Nationale ale Romaniei, ANIC, fond *CC al PCR – Secţia Propagandă şi Agitaţie*, dosar 54/1966, f. 3.
12. Riordan, *Sport in Soviet Society*.
13. Necula, "Daciada- un bun al intregului popor." The term 'Daciada' highlighted the 'dacique' origins (people from north of the Danube) of the Romanian people.
14. *Sportul Românesc*, January 21, 1992, Year II, no. 103.
15. Lia Manoliu (1932–1998), Olympic champion (discus) in the Mexico Olympic Games in 1968 and two times bronze medal winner (Rome Games, 1960 and Tokyo Games, 1964) participated in six consecutive Olympic Games (Helsinki 1952–Munich 1972).
16. Letter from A. Siperco to J.A. Samaranch, October 30, 1980, IOC Archives, Lausanne, File 6832.
17. Ibid.
18. Ibid. On this point, see Ousterhoudt, "Capitalist and Socialist Interpretations."
19. Arhivele Nationale ale Romaniei, ANIC, fond *CC al PCR – Secţia Propagandă şi Agitaţie*, dosar 5/1975, f. 146.
20. Arhivele Naţionale ale Romaniei, ANIC, fond *CC al PCR – Secţia Propagandă şi Agitaţie*, dosar 54/1966, f. 3.
21. He presided over the ROC from 1966 to 1974.
22. Anghel Alexe, ROC President, and Alexandru Siperco, IOC member for Romania, to Avery Brundage, IOC President, July 8, 1968, IOC Archives, Lausanne, File no. 12823.
23. Letter from Ioan Paun, ROC Secretary General, to Monique Berlioux, IOC Director, May 13, 1972, IOC Archives, Lausanne, File 12824. Reply from the IOC (Letter from Monique Berlioux to Ioan Paun, April 20, 1972, IOC Archives, Lausanne, File 12824, recalled that, according to Rule 35, 'the maximum number of competitors entered by each NOC and for each event is fixed by the IOC, following agreement with the international federation concerned. The number of competitors entered may not exceed: a. for individual events, 3 competitors per country (without substitutes) for Summer and Winter Olympic Games; b. for team sports, one team per country, with the IOC fixing the number of substitutes in agreement with the international federation concerned').
24. Letter from Ioan Paun, ROC Secretary General, to Monique Berlioux, IOC Director, May 13, 1972, IOC Archives, File 12824.
25. Letter from Anghel Alexe, ROC President, and Alexandru Siperco, IOC member for Romania, to Avery Brundage, IOC President, July 8, 1968, IOC Archives, File 12823.
26. Wood, "Superpower;" and Kerr, "The Impact of Nadia Comaneci."
27. Wilson, "The Golden Opportunity;" and Ionescu and Terret, "A Romanian Within the IOC."
28. Zyser, "Phone Call From China." In 1984, however, the press suspected the LAOOC of having paid all the costs, to encourage Romania to participate and thus break the boycott called for by the USSR. Cf. Peter Ueberroth to A. Samaranch, July 30, 1984, IOC Archives, File 12824.
29. "The Telegram Sent by the RSR Olympic Delegation to the PCR Central Committee, to Comrade Nicolae Ceausescu – PCR Secretary General and to the RSR President" (*Sportul*, no. 10 783, August 15, 1984).
30. In Moscow, the Romanian medal winners belonged to 20 sports clubs located in 11 provinces, in addition to the capital.
31. "Statistics and Observations Following the Participation of Romanian Athletes in the Los Angeles Summer Olympic Games. Growth of Olympic Potential is Secured by the General Resources of the Sport Movement" (*Ziarul Sportul*, no. 10 794, August 29, 1984).
32. "Parade of Athletes on the Anniversary of 23 August" (*Sportul*, no. 10 791, August 23, 1984).
33. "Romania Created Modern Gymnastics" (*Sportul*, no. 10 697, May 7, 1984).
34. "Ceausescu and Sport" (*Evenimentul Zilei*, June 20, 2011).

35. His brother had illegally left Romania for Germany during the dictatorship.
36. Law nr. 1/1985 concerning the self-monitoring, economic—financial self-management and self-financing of territorial administrative units.
37. "The Political Concept and Actions of the President Nicolae Ceausescu: The Noble Mission of Sport in the Struggle for Peace" (*Sportul*, no. 11 846, January 25, 1988).
38. Letter from General Marin Dragnea, ROC President, to J.A. Samaranch, November 13, 1981, IOC Archives, Lausanne, File 12824.
39. Samaranch to Ceausescu, July 21, 1981, IOC Archives, Lausanne, File 12824.
40. Coubertin's formula that out of 100 people involved in physical culture, only 50 would continue doing sport, 20 of them would specialise and only 5 would be capable of achieving remarkable results (widely acknowledged because of its famous geometrical symbol of the pyramid), has clearly served as a symbol for the way Olympic sport and many national sport systems have been organised for nearly 100 years.
41. Riordan, "The Impact of Communism on Sport;" and Girginov, "Capitalist Philosophy and Communist Practice."
42. Courtney and Harrington, *Relații româno-americane*.
43. National press at the time felt that the result was satisfactory, but also that it could be improved. "The Results of the Games Could be Much Better" (*Sportul*, October 4, 1988).
44. Riordan, "Sports After the Cold War."
45. "Supra licit ROC" (*Sportul Românesc*, January 21, 1992, Year II n°103).
46. Riordan, "Sports After the Cold War."
47. Law for physical education and sport, no. 69/2000, Title X.
48. Decision of Romanian Government, no. 1447 of November 28, 2007, concerning the acceptance of financial norms for sport, published in: MONITORUL OFICIAL No. 823 of December 3, 2007.
49. "Adrian Nastase has Received the Mercedes he Won in a Wager With Ioan Tiriac" (*Adevărul*, November 5, 2004). http://www.adevarul.ro/actualitate/Adrian-Nastase-Mercedesul-Ion-Tiriac_0_65993842.html# (accessed November 3, 2012).
50. Special Eurobarometer 334 /Wave 72.3, Sport and Physical Activity, http://ec.europa.eu/sport/news/eurobarometer-survey-on-sport-and-physical-activity_en.htm
51. Decision of Romanian Government no. 994 of September 3, 1990.
52. "Tăriceanu Does Not Wish to Have a Ministry for Sport" (*Prosport*, August 30, 2008). http://www.prosport.ro/alte-sporturi/alte-sporturi/tariceanu-nu-vrea-minister-pentru-sport-3084125 (accessed November 1, 2012).
53. "Băsescu Wishes to Have a Ministry for Sport, Tăriceanu Thinks it is Too Late" (*Gândul*, August 28, 2008). http://www.gandul.info/news/basescu-vrea-minister-al-sportului-tariceanu-crede-ca-este-tarziu-3017330 (accessed November 1, 2012).
54. Grosset and Attali, "The French National Olympic and Sports Committee."
55. "Ion Tiriac and Octavian Morariu Ask Adrian Năstase to Disband the National Agency for Sport" (*Adevărul*, February 3, 2004). http://www.adevarul.ro/sport/Octavian-Morariu-Nastase-Agentia-Nationala_0_70793929.html# (accessed November 3, 2012).
56. The President of the Romanian Wrestling Federation is a politician.
57. "Who is Afraid of the Reform of the COSR?" (*Jurnalul Național*, August 19, 2012). http://m.jurnalul.ro/editorial/cui-ii-este-frica-de-reforma-cosr-621479.html (accessed November 1, 2012).
58. http://www.tolo.ro/2012/08/11/cosr-vrea-tot-sportul-de-performanta-recunosc-de-bunavoie-ca-sint-pucist/
59. The study has been widened on an ad hoc basis to include more newspapers.
60. *Jurnalul Național*, July 23, 2012.
61. *Prosport*, July 27, 2012.
62. *Prosport*, July 26, 2012.
63. The referendum was the result of conflict between President Traian Băsescu and his Prime Minister Victor Ponta, appointed in May 2012. The disagreement concerned, more particularly, management of the economic crisis. Băsescu was accused of having breached the Romanian Constitution and imposed austerity measures. The Constitutional Court finally invalidated the referendum on account of too low a turnout. Traian Băsescu was reinstated on August 28, 2012. See "Roumanie: le président Traian Băsescu sauve son siège", (*Le Monde*, August 21, 2012).
64. *Gândul*, July 28, 2012.

65. *Gândul*, August 9, 2012.
66. *Gazeta Sportului*, August 3, 2012.
67. *Adevărul*, August 5, 2012.
68. *Jurnalul Naţional*, August 8, 2012.
69. *Gândul*, August 14, 2012.
70. For example, Maguire, "Sport, Identity Politics, and Globalization." The article particularly explores the British case.
71. Todovora, "Introduction."
72. Jameson, "Nostalgia for the Present."
73. Hutcheon, "Irony, Nostalgia, and the Postmodern."
74. Berdhal, *On the Social Life of Postsocialism*; Hann, *Postsocialism*; and Todorora and Gille, *Post-Communist Nostalgia.*
75. Bartmanski, "Successful Icons of Failed Time."
76. Popescu-Sandu, "Let's All Freeze Up Until 2100 or So."
77. Georgescu, "Ceausescu Hasn't Died."
78. Ionescu and Terret, "A Romanian Within the IOC."
79. After Nadia Comaneci's retirement from competition, she was forbidden to leave Romania, even though she was invited to numerous competitions and international sports events. She decided to leave the country illegally in December 1989, shortly before the revolution and fall of the communist government. She now lives in the United States.
80. *Prosport*, July 26, 2012.

References

Andreff, M., and W. Andreff. "Economic Prediction of Sport Performances: From Beijing Olympics to 2010 FIFA World Cup in South Africa." Working Paper Series, Paper No. 10–08 2010.

Bartmanski, D. "Successful Icons of Failed Time: Rethinking Post-Communist Nostalgia." *Acta Sociologica* 54 (2011): 213–231.

Berdhal, B., ed. *On the Social Life of Postsocialism: Memory, Consumption, Germany.* Bloomington: Indiana University Press, 2010.

Courtney, B., and J. Harrington. *Relaţii româno-americane, 1940–1990.* Iaşi: Polirom, 2002.

Georgescu, D. "'Ceausescu Hasn't Died': Irony as Counter-Memory in Post-Socialist Romania." In *Post-Communist Nostalgia*, edited by M. Todorora, and Z. Gille, 155–176. New York: Berghahn Books, 2012.

Girginov, V. "Capitalist Philosophy and Communist Practice: The Transformation of Eastern European Sport and the International Olympic Committee." *Culture, Sport, Society: Cultures, Commerce, Media, Politics* 1, no. 1 (1998): 118–148.

Grosset, Y., and M. Attali. "The French National Olympic and Sports Committee: A History of the Institutionalization of Sport and Olympism (1908–1975)." *Olympika: The International Journal of Olympic Studies* 17 (2008): 133–152.

Hann, C. M., ed. *Postsocialism: Ideals, Ideologies and Practices in Eurasia.* Routledge: London, 2002.

Hutcheon, L. "Irony, Nostalgia, and the Postmodern." *Studies in Comparative Literature* ("Methods for the Study of Literature as Cultural Memory," edited by A. Estor and R. Vervliet) 30 (2000): 189–207.

Ionescu, S., and T. Terret. "A Romanian Within the IOC: Alexandru Şiperco, Romania and the Olympic Movement." *The International Journal of the History of Sport* 29, no. 8 (2012): 1177–1194.

Jameson, F. "Nostalgia for the Present." *The South Atlantic Quarterly* 88, no. 2 (1989): 517–537 (reprinted in *Postmodernism, Or, the Cultural Logic of Late Capitalism*, Duke University Press, 1991).

Kerr, R. "The Impact of Nadia Comaneci on the Sport of Women's Artistic Gymnastics." *Sporting Tradition* 23, no. 1 (2006): 87–102.

Maguire, J. "Sport, Identity Politics, and Globalization: Diminishing Contrasts and Increasing Varieties." *Sociology of Sport Journal* 11, no. 4 (1994): 398–427.

Necula, L. "Daciada- un bun al intregului popor." *Revista Eramus* 12 (2001): 232–241 (Bucureşti: Editura Ars Docendi).

Ousterhoudt, R. G. "Capitalist and Socialist Interpretations of Modern Amateurism: An Essay on the Fundamental Difference." In *Olympism*, edited by J. Segrave, and D. Chu, 42–47. Champaign, IL: Human Kinetics, 1981.

Popescu-Sandu, O. "'Let's All Freeze Up Until 2100 or So': Nostalgic Directions in Post-Communist Romania." In *Post-Communist Nostalgia*, edited by M. Todorora, and Z. Gille, 113–128. New York: Berghahn Books, 2012.

Postolache, N. *Din istoria mişcării sportive muncitoreşti şi de mase*. Bucureşti: Editura Sport-Turism, 1975.

Riordan, J. *Sport in Soviet Society: Development of Sport and Physical Education in Russia and the U.S.S.R.* Cambridge: Cambridge University Press, 1977.

Riordan, J. "Sports After the Cold War: Implications for Russia and Eastern Europe." In *East Plays West*, edited by S. Wagg, and D. L. Andrews, 271–278. London: Routledge, 2007.

Riordan, J. "The Impact of Communism on Sport." *Historical Social Research* 32, no. 1 (2007): 110–115.

Tismaneanu, V. *Stalinism for All Seasons: A Political History of Romanian Communism*. Berkeley/Los Angeles: University of California Press, 2003.

Todovora, M. "Introduction: From Utopia to Propaganda and Back." In *Post-Communist Nostalgia*, edited by M. Todorora, and Z. Gille, 1–16. New York: Berghahn Books, 2012.

Todorora, M., and Gille, Z., eds. "Post-Communist Nostalgia." New York: Berghahn Books, 2012.

Trond, G. *Nationalism and Communism in Romania: The Rise and Fall of Ceausescu's Personal Dictatorship*. Boulder, CO: Westview Press, 1990.

Wilson, H. E. "The Golden Opportunity: Romania's Political Manipulation of the 1984 Los Angeles Olympic Games." *Olympika: The International Journal of Olympic Studies* III (1994): 83–97.

Wood, M. A. "Superpower: Romanian Women's Gymnastics During the Cold War." Dissertation, University of Illinois at Urbana-Champ 2010.

Zyser, L. "Phone Call From China Transformed 84' Games." *The New York Times*, July 14, 2008.

The Olympic Games in London 2012 from a Swedish Media Perspective

Susanna Hedenborg

Department of Sport Studies, Malmö University, Malmö, Sweden

The purpose of this article is to analyse the cultural information on (Olympic) sports presented in Swedish media coverage of the London Games 2012. A starting point for the analysis is that the media plays an important part in shaping a majority of the viewers' ideas about what sport is, and who is a real sportsman or sportswoman. In that way, the media gives cultural information on sports. The article focuses on a quantitative analysis of media representations, exploring how coverage intersects with gender and nationality, and devotes special attention to a comparison between the ways in which Sweden and Britain are represented in the media. The study demonstrates that there was a higher percentage of articles on Swedish sportswomen participating in the London Olympic Games compared to previous Olympics. A possible explanation is that the Swedish gender equality discourse has permeated the Swedish media, influencing it to cover sportswomen more than before. In addition, the cultural information presented to the Swedish readership about the London Olympic Games is, in short and oversimplified, nationalism rather than internationalism; that women, and especially Swedish women, practise sport; that track and field, swimming, handball, equestrian sports and football are very important and that they are performed by both men and women; and, finally, that in Britain, men play football and women are not involved in many sporting activities.

Introduction

The core values of the Olympic Movement are sport for all, development and education through sport, women and sport (increasing participation), peace through sport and environment and sport.[1] These values attest to the Olympic Movement's aims for social responsibility, and may be interpreted as demonstrating the movement's concern with issues of internationalism (an important goal since the founding of the Movement), gender equity and sustainability (goals that were added later). While these aims can be read as proof of a socially responsible movement, it is uncertain whether the actual event, the Olympic Games, increases the social responsibility of its participants and audience.

In London's bid to host the Olympic Games 2012, the Olympic legacy played an important part. It was promised that the London Olympic Games would inspire the population to become more physically active, and tackle wider social and economic issues such as exclusion, obesity and unemployment.[2] Whether the London Games 2012 will in fact have such an effect in London, Great Britain or anywhere else, is debated. As the media is a significant actor in the majority of viewers' experience of the Games, the legacy is likely to be influenced by media representations. Sociologist Pirkko Markula claims: 'media preserve, transmit and create important cultural information, they powerfully shape how and what we know about sport in general and women's sport in particular'.[3] Media representations are an interesting area of study. The purpose of this article is therefore to analyse the cultural information on (Olympic) sports presented in Swedish media coverage of the London Games 2012. The article will focus on how these representations intersect with gender and nationality, and devote special attention to a comparison between the ways in which Sweden and Britain are represented in media. This comparison is relevant as the 2012 Olympic Games took place in London. Did the location of the Games affect the Olympic legacy presented to the Swedish readership? Conclusions will be drawn in relation to Markula's points about the media's creation and transmission of important cultural information.

Materials and Methods

Articles from a daily newspaper, *Dagens Nyheter*, and a tabloid paper, *Aftonbladet*, will be used as source material to enable an analysis of how the Olympic Games 2012 are presented to the Swedish media audience. Sweden has two daily national newspapers. *Dagens Nyheter* is the biggest of these two and its printed edition has a daily circulation of approximately 350,000.[4] Sweden has three national tabloids, of which *Aftonbladet*, the printed edition, has a daily circulation of 235,000.[5] However, the real number of readers is difficult to establish precisely; a single copy of the paper may be read by more than one person, as a family or a workplace may share one paper. Many readers also access the papers online. According to *Dagens Nyheter*'s website, the paper is read by 858,000 people everyday (this amounts to approximately 10% of the Swedish population). *Aftonbladet* reaches 2.6 million people through their paper (more than 25% of the population), website and the Aftonbladet TV.

The analysis is primarily built on a quantitative study in which articles on the Olympic Games 2012 were collected from July 6, 2005, when London was chosen to host the Olympic Games 2012, up until the end of the Olympic Games on August 12, 2012. Articles were then categorised by the nationality and sex of the athletes (and/or coaches) presented, or as 'others', and by the sport portrayed. Information on the journalists was also collected. Data collection was conducted by means of an Internet search on the two papers' websites, using the following keywords: 'London' + 'OS' and 'London' + 'Olympiska spelen' (Olympiska spelen (OS) = Olympic Games). The online search enabled an analysis of a longer period than otherwise had been possible, and brought up a wider range of articles as the search was not limited to the respective papers' sport pages.[6] The choice to study articles throughout this lengthy time period is based on the fact that 'legacy-building' is likely to start as early as when the hosting country is selected. The gathered material was subsequently divided into two periods: before (from July 6, 2005 to July 26, 2012) and during the games (from July 27, 2012 to August 12, 2012). This was done because expected performance and actual performance are likely to influence number of articles.

Table 1 shows that there were a total of 1881 articles in the two papers; 900 in *Dagens Nyheter* and 981 in *Aftonbladet*. The total number of articles published before the Games was somewhat less than the number of articles during the Games, 842 and 1039, respectively. However, *Dagens Nyheter* published more articles before (488) than during

Table 1. Number of articles on the Olympic Games in the Swedish newspapers *Dagens Nyheter* and *Aftonbladet* before and during the Olympic Games 2012.

Period	*Dagens Nyheter*	*Aftonbladet*	Total
Before the Olympic Games	488	354	842
During the Olympic Games	412	627	1039
Total	900	981	1881

Note: Search was conducted through search engines on the respective papers' websites, using the keywords: 'London' + 'OS' and 'London' + 'Olympiska spelen' (Olympiska spelen (OS) = Olympic Games). *Source*: *Aftonbladet* and *Dagens Nyheter*, before the Olympic Games (from July 6, 2005 to July 26, 2012) and during the Olympic Games (from July 27, 2012 to August 12, 2012).

the Games (412), whereas *Aftonbladet* published 354 articles before the Games and 627 during the Games. The greater number of articles in *Aftonbladet* during the Games can be explained by the fact that this newspaper published short updates several times daily, while *Dagens Nyheter* did not report on the Games in this manner. *Dagens Nyheter* had 10 journalists stationed in London during the Games: eight sports journalists, one correspondent and one photographer.[7] *Aftonbladet* had a larger number of reporters covering the games, both employees and freelancers.[8] Both journals published articles taken from TT (*Tidningarnas Telegrambyrå*, i.e. the Swedish Central News Agency), with *Aftonbladet* taking more articles than *Dagens Nyheter*. Only 3% of the sports journalists from TT whose articles were quoted in *Dagens Nyheter* or *Aftonbladet* were women. A majority of the journalists whose names were provided were men (85%), more so in *Aftonbladet* than in *Dagens Nyheter*.[9] However, almost half of the articles in *Aftonbladet* (42%) were short pieces by anonymous journalists, and thus it is difficult to draw any definitive conclusions in the matter.

Previous Research

An important conclusion drawn from previous research on sports journalism and the Olympic Games is that women are under-represented in media coverage of sports events in general. In the anthology *Sportswomen at the Olympics*, it is demonstrated that articles on sportswomen comprise between 0% and 23% of global routine media coverage, or normal day-to-day coverage, and that in general women received less than 10% of the newspaper sport coverage.[10] During major international events, however, sportswomen receive more attention. In addition, some studies indicate that successful athletes, regardless of gender, are covered more than others in national reporting. In that sense, interest in successful native athletes seems to sometimes overrule the concept of gender.[11]

Another conclusion in previous research has been that the share of articles on women and sport in routine sport coverage does not seem to have changed over time. Studies of Denmark, Iceland, the Netherlands, Germany, Norway and Sweden show that sport media coverage has not exceeded 10% since the 1970s, despite the fact that an increasing number of women participate in sports activities.[12] In Sweden, men's football and ice hockey are the most media-covered sports. In the biggest daily newspaper, more than 80% of the routine sports coverage concerns men's football or hockey.[13]

When it comes to the sports media coverage of women in the Olympic Games, however, this coverage has grown from below 20% in the 1980s to about 30% since then.[14] A study of two newspapers in Denmark covering the Olympic Games in Athens 2004 demonstrated that 26% of the sport articles were about women.[15] During the same

Olympic Games, 33% of the articles in one Norwegian newspaper covered sportswomen.[16] A study of one of the Swedish newspapers shows a similar situation, sportswomen in this case receiving 31% of the sports coverage. However, the study emphasises that not all sportswomen were covered to the same degree. During these Games, articles on one female athlete amounted to 25% of the coverage measured in space.[17] In a similar study, Kelly Redman, Lucy Webb, Judy Liao and Pirkko Markula demonstrate that in the British papers *The Sun* and *The Mirror*, sportswomen got 20% of the coverage in the Olympic Games 2004.[18]

Background: Women and Men in the Olympic Games

Over time, women have gained access to an increasing number of events in the Olympic Games.[19] The history of the Olympic Games is, however, complex. The official narrative states that women were not allowed to compete. Nonetheless, in practise, women participated in several events as early as 1900.[20] Regulations notwithstanding, however, the percentage of male competitors has consistently been higher than the percentage of female competitors in the Olympic Games (Figure 1).

In 1928, the proportion of female participants was 9.6% and 70 years later, in 2004, the percentage of female athletes had risen to 40.7%.[21] In the Olympic Games in London 2012, there were 10,528 athletes; the share of women had grown since the last Games, and now amounted to 44% (see Table 2). The share of women in the national teams differed between the nations. As Sweden and Britain will be given special attention in this article, it is relevant that there were five times more British athletes than Swedish this year, but that sportswomen amounted to a higher share (59%) of the Swedish team than the British sportswomen (44%). The article will now address the question whether the increased participation of women and the varying participation rates of sportswomen in different national teams are reflected in media coverage.

Sportswomen and Sportsmen in Media

In *Sportswomen at the Olympics*, it is hypothesised that female and male athletes may receive coverage relative to their participation.[22] The studies of different national contexts

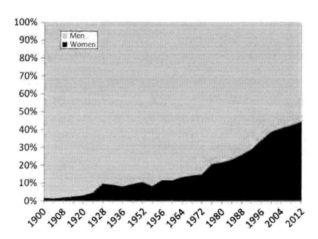

Figure 1.   Share of men and women (in %) participating in the Olympic Games, 1900–2012.
Source: http://www.sports-reference.com/olympics/summer/20120928

Table 2.   Total number of men and women and number of Swedish and British women and men competing in the London Olympic Games 2012 and share of female and male athletes (%).

Sex of athletes	Total number of athletes in the Olympic Games	Swedish athletes	British athletes
Women	4662 (44)	78 (59)	257 (44)
Men	5866 (56)	55 (41)	273 (56)
Total	10,528 (100)	133 (100)	530 (100)

Source: http://www.sports-reference.com/olympics/summer/20120928

in the book demonstrated that this was not true of the Olympic Games in 2004. Generally, women were under-represented and men were over-represented in the media in relation to their participation. This also holds true of the London Olympics 2012. As has been demonstrated in previous research conducted on other Olympic Games, male athletes received more media coverage than female athletes, somewhat more so in *Aftonbladet* than in *Dagens Nyheter*. Of the articles in *Aftonbladet*, 51% treated male athletes and 34% treated women. In *Dagens Nyheter*, 45% of the articles treated male athletes, whereas 37% treated female athletes. The rest of the articles covered either both sexes or other subjects (about 7% in *Aftonbladet* and 9% in *Dagens Nyheter*; Figure 2). Since the Olympic Games 2004 in Athens, however, there has been an increase in coverage of sportswomen in the Swedish papers. In her study, Helena Tolvhed showed, that 31% of the articles in *Dagens Nyheter* covered sportswomen,[23] in comparison to 37% in *Dagens Nyheter* in 2012 (36% in both papers together).

The increase in the share of articles on female athletes competing in the Olympic Games may indicate that the growing number of sportswomen has had some effect on media representations.[24] It is impossible to say for certain whether increased female participation is really the reason for the greater share of articles on women, or if other factors have had a greater impact. One such factor could be a growing awareness of gender equality among journalists and editors, although interviews with journalists and editors are

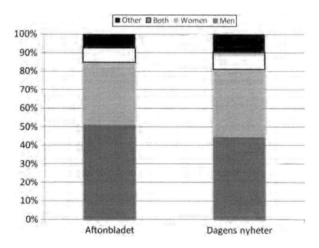

Figure 2.   Share of articles in the Swedish newspapers *Aftonbladet* and *Dagens Nyheter* about the Olympic Games 2012, covering sportsmen, sportswomen, both or other subjects. *Source*: *Aftonbladet* and *Dagens Nyheter*: before the Olympic Games (from July 6, 2005 to July 26, 2012) and during the Olympic Games (from July 27, 2012 to August 12, 2012).

necessary to verify this. Sweden is ranked as number four in The Global Gender Gap Report 2012. This suggests that Sweden is among the most gender-equal countries in the world, although the country has actually weakened its relative position, being ranked as number one in 2006. Nonetheless, the level of gender equality in Sweden compared to most other countries is high.[25]

Media logics may also explain the development, and logics favouring nationality and number of medals will be discussed in the following section. However, the increase in the share of articles is interesting in itself, as it well results in female athletes having a more prominent position in the Olympic legacy presented to the readership.

Gender, Nationalism and Internationalism in Media Coverage

The idea of internationalism has a long history in the Olympic movement. The number of participating athletes has grown, and the same is true of the number of competing nations. Today, the Olympic Games is a true mega event with 10,528 athletes from 205 different nationalities competing in 32 different sports.[26] It has, however, been pointed out that although the Olympic Games is a global event, it can be represented in the media in many different ways depending on cultural contexts.[27] Not least, newspapers tend to be biased towards their own nation.[28] National newspapers are inclined to focus on their own sportsmen and sportswomen, as well as sports that are popular in their home countries. A study of the articles published before the Olympic Games in 2012 endorses these findings. During the Games, however, there is another pattern. A majority of the articles on the Olympic Games in *Aftonbladet* and *Dagens Nyheter* before the Games covered Swedish sportsmen and sportswomen (Figure 3). Of the articles, 61% were about Swedish sportsmen and sportswomen, 34% treated international athletes and 4% covered both Swedish and international athletes. During the Games, there were more articles on international sportsmen and sportswomen. The coverage of the international athletes had

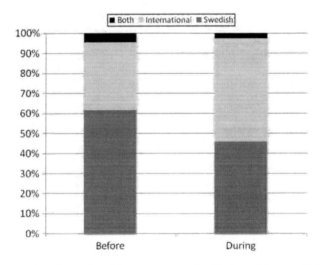

Figure 3.   Share of articles in the Swedish newspapers *Aftonbladet* and *Dagens Nyheter* on Swedish or international sportsmen and sportswomen before and during the Olympic Games 2012. *Source*: *Aftonbladet* and *Dagens Nyheter*: before the Olympic Games (from July 6, 2005 to July 26, 2012) and during the Olympic Games (from July 27, 2012 to August 12, 2012).

then increased to 52%. During this period, articles on Swedish sportsmen or sportswomen in the Olympic Games amounted to 46%, and articles where both Swedish and international athletes were featured in the same piece amounted to 3%.

Even though the coverage of the international athletes in the Olympic Games amounted to a higher portion than the Swedish athletes during the Games, it is difficult to speak about true internationalism as most of the international athletes covered in the Swedish papers came from the United States or Western Europe. In addition, if the number of articles is compared with the number of athletes competing for different countries, Swedish athletes are greatly over-represented in the media coverage. This is clearly seen also in relation to the representation of British athletes. In the Swedish papers, articles on British athletes amount to 8% of all articles on international athletes or 3% of all articles. The coverage is neither related to number of athletes nor to medals won in the Olympic Games. Whereas Sweden was ranked as number 29 with 4 medals, Britain was ranked as number 4 with 64 medals. Media logics oriented towards the concept of 'victory' or general patterns in the relative prominence of different sports in media coverage do not seem to apply to Swedish media representations. The latter logic will be discussed more thoroughly below. The over-representation of Swedish athletes indicates the unimportance of the victory logic in this source material, and suggests that the Olympic mission of internationalism has not rubbed off on the Swedish papers.

A study of the media coverage of Cathy Freeman during the 2000 Sydney Olympic Games demonstrated that gender was less important than the representation of a national symbol.[29] Freeman received a lot of media coverage, far more than what could have been expected, as female athletes were generally under-represented. Hence, Wensing and Bruce stress that the principle of nation can overrule that of gender. Depictions of the 2012 Olympic Games in Swedish papers are not as clear. If all the collected articles are analysed as one group, it becomes evident that the share of articles on international male athletes is slightly higher (25%) than the share of articles on Swedish male athletes (22%; see Table 3). For female athletes, the pattern is different; the articles on Swedish female athletes amount to 23%, i.e. about the same share as the international and Swedish male athletes, whereas the articles on international female athletes only amount to 12%.

These results indicate the relevancy and importance of studying the intersection of gender and nationality. Evidently, Swedish women received approximately the same amount of coverage as the two other male groups. It is not possible to pinpoint a specific

Table 3.   Share of articles on Swedish male and female athletes and international male and female athletes (in %), in the Swedish newspapers *Aftonbladet* and *Dagens Nyheter* before and during the Olympic Games 2012.

Articles on . . .	Percentage (%)
Swedish male athletes	22
International male athletes	25
Swedish and international male athletes	1
Swedish female athletes	23
International female athletes	12
Swedish and international female athletes	2
Swedish male and female athletes	9
International male and female athletes	6
Total	100

Source: *Aftonbladet* and *Dagens Nyheter*: before the Olympic Games (from July 6, 2005 to July 26, 2012) and during the Olympic Games (from July 27, 2012 to August 12, 2012).

Swedish sportswoman as was done by Tolvhed for the Olympic Games in Athens.[30] Instead, there is a wider range of Swedish sportswomen being covered. Admittedly, the result could be read as an under-representation of Swedish sportswomen in media coverage as a greater number of Swedish female athletes than Swedish male athletes competed. Nonetheless, I believe this pattern indicates something important; that, perhaps, Swedish media representations of the Olympic Games 2012 can be interpreted as indicating that media coverage is starting to reach gender equity in share of articles on Swedish sportsmen and sportswomen in coverage of the Olympic Games.[31]

Gender and Type of Sport in the Media Coverage

The most globally widespread sport of British origin is most likely football, both in reality, counted in the number of countries where football is played and as a media phenomenon. Interestingly, English football – the (men's) English Premier League – dominates the media in many countries outside the UK, indicating the prominence of the British sports legacy. As stated above, men's football and ice hockey are the most frequently mentioned sports in everyday coverage in *Dagens Nyheter*.[32] Nevertheless, sports coverage in relation to the Olympic Games is wider, even though not all of the 32 Olympic sports, and far from the 302 different events, were reported on or covered. Before the Games, *Dagens Nyheter* published articles on 25 different Olympic sports, and during the Olympic Games, 27 different Olympic Sports were covered. A similar pattern is found in *Aftonbladet* (Table 4).

Although sports journalism during the Games covers a wider spectrum of sports than routine sports coverage, it is generally the case that sports that receive more everyday coverage tend to be covered more during the Olympics as well.[33] In the Swedish papers, football is one of the most frequently covered sports. However, track and field events received the most coverage (262 articles). The second most covered sport was swimming (133 articles), and football came in third place (131 articles). Fourth was handball (90 articles) and equestrian sport was the fifth most covered sport (65 articles).

Generally, the amount of media coverage received by male and female athletes is related to which sports are considered masculine and feminine; most media coverage focuses on sports that are traditionally considered masculine.[34] This was true of the 2012 Olympic Games as well, and may be connected to the fact that most sports journalists are men.[35] However, both male and female sports journalists covered a variety of sports during the Games.

In addition, the sports that are perceived as masculine and feminine vary between different cultural contexts. Handball is a good example of this, and is seen as a women's sport in Norway, a gender-neutral sport in Denmark and as a masculine sport in Germany.[36] In a study of the European championships for women's handball, sociologist Gerd von der Lippe demonstrates the connection of sport to gender and nationality. In Norway, women's handball received 30% of the media coverage, whereas handball

Table 4. Number of Olympic sports covered in the articles in *Aftonbladet* and *Dagens Nyheter* before and during the Olympic Games 2012.

Period	*Dagens Nyheter*	*Aftonbladet*
Before the Olympic Games	24	22
During the Olympic Games	27	27

Source: *Aftonbladet* and *Dagens Nyheter*: before the Olympic Games (from July 6, 2005 to July 26, 2012) and during the Olympic Games (from July 27, 2012 to August 12, 2012).

only received 10% in the German newspapers.[37] Furthermore, male dominance in sport is seen in media as female athletes are marginalised, trivialised and sexualised.[38]

In a study of media coverage and gender in relation to the 2004 Athens Olympic Games, it was demonstrated that articles on athletics and women's football comprised half the media coverage of sportswomen in Sweden.[39] In Norway, sailing, mountain biking, athletics and beach volleyball were the sports in which sportswomen were most frequently covered.[40] In a study of Danish media coverage of the Olympic Games in Athens 2004, sociologist and historian Gertrud Pfister showed that in the newspaper *Politiken*, sportsmen were most often mentioned in articles on athletics, football, cycling and tennis. Sportswomen, on the other hand, were most frequently reported on in connection to handball, gymnastics, swimming and sailing. In the second newspaper, the tabloid *BT*, that was a part of Pfister's study, sportsmen were most frequently covered the sports athletics, handball, cycling and sailing, while sportswomen were most often featured in articles on handball, running, swimming and sailing.

Hovden and Hindenes as well as Pfister are wary of drawing any definitive conclusions about gender coding of the sports covered in the papers. Sailing, mountain biking and athletics are not usually regarded as feminine sports, and Hovden and Hindenes conclude that the performance of individual athletes in those cases is more important than notions of emphasised femininity or heterosexuality.[41] Nonetheless, Hovden and Hindenes suggest that the connection between sportswomen and beach volley may be interpreted otherwise. Pfister adds a further dimension, and emphasises that sports journalism is aimed at a male audience.[42] Another hypothesis presented by the researchers behind the book *Sportswomen at the Olympics* is whether the coverage received by female athletes is in proportion to the number of medals they win in the Olympic Games. Pfister concludes that the greater number of medals won by the male athletes may partly explain the disparities in coverage, but that this alone does not adequately explain the male dominance in media representation.[43] The study of Norway showed a slightly different pattern, where men received less media attention in relation to the medals they won (67% of the medals and 56% of the coverage).[44]

In order to discern patterns in the gender representations in the 2012 Olympic Games, this article will now proceed to clarify which sports were the most frequently covered in relation to gender (Table 5). The five sports in which male athletes received the most coverage were athletics (178), handball (73), football (72), swimming (53) and equestrian sports (40). The fact that men's football gets less media attention during the Olympic Games than in routine coverage is usually explained by the fact that the men's teams do not consist of the best players. According to the FIFA regulations for men's football in the Olympics, the associations affiliated with FIFA are invited to send their men's U-23 teams. In addition, regulations for the 2012 Olympic Games stated that all players participating in

Table 5. The five most covered sports in the Olympic Games 2012, for male and female athletes, respectively, in *Aftonbladet* and *Dagens Nyheter* (number of articles).

Men	Women
Track and field (178)	Track and field (84)
Handball (73)	Swimming (80)
Football (72)	Football (59)
Swimming (53)	Equestrian sports (25)
Equestrian sport (40)	Gymnastics (19)

Source: *Aftonbladet* and *Dagens Nyheter*: before the Olympic Games (from July 6, 2005 to July 26, 2012) and during the Olympic Games (from July 27, 2012 to August 12, 2012).

the preliminary and final competitions of the tournament had to be born on or after January 1, 1989, although regulations allow a maximum of three older male players to be included in the official list of players for the final tournament.[45] While men's football does not dominate Olympic media coverage in the way it does routine coverage, however, it was still the third most covered sport in the source material for this article.

The sports in which female athletes received the most media coverage were athletics (84), swimming (80), football (59), equestrian sport (25) and gymnastics (19; Table 4). FIFA regulations for the women's football tournament do not prevent the best players from participating, as no age restrictions are enforced in the women's tournament.[46] An interesting fact is that athletics, football and equestrian sports were among the most covered sports for both male and female athletes. This makes it difficult to draw any definitive conclusions regarding media representation of the Olympic Games 2012 in relation to feminine and masculine sports. Men's handball and women's gymnastics are different cases; gymnastics, in particular, is usually considered a feminine sport.

A different pattern emerges when the number of articles on male and female athletes competing in different sports are divided on the basis of nationality (Table 6). The four most covered sports in relation to international male athletes are track and field, handball, football and swimming, while the most covered sports in relation to Swedish male athletes are handball, shooting, track and field and equestrian sports. The fact that Swedish men's football was not among the most frequently covered sports, and actually received no mention at all, is unsurprising in the light of the fact that Sweden did not send a men's football team to compete in the Olympics this year. The four sports where international female athletes received the most coverage are track and field, swimming, football and equestrian sport, while the most frequently covered sports in relation to Swedish female athletes are swimming, track and field, football and equestrian sports. The coverage of Swedish male and female athletes may partly be explained by individual or team accomplishments (medals won by male athletes in handball, shooting, sailing and wrestling, and by female athletes in equestrianism and triathlon), and partly by performance expectations. The high coverage of international women's football by Swedish media can partly be attributed to the winning US team's Swedish female head coach, Pia Sundhage. Several articles detailed the US team's performance from a coaching point of view.

A comparison between the representation of Swedish and British male and female athletes shows that football was the most covered men's sport in connection to Great Britain (see Table 7). This is not explainable by the British football team's performance, as they were defeated in the quarter-finals. Instead, as Tolvhed pointed out in the case of

Table 6. The four most covered sports for international and Swedish male and female athletes in the London Olympic Games 2012 in *Aftonbladet* and *Dagens Nyheter*. Share of articles (%).

Articles on . . .			
International sportsmen	Swedish sportsmen	International sportswomen	Swedish sportswomen
1. Track and field (25)	1. Handball (20)	1. Track and field (18)	1. Swimming (21)
2. Handball (10)	2. Shooting (11)	2. Swimming (18)	2. Track and field (16)
3. Football (10)	3. Track and field (11)	3. Football (13)	3. Football (14)
4. Swimming (7)	4. Equestrian sports (11)	4. Equestrian sports (5)	4. Equestrian sports (7)

Source: *Aftonbladet* and *Dagens Nyheter*: before the Olympic Games (from July 6, 2005 to July 26, 2012) and during the Olympic Games (from July 27, 2012 to August 12, 2012).

Table 7. The four most covered sports for British sportsmen and sportswomen, and Swedish sportsmen and sportswomen in the London Olympic Games 2012. Share of articles (%) of British and Swedish sportsmen and sportswomen, respectively.

Articles on...			
British sportsmen	Swedish sportsmen	British sportswomen	Swedish sportswomen
1. Football (51)	1. Handball (20)	1. Athletics (60)	1. Swimming (21)
2. Cycling (11)	2. Shooting (11)	2. Swimming (20)	2. Athletics (16)
3. Athletics (6)	3. Athletics (11)	3. Weightlifting (20)	3. Football (14)
4. Tennis (7)	4. Equestrian sports (11)	4. –	4. Equestrian sports (7)
$N = 51$	$N = 323$	$N = 5$	$N = 325$

media coverage of Swedish athletes, one particular athlete received a large amount of coverage.[47] Despite the fact that he did not participate in the Olympic Games, 42% of the articles on British men's sports in the Olympic Games concerned David Beckham. For the most part, these articles debated whether Beckham would be selected to participate in the Games. Cycling, athletics and tennis were also covered, as British sportsmen won medals in these sports. Intriguingly, British horse riders were hardly mentioned at all, regardless of the fact that equestrianism, in general, received a lot of coverage in Swedish media in connection to the Olympic Games 2012, and the fact that the British equestrian team won an individual gold medal and an individual bronze medal in dressage, a team gold medal in dressage, a team gold medal in show jumping and a team silver medal in three-day eventing. Despite several medals being won by British female athletes, British sportswomen were only featured in five articles. Clearly, the number of medals won is not related to the amount of media coverage received in these cases.

A different pattern emerges when coverage of Swedish athletes is studied. Coverage of Swedish sportsmen focused on handball, which can partly be explained by the fact that the Swedish team won the silver medal. Articles on shooting and athletics covered expected results, actual results and injuries. Women in athletics received similar coverage, and so did the female swimmers. Articles are loaded with medal hopes, and express disappointment when athletes fall short of expectations. Articles on the female football players not only detailed their injuries, but also stressed their great potential as sportswomen. Coverage of equestrian sport was somewhat different. In articles before the Games, journalists expressed great hopes for especially the Swedish male competitors in jumping and dressage. During the Games, the coverage changed somewhat as a woman won silver medal in three-day eventing, and subsequently received a lot of media attention. The men who were expected to win medals did not perform as well as had been anticipated. One example is the show jumping rider Rolf-Göran Bengtsson who was given special attention in Swedish media, and whom journalists expected to win medals during the Games. At the time of the London Olympics, he had won silver medal in the individual jumping competition during the 2008 Beijing Olympic Games, as the first Swedish silver medallist in show jumping since 1932. In September 2001, he became the first Swedish rider to win the European Championships in Madrid. In 2011, Bengtsson was also awarded the 'Jerring Prize' (Jerringpriset), a Swedish people's choice award where the public votes for the best sportsman of the year. He was also Sweden's flag bearer in the London Olympic Games. When Bengtsson elected not to compete in the finals due to an injury sustained by his horse, he was not portrayed as having fallen short of expectations, but as a champion of 'fair play' towards his horse.[48]

Concluding Discussion

The purpose of this article was to analyse cultural information on (Olympic) sports presented in Swedish media representations of the 2012 London Olympic Games. Methodologically, the article is based on quantitative data. Articles about the Olympic Games 2012 in two papers: one daily newspaper, *Dagens Nyheter*, and one tabloid paper, *Aftonbladet*, have been counted and studied from July 6, 2005 when London was selected to host the Games until the Games were over, on August 12, 2012. A starting point for the analysis was that the media plays an important part in shaping a majority of the viewers' ideas about what sport is, and who is a real sportsman or sportswoman. In order for the Olympic Movement to attain its goals regarding internationalism and women's sport, media representations must be taken into consideration. Although significant progress has been made, this study demonstrates that these aims have not been entirely accomplished.

In everyday coverage of sport in Sweden, men's football and ice hockey dominate. As proven by previous research on other Olympic Games, however, coverage during the 2012 Games featured a wider variety of sports, and sportswomen received more attention than in day-to-day sports coverage. A majority of the journalists behind the articles that were used as source material for this study were men (more so in *Aftonbladet* than in *Dagens Nyheter*). Along with gender-coded expectations for athletes, this may explain why male athletes received more coverage. In many of the articles, it was not possible to determine whether the journalists were men or women, and an analysis of the cases where the journalists' names were provided showed that both male and female reporters covered many different sports and athletes of both sexes. International and Swedish athletes received almost equal shares of the coverage; Swedish athletes received more attention before the Games, but less once the Games had commenced. In that sense, the Olympic mission of internationalism has not been accomplished in Swedish papers, although it is questionable whether such a simple conclusion can be made about the Olympic missions of internationalism. The article also shows that Swedish athletes were over-represented if the number of competing athletes and medals won are considered, and few of the 205 competing countries were covered at all. Even Britain, the hosting nation that finished fourth in the Olympic medal table was only sparsely covered, which suggests that the Swedish readership was provided with comparatively little international cultural information.

Interestingly, female athletes received more coverage than in previous Games. The fact that the Nordic countries have long ranked highly in reports on gender equality may explain why Nordic media covered sportswomen to a greater extent than many other countries, although female athletes were still under-represented.[49] According to The Global Gender Gap Report 2012, Sweden is the world's fourth most gender-equal country.[50] The report measures women's economic participation and opportunities, educational attainments, health and survival and political empowerment in relation to men. Swedish women are highly educated, and have a high level of labour force participation. Moreover, salary gaps between men and women in Sweden are among the lowest in the world, and parents are able to combine labour and raising children. All these factors contribute to Sweden's high rank, though it must be re-emphasised that Sweden has dropped from number one to number four since 2006. Still, other factors must be considered in relation to media coverage of female athletes in the 2012 Olympic Games. A study of the intersections between gender and nationality in media representation has demonstrated that although Swedish male and female athletes, together with international male athletes received almost equal shares of the coverage, international female athletes were covered much less frequently.

Previous research has indicated that the Olympic Games are represented differently in different countries, and that native athletes receive the most coverage. This holds true of the Swedish female athletes, but does not apply to male athletes during the Games. During the Games, Swedish and international sportsmen were featured in an almost equal number of articles. When the number of participating athletes from different nations and the number of medals won are taken into account, it is clear that Swedish male and female athletes were over-represented. Male and female athletes also received varying amounts of coverage depending on the sport in which they competed. As of yet, no definitive conclusions can be made regarding how this is connected to notions of feminine or masculine sports.

This article focused especially on representations of Sweden and Britain, in order to discern what cultural information about the hosting country was presented to the Swedish readership. This comparison renders interesting conclusions. Although female athletes in general and Swedish ones in particular received more coverage than in previous Olympic Games, very little was written about British female athletes. Furthermore, articles on British athletes focused mainly on men's football, especially whether David Beckham would be selected to participate. Articles on Swedish athletes targeted a far wider range of issues. The coverage of Swedish athletes cannot be fully explained by their accomplishments, but possibly by a combination of expectations and medals won. The coverage of David Beckham should more likely be attributed to media expectations of British sports.

To use Markula's concept, the cultural information presented to the Swedish readership about the London Olympic Games is, in short, nationalism rather than internationalism; that women, and especially Swedish women, practise sport; that track and field, swimming, handball, equestrian sports and football are very important and that they are performed by both men and women; and, finally, that in Britain men play football and women are not involved in many sporting activities. Naturally, this is an oversimplified reading of the results. Another issue is that these findings are mainly based on the number of articles, rather than on their content. A study of the contents of the articles about the 2012 Olympic Games would enable further insights about the cultural information presented to the Swedish readership. However, that challenge must be addressed in a future article.

Acknowledgements

I am grateful to Manon Hedenborg-White and Jens Radmann, who collected the data for this study. Without your work this article could not have been written! I also want to thank the reviewers of the article who made me clarify some of the results and be more modest in relation to other conclusions.

Notes on Contributor

Susanna Hedenborg, Professor of Sport Science, Malmö University.

Notes

1. Olympic Movement, "Olympism in Action."
2. Girginov and Hills, "Political Process of Constructing."
3. Markula, Bruce, and Hovden, "Key Themes in the Research on Media Coverage," 2; cf. Pedersen, Whisenant, and Schneider, "Research and Reviews."
4. *Dagens Nyheter*, "DN i siffror."
5. *Aftonbladet*, "I siffror."

6. An analysis of the printed edition would have enabled further interesting questions regarding the position of the articles in the papers (e.g. editorials, news articles and sports pages). As the online edition is used as source material in this article, however, this question has not been explored.
7. Email from Göran Lowgren, *Dagen Nyheter*, November 23, 2012.
8. The names of the journalists were noted and checked against *Aftonbladet*'s presentations of its reporters. Journalists without their own presentations were identified by an online search for their names. Around 50 journalists were found.
9. Although the exact length of the articles could have been measured (cf. Tolvhed, "Swedish Media Coverage"), this has not been the aim here. Instead, the number of articles has been the result of the main focus.
10. E.g. Markula, Bruce, and Hovden, "Key Themes in the Research on Media Coverage"; Bernstein, "Is It Time for a Victory Lap?" 415–428.
11. Wensing and Bruce, "Bending the Rules."
12. Markula, Bruce, and Hovden, "Key Themes in the Research on Media Coverage."
13. Tolvhed, "Swedish Media Coverage."
14. Markula, Bruce, and Hovden, "Key Themes in the Research on Media Coverage."
15. Pfister, "Women in Sport."
16. Hovden and Hindenes, "Gender in Olympic Newspaper Coverage."
17. Tolvhed, "Swedish Media Coverage."
18. Redman et al., "The United Kingdom: Women's Representation in British Olympic Newspaper Coverage 2004."
19. Pfister, "Women in Sport," 236–37; Teetzel, "Rules and Reform," 386–98.
20. Pfister, "Women in Sport," 236–37.
21. Ibid.
22. Markula, Bruce, and Hovden, "Key Themes in the Research on Media Coverage," 7.
23. Tolvhed, "Swedish Media Coverage."
24. Cf. Tolvhed, "Swedish Media Coverage."
25. Hausmann, Tyson, and Zahidi, "Global Gender Gap Report," Table 3a, 8.
26. Sports-Reference: Olympic Sports, "2012 London Summer Games."
27. E.g. Puijk, "A Global Media Event?."
28. Bernstein, "Things You Can See."
29. Wensing and Bruce, "Bending the Rules." There are additional media logics that are relevant to the Cathy Freeman case, such as the focus on victory and 'story telling'.
30. Tolvhed, "Swedish Media Coverage."
31. If the share of articles is calculated in relation to the period before and during the Games, the result is very close to what is presented in Table 3.The share was slightly higher for international and national female athletes during the games in comparison to before the Games; for the Swedish male athletes, the share of articles was slightly lower during the Games in comparison to share of articles before the Games.
32. Tolvhed, "Swedish Media Coverage." In the book *Europe, Sport, World: Shaping Global Societies*, historian Tony Mangan writes that England was the birthplace of several significant modern sports, and that the British Empire exported these sports to countries in the Empire as well as other European countries. During the globalisation process, European and, somewhat later, American sports spread and became the 'property' of new nations; see Mangan, *Europe, Sport, World*, 1–4. Mangan also underlines that the process is not only working in one direction – sports from other parts of the world influence European sports too.
33. Bernstein, "Things You Can See."
34. Koivula, *Gender in Sport*; Koivula, "Gender Stereotyping in Televised Media."
35. Cf. Pfister, "Denmark: Nationalism, Gender and Media Sports."
36. von der Lippe, "Media Image."
37. Ibid.
38. E.g. Tolvhed, *Nationen på spel*; Markula, *Olympic Women and the Media*.
39. Tolvhed, "Swedish Media Coverage."
40. Hovden and Hindenes, "Gender in Olympic Newspaper Coverage."
41. Ibid.
42. Pfister, "Denmark: Nationalism, Gender and Media Sports."

43. Ibid.
44. Hovden and Hindenes, "Gender in Olympic Newspaper Coverage."
45. FIFA, "Regulations of the Olympic Football Tournament."
46. Ibid.
47. Cf. Tolvhed, "Swedish Media Coverage."
48. The media narrative around the Swedish equestrian team is analysed in an article by Anna Maria Hellborg and Susanna Hedenborg, "Mediated gender relations in a gender mixed sport."
49. Tolvhed, "Swedish Media Coverage."
50. Hausmann, Tyson, and Zahidi, "Global Gender Gap Report."

References

Aftonbladet. "I siffror." *Aftonbladet.* Accessed October 28, 2012. www.aftonbladet.se/siffror
Bernstein, Alina. "Things You Can See From There You Can't See From Here: Globalization, Media, and the Olympics." *Journal of Sport and Social Issues* 24, no. 4 (2000): 351–369.
Bernstein, Alina. "Is It Time for a Victory Lap?" *International Review for the Sociology of Sport* 37 (2002): 415–428.
Dagens Nyheter. "DN i siffror." *Dagens Nyheter.* Accessed October 28, 2012. www.dn.se/diverse/diverse--hem/dn-i-siffror
FIFA. "Regulations of the Olympic Football Tournaments: Games of the XXX Olympiad London, 27 July to 12 August 2012." FIFA. Accessed October 28, 2012. http://www.fifa.com/mm/document/tournament/competition/01/33/73/30/regulationsoft2012_updatedjune2012_en.pdf
Girginov, Vassil, and Laura Hills. "The Political Process of Constructing a Sustainable London Olympics Sports Development Legacy." *International Journal of Sport Policy and Politics* 1, no. 2 (2009): 161–181.
Hausmann, Ricardo, Laura D. Tyson, and Saadia Zahidi. "The Global Gender Gap Report." World Economic Forum. Accessed October 28, 2012. http://www3.weforum.org/docs/WEF_GenderGap_Report_2012.pdf
Hellborg, Anna Maria and Susanna Hedenborg. "Mediated Gender Relations in a Gender Mixed Sport – Representations of Gender in Equestrian Sports During the Olympic Games in 2012." Accepted for publication in *Sport in Society*, forthcoming.
Hovden, Jorid, and Aina Hindenes. "Norway: Gender in Olympic Newspaper Coverage: Towards Stability or Change?" In *Sportswomen at the Olympics: A Global Content Analysis of Newspaper Coverage*, edited by Toni Bruce, Jorid Hovden, and Pirkko Markula, 47–60. Rotterdam: Sense Publishers, 2010.
Koivula, Nathalie. *Gender in Sport.* Stockholm: Department of Psychology, Stockholm University, 1999.
Koivula, Nathalie. "Gender Stereotyping in Televised Media Sport Coverage." *Sex Roles* 41, no. 7–8 (1999): 589–604.
Mangan, Tony. *Europe, Sport, World: Shaping Global Societies.* London: Frank Cass, 2001.
Markula, Pirkko. *Olympic Women and the Media: International Perspectives.* Basingstoke: Palgrave Macmillan, 2009.
Markula, Pirkko, Toni Bruce and Jorid Hovden. "Key Themes in the Research on Media Coverage." In *Sportswomen at the Olympics: A Global Content Analysis of Newspaper Coverage*, edited by Toni Bruce, Jorid Hovden, and Pirkko Markula, 1-18. Rotterdam: Sense Publishers, 2010.
Olympic Movement. "Olympism in Action: Olympic Values and Programmes." Accessed June 5, 2012. http://www.olympic.org/olympism-in-action
Pedersen, Paul M., Warren A. Whisenant, and Ray G. Schneider "Research and Reviews: Using a Content Analysis to Examine the Gendering of Sports Newspaper Personnel and Their Coverage." *Journal of Sport Management* 17, no. 4 (2003): 376–393.
Pfister, Gertrud. "Denmark: Nationalism, Gender and Media Sports: A Content Analysis of Danish Newspapers." In *Sportswomen at the Olympics: A Global Content Analysis of Newspaper Coverage*, edited by Toni Bruce, Jorid Hovden, and Pirkko Markula, 33–46. Rotterdam: Sense Publishers, 2010.
Pfister, Gertrud. "Women in Sport: Gender Relations and Future Perspectives." *Sport in Society* 13, no. 2 (2010): 234–248.
Puijk, Roel. "A Global Media Event? Coverage of the 1994 Lillehammer Olympic Games." *International Review for the Sociology of Sport* 35, no. 3 (2000): 309–330.

Redman, Kelly, Lucy Webb, Judy Liao, and Pirkko Markula. "The United Kingdom: Women's Representation in British Olympic Newspaper Coverage 2004." In *Sportswomen at the Olympics: A Global Content Analysis of Newspaper Coverage*, edited by Toni Bruce, Jorid Hovden, and Pirkko Markula, 73–90. Rotterdam: Sense Publishers, 2010.

Sports-Reference: Olympic Sports. "2012 London Summer Games." Accessed October 28, 2012. http://www.sports-reference.com/olympics/summer/2012/

Teetzel, Sarah. "Rules and Reform: Eligibility, Gender Differences, and the Olympic Games." *Sport in Society* 14, no. 3 (2011): 386–398.

Tolvhed, Helena. *Nationen på spel: Kropp, kön och svenskhet i populärpressens representationer av olympiska spel 1948–1972*. Umeå: H:ström-Text & kultur, 2008.

Tolvhed, Helena. "Sweden: Swedish Media Coverage of Athens 2004." In *Sportswomen at the Olympics: A Global Content Analysis of Newspaper Coverage*, edited by Toni Bruce, Jorid Hovden, and Pirkko Markula, 61–72. Rotterdam: Sense Publishers, 2010.

von der Lippe, Gerd. "Media Image: Sport, Gender and National Identities in Five European Countries." *International Review for the Sociology of Sport* 37, no. 3–4 (2002): 371–395.

Wensing, Emma H., and Toni Bruce. "Bending the Rules: Media Representations of Gender During an International Sporting Event." *International Review for the Sociology of Sport* 38, no. 4 (2003): 387–396.

Close Strangers or Strange Friends? The London Olympics and Anglo-Norwegian Sports Relations in a Historical Perspective

Matti Goksøyr

The Norwegian School of Sport Sciences, Sognsveien, Norway

This article studies similarities and disparities between the two nations England and Norway as they could be observed before and during the London 2012 Olympics, and discuss them in the historical perspective of geopolitical and sportive relations. The main perspective is how these relations have been seen and experienced from Norway. The article also studies whether the London Olympics of 2012 did present new forms of relationships between the two geographical neighbours. The article discusses the role of ball games, preferably team handball at the 2012 Games, as one example of where sporting interests differ. The article reflects upon these matters in a historical context. It builds upon traditional historical methods, document and media analysis. It also looks at the 2012 London Olympics against the background of the former London Games of 1908 and 1948, and the overall historical sports relations between England, 'land of sport' and a small country like Norway, who generally has been on the receiving end of these interchanges. Such asymmetric relationships invite to a critical use of perspectives like cultural imperialism and post-colonialism. The article discusses whether such perspectives can be fruitful also when one discusses matters between the so-called First World nations. As the title of the article indicates, Norway and England are both close, politically and culturally, while also being strangers to one another, e.g. in parts of the sports culture. The 2012 Olympics seemed to reinforce this impression.

Introduction

When it comes to Olympic Games, Norway is a winter sports nation. Together with Austria and Lichtenstein, it is the only country with a better medal record from the Winter Games than from the Summer Games.[1] It is perhaps one of those slightly ironic cases of history then, that the only 'winter' event that has been presented at any London Games; the ice skating of 1908 happened without Norwegian participation. Yet, Norway's relation to the three London Olympic (Summer) Games and to the English sport, in general, provides special cases of cultural and geopolitical links between two politically and culturally close, albeit very different sporting nations. In 1908, the difference came out on the ice; the English favoured figure skating, which was the Olympic event, while the Norwegians preferred speed skating and stayed home. In 2012, the Norwegians dominated (women's) team handball, while the English fancied other ball games. Behind it all is the Norwegian *anglofilia*; the uncritical idolisation of English football, and the distinction between Englishmen playing cricket and Norwegians who like skiing.

113

This article will attempt to analyse similarities and disparities between the two nations England and Norway as they could be observed historically and during the London 2012 Olympics and discuss them in the perspective of geopolitical and sportive relations. Did the London Olympics of 2012 present new forms of relationships between the two geographical neighbours? The main perspective will be the bilateral relations – 'the bridge over the North Sea'[2] – as seen and experienced from Norway. The article is based upon primary and secondary literature and recent media observations.

Theoretical and Methodical Perspectives on an Uneven Relationship

In the history of sport, England has been the recognised epicentre for centuries. England was the 'land of sport', the inventor of modern sports and the governing body of many sports. The British sports club became a model for organising local-level sports in several countries, if not all. In sport, Britain was the nation to look up to, to admire, to emulate, to be recognised by and eventually to challenge and demand some respect from. Most of the world's sports nations can relate to an asymmetric history of that kind. Also Norwegians came to find themselves at the receiving end of their relations with the English.

However, the Norwegian sports movement emerged from the late nineteenth century in much the same way as it grew up in other nations, as a mix between homemade, traditional physical exercises and impulses from abroad. In Norway, this meant that the local *idrett*, in the form of winter activities such as skiing and ice-skating, together with maritime exercises such as rowing and sailing, plus rifle shooting, met with *gymnastics* from Sweden, *turnen* from Germany and most notably *sport* from England.[3]

The process when impulses from abroad are introduced, integrated or rejected in new cultures is a familiar topic in history and social sciences, and has been studied through all sorts of theoretical perspectives. The spread of modern, competitive sport in its Western form has been portrayed as cultural diffusion, cultural imperialism, cultural hegemony or the broader modernisation, globalisation or simply development. Allen Guttmann has discussed the use of these terms, but mostly applied to developing – or Third World – countries, as they were once called.[4] One question implicit in this article is whether such perspectives can also be used to understand sports relations between the so-called First World nations. One argument for attempting this would be that inside the field of sport, England held a particularly dominating role, and that small countries such as Norway, in the late nineteenth and early twentieth century, can be said to have been in an extremely one-sided relationship with England. Although the Norwegian situation was neither post-colonial nor post-imperial, such perspectives could provide interesting questions. For example, what were the long-term effects of this cultural meeting with the English sport? What happened after the dominance was gone, or not longer so obvious? Is there a legacy, a 'colonisation of meaning'?[5]

For England, Norway was obviously not the 'significant', in the meaning relevant, 'other'. Norway was too small and insignificant. What if we turn the question around? England held a special role for all sporting nations. But the contrast was too big for England to be called relevant in that sense for the Norwegians. For Norway, the significant others were their Scandinavian neighbours, Sweden and Denmark, by whom they could be accepted as a challenger and hope to beat, occasionally. The English were in another league, looked upon as a master to be treated respectfully.

Hence, in general, the Norwegian relation to the English in sports were characterised by attitudes of inferiority. The English were the experts and authorities who knew it all, while the Norwegians were the students, eagerly admiring their masters.[6] This general impression was arguably valid for most sports, except for winter sports on snow and ice, where the Norwegians felt they had less reason for feeling secondary. The superior–inferior relationship is obviously a historical relationship.

The Geo-Political History

Norway and England are geographical neighbours with a very different historical impact on the world. One is a former world power, although the last half century in relative decline. The other is a small nation, poor at the time the other was great, the last hundred years, however, economically prosperous and regularly scoring high in United Nations (UN) and Organisation for Economic Co-operation and Development (OECD) polls on where the 'better life' is.[7] England/Great Britain and Norway share the North Sea as border area and a field of economic interest (oil, fisheries). They cover somewhat uneven geographical areas: Norway, stretching far to the North, is clearly the larger,[8] covering $323,802 \, km^2$ and England covering $130,395 \, km^2$. In all other respects, population size, political, economic and military power, England has been the bigger and the dominant.

After close cultural contacts during the early Medieval Ages,[9] Norway bore less strategic interest for England until the Napoleonic wars, when they ended up as enemies. Denmark/Norway was pitted against Sweden/England in 1812. That was, however, the last time war waged between the two nations. The last two hundred years have been characterised by peaceful coexistence and political alliances.

At the same time, the two countries experienced a very different political and economical development. While England saw industrial revolutions on its land and grew to become the world's leading military, economic and political power during the eighteenth and nineteenth centuries, Norway remained a poor and sparsely populated place on earth. England had 8.3 million inhabitants in 1801, 53 million in 2011, while Norway only had 0.880 million in 1801 and reached 5 million in 2012.[10] Politically Norway became a subject of the Kingdom of Denmark until it gained a political independence in 1814. From then on till 1905, Norway found itself in junior role in a royal alliance with Sweden. There have, however, been areas where Norway has scored higher than their population should indicate. Norway was a major shipping nation during most of the twentieth century. The merchant fleet was the fourth largest in the world at the outbreak of the Second World War and played a vital role in bringing supplies to the isolated Britain during the war.

The general cultural development in Norway during the late nineteenth and early twentieth centuries had seen broad German-friendly tendencies: after all, the nation had presented the great philosophers, composers, poets and scientists to the world. In Norwegian schools, German was the most taught foreign language, and in science, it was the lingua franca. However, this did not hinder Norway and England from being on friendly terms, and cultural impulses like the Boys' Scouts, the Salvation Army – and the sport – from reaching Norway.

Through the first half of the twentieth century, the English connection grew visibly stronger. It was part of this picture that in 1905, when Norway gained full independence after the dissolution of the union with Sweden, and Norwegians had voted for monarchy as their constitutional form and a new royal family had to be established, that the candidates to this coming Norwegian royalty were found in Denmark and England. The new Queen of Norway was the daughter of the English King Edward VII. This strengthened the already existing historical relationship; the Norwegian royal family was and has continued to be kin to the English royal family. Of symbolic interest in some cases maybe, however, sport is a field where precisely the presence of royalties as national symbols can give the occasion a different level of meaning.

The Second World War and the German occupation of Norway from 1940 linked Norway to England stronger than ever before.[11] After the war, Norway and England continued to be political allies in the North Atlantic Treaty Organisation (NATO). During the first post-war decades, they also shared scepticism to the European Union (EU). This is, however, where they have parted company. Britain became a member in 1973, while Norway is still on the outside. Related to this is a geopolitical situation that makes control over the seas and their natural resources a key point. Possible conflicts on fisheries and oil/gas have made borders on the ocean important. However, the bilateral relations have been mostly harmonious, with a slight exception of environmental issues.[12]

The EU question has, however, made the political atmosphere of 2012 less tight than the case was in 1948 when both nations were members of the European trade organisation European Free Trade Association (EFTA), both were heading for NATO membership, and both had just come out of the Second World War as close friends and allies. Still, the overall relationship has been one of neighbourly friendliness, familiarity, mutual understanding and cultural contrasts; for example, do the English distinctions of social class appear to be oceans apart from Norwegian equalitarian social democracy? This has enabled all kinds of relations in the fields of sport – ranging from Norwegians performing pilgrim travels to English football grounds to mutual ignorance of many other sports.

Norway at the London Olympics 2012: Historical Context and Present Challenges

After some initial reservations more than a hundred years ago, Norway has shown great interest in the Olympic Games, both as applicant to be host, and as host and participant. It is the only Nordic nation that has accommodated the Olympic Games more than once (though Winter Games; 1952 and 1994), and Oslo, the capitol, is currently involved in a public debate on whether to announce its candidacy as host city of the Olympic Winter Games of 2022. The London 2012 Olympics led to a rising interest for another Norwegian application. A growing curiosity for the ideas, plans and strategies that made the London Olympics relatively successful could be observed. In other words, were there yet again things to be learned from the English? This is an ongoing debate, the end of which is unclear at the moment.

Although Norway was a keen Olympic participant nation with close connections to England, the two nations split sides in 1980, when the Norwegians joined the American-led boycott of the Moscow Olympics, while the British chose to take part. On a large scale, this is the only time the two nations have gone separate ways.

For the 2012 London Olympic Games, the Norwegian Olympic Committee selected 64 athletes (31 women and 33 men). They came home with a disappointingly modest medal harvest (2-1-1).[13] Seen numerically, in participants and medals, the 2012 Games did not differ dramatically from the former London Games.[14] However, the three contingents did not only represent very different historical versions of the Norwegian society and three different sport systems regarding the organisation of top level sport. They also came to London in three different international situations. The 1908 Games took place only three years after a dramatic dissolution of a very unpopular union with Sweden. The 1948 Games came just 3 years after the Second World War. The 2012 Games, for Norway's part, were the first to happen in 'normal' times, without dramatic political events preceding the Games.

Former London Olympic Games

More than a hundred years ago, the Norwegians' self-perception in most sports was that of a keen beginner. Sports leaders realised they were inexperienced newcomers; hence, they were eager to learn, especially from the English. They established relations, travelled to see and study, and invited clubs and coaches in a variety of sports. The first national association to do so was the Norwegian Rowing Association, who hired a coach to prepare for the London Olympic Games 1908.[15] At that time, Norway was a fresh nation on the international scene, after in 1905 having come out of an unpopular union with Sweden. The main concerns of the union, seen from the Norwegian side, had been that Swedish authorities were responsible for foreign politics and that the Swedish king also was king of Norway. The London Olympics in this situation was a chance to display the Norwegian flag among equals. That is also the reason why the extra-Olympic Games of 1906 have been given prominent place in early Norwegian sports history; it was the first time Norway participated as a totally independent nation. It was also the first time Norwegian athletes came home with Olympic gold medals. Norway had attended the 1900 Olympics in Paris, demonstrating the difference between political geography and sports geography, while showing that Norway had established a fair degree of autonomy in the union with Sweden, perhaps also illustrating that sport was not an overwhelmingly important matter for Swedish foreign relations.[16]

However, in 1908, the aftermath of the dissolution of the union with Sweden was still visible and alive, even though the separation ended peacefully, after threats and military mobilisation had been a heated issue on both sides. Nevertheless, a fierce rivalry with the former union partner emerged, above all in sports.[17] Antagonisms before the dissolution had provoked a first Norwegian sports boycott on political grounds, when Norwegian skiers refused to travel to Sweden to compete in the Nordic Games in the winter 1905 – an action that prompted a Swedish response in the form of a boycott of Swedish–Norwegian sporting collaboration in the years to come. This last boycott was mostly enacted in the nationally symbolic-laden winter sports; hence, the 1908 Games became an international scene on which this rivalry could be displayed. The importance of the performance in London was perhaps more emphasised on the Swedish side than the Norwegian. According to historian Jan Lindroth, Swedish politicians on a broad scale were eager to provide conditions so that Swedish athletes could demonstrate who was the 'big brother' in Scandinavia. State economic support for Olympic participation was increasing in both nations, although not rising particularly above the symbolic gesture level. With clear national arguments, Swedish politicians had voted to grant 15,000 Swedish Crowns, many times the amount their Norwegian colleagues agreed upon. 'We do not wish to be passed by Norway in such a matter, do we?' Swedish minister of ecclesial affairs Å.H. Hammarskjöld argued.[18]

Norwegians too, with some exceptions, were eager to participate in London. However, after a hammering by the Swedes 11-3 in the first football international ever played by both nations, a more sombre and realistic tone seems to have dawned upon the otherwise highly patriotic Norwegians. Alas, expectations were not very high, and disappointment was not too big, when the Swedes could triumph in the Olympic sports, by being ranked the third best nation in the medals table. The Norwegians placed eight best and seemed to be happy to be allowed to show their flag at the Olympic arena. The outcome was still that the Norwegian athletes had made a performance of which the nation could be proud. Two gold medals were won in rifle shooting, a coming Olympic stronghold for Norwegian Olympians, and six other medals were also conquered. Sports officials claimed, with a certain impact, that it, also in the future, would be important for a small nation to be present when youth of the world was gathering. Hence, during the next four years, Norwegians tried to collect their athletic strength; Parliament granted three times more money for the next Games, money that amongst others was spent by hiring more British coaches and by presenting the third largest contingent of all participating nations in the Olympic Games in 1912 – which by the way took place in Sweden.[19]

However, not everybody inside sports had been ardent supporters of Olympic participation. Especially among sports officials who feared for the development of the Norwegian 'idrett',[20] there was both reluctance and resistance to the idea of staging Olympic Games every fourth year. Sports leaders from the gymnastic and rifle shooting associations controlled the existing umbrella organisation for Norwegian sports.[21] One of them, Johan Martens, the gymnasts' leader, meant that Olympics every fourth year was 'too frequent'.[22] Instead, he and others aimed for a sport in the service of overall physical health and not the least; defence of the fatherland. Another opponent, Jacob Grøttum stated that at the Olympics, 'there are no requests for the participant's physical development in a healthy and harmonious direction'.[23] Olympic Games were portrayed as sensationalism, unhealthy specialisation and record hysteria causing immoral prioritising inside sports. These military-oriented sports leaders were on the losing side, however. The positive impressions from the first London Olympic Games would instead contribute to growing discontent with the way Norwegian sports had been organised and lead to the foundation of a new national sports federation – an organisation that was quite differently positive to international competitive sport – in 1910.[24] In that sense, the first London Olympics contributed to the argument of national honour gaining terrain.

The next London Olympics in 1948 also came at a special time. The London connection had grown strong during the Second World War. The Norwegian government and the Royal family had managed to escape from occupant German soldiers in 1940 and lived in the English capital as refugees for the rest of the war. The 'London government' was the name of the Norwegian exile authorities. The state-run Norwegian Radio broadcasted from London, and 'the voice from London' became an important and well-known symbol for the resistance movement. Many personal relationships with British culture were also established. For example, Prince, later King, Olav V, who also was a former student of Balliol College at Oxford, strengthened his sympathies for the Arsenal Football Club.

That only three years had passed since the Second World War was valid for (almost) all participating nations. However to Norway, this held a special relevance. Norwegian sport had come out of the war, arguably more marked and weakened than other nations, since it, in addition to war's 'normal' ordeals, had carried through a five-year sports strike – a boycott of and a protest against the German occupiers and the Nazi rule of Norway. The 'sports' strike' meant no competitions and no training for the overwhelming majority of Norwegian sportsmen and women from late autumn 1940 till May 1945. This obviously handicapped their sports performances the first years after the war. And it made the London Games even more welcome, as an international return to normality among friends – an amity that was felt stronger not only by the absence of the Axis powers in 1948, but also by the fact that Norwegian relations to Britain, due to the alliances made during the war, were closer than ever before. It was hardly accidental that Crown Prince (later King) Olav, cousin of the English King George VI, had a prominent position in the Olympic contingent, as leader for the relatively successful sailors – another traditional Norwegian stronghold in Summer Olympics – who came home with Norway's only gold medal.[25] Among friends, one could live with achievements that were not always as wanted. Hence, any medals that Norwegians could bring home were welcomed. The London Games cemented the friendly relations, which were demonstrated also during the coming Winter Olympics in Oslo 1952. Then, the death of King George VI just before the Games were about to start – a death in the family so to say – prompted a court mourning in Norway. At the opening ceremony in Oslo, there was a 2-min silence to honour the English King, and neither the Norwegian King nor Crown Prince was present, something that made an impression on the English audience, according to the London correspondent of the newspaper Aftenposten.[26]

London 2012

When London invited to Olympic Games for the third time in 2012, the situation obviously was different. But what had changed? Did the London Olympics of 2012 present new forms of relationships between the two geographical neighbours, and if so how? The two had lived through the Cold War as NATO allies. England had, in contradiction to Norway, joined the 'new Europe', the EU. Regarding their economic and geopolitical situations, England, the former dominant of the world, was no longer a world power, in all or most areas, although it was a member of the UN's Security Council and a self-evident member of the G-7 and G-20 groups. Norway on the other side, as an oil producer, had become more affluent and managed to maintain a welfare state. The fact that it is not a member of the EU – regardless of the prospects concerning Britain's relations to the EU – has not impacted its situation in the world to a degree one could perhaps expect. Today, its non-membership is more a sign of sovereignty on the symbol-level than it is an impact on real geopolitics.

Another element that had been added to the bilateral relations was the popular cultural dimension. This became particularly evident during the closing ceremony on the final day of the Games, when symbols of 'Englishness' of all sorts and branches of popular culture were distributed to the world. The Norwegian TV audience was indeed a grateful assembly of receivers, a great part of them having lived with these trademarks of English culture since the 1960s, when television came to Norway. TV was in itself one of those new inventions established between the second and the third London Games that substantially reinforced Anglo-Norwegian relations. English TV has – perhaps until it was challenged by American youth series during the last two decades – been dominant in the TV market in Norway. Humour programmes especially, but also drama series and children's programmes were transmitted on what could be called a common cultural wavelength and became immensely popular. Not to mention pop music, where the influence has been overwhelming.

To this body of popular cultural influences, one can also add sports. Norwegian TV in its early years (the 1960s) annually televised the Grand National steeplechase from the Aintree Racecourse and the Oxford versus Cambridge Boat Race at the Thames; two significant signs of spring on the Norwegian TV menu, and two introductions to a manifold and different English sports culture. More influential, however, from 1969 the Norwegian state broadcaster Norsk Rikskringkasting (NRK) directly transmitted English football games. Every Saturday afternoon in the half year of winter (so as not to collide with the Norwegian football season), an English league game could be watched by Norwegian TV viewers. This established a firm bond of interest across the North Sea – in one direction, from Norway to England.

The common interest in football was, however, the big exception. Although the two countries were on friendly terms politically and in many ways culturally close, they also displayed dissimilar sports cultures. Hence, the two nations very rarely have been rivals on particular sports fields. This was demonstrated also in London 2012. One of the two gold medals for Norway in the 2012 Olympics came in women's team handball. This sport can serve as an example of the lacking similarities in the practice field between the two neighbours, also when it comes to ball games, football apart. While Britain cultivates cricket, net ball, rugby and field hockey as natural games to play, these sports are more or less absent in Norway. Norway on the other side nurtures team handball – a ball game that is rather non-existent in Britain, but quite popular in Continental Europe. Although clearly not the biggest ball game in the world, it has substantial international following: Korea, Russia, Eastern and Central Europe, Scandinavia, Germany, France (who won the two last Olympic gold medals in the men's game), Spain and Northern Africa are international strongholds. To a surprising degree, Norway, in the women's game, the last − 25 years has been an international championship contender with gold medals from the last two Olympics, 2008 and 2012. The 'handball girls' have become immensely popular Norwegian icons, winning national sports awards regularly. The sport has also become a popular children's, hence, mass sport in Norway.

The English situation in this sport was markedly different. The British Handball Association had to engage in active recruiting, also internationally, to be able to field the national team expected from an Olympic host nation. This even gave Norwegian handball players from the lower divisions a chance to become Olympians, not for Norway, but for Great Britain, if they could provide some sort of British origin.[27] British media also had to try to educate the local spectators in the basics of the game and what to expect.[28] Such predispositions gave the Norwegian media a chance to be not just slightly patronising over the British, who simply did not know or understand this game. Media reports amused themselves and their readers over English spectators who obviously had no clue of the game, and hence displayed the uncorrect kind of reactions at the 'wrong' situations of the game.[29] This was a rare occasion which the Norwegian media could not let slip away. Better though, the even rarer appreciations – handball became a spectator success in London – of a sport many Norwegians due to the success of the women, to a certain degree tend to see as 'ours', or at least partly ours, disregarding the fact that the game was a German/Danish invention, and that the Soviet bloc dominated, particularly the women's game, for decades.

Nonetheless, the 'handball girls' salvaged the London Olympics for the Norwegians, by defending their Olympic title from 2008. By doing so, they also contributed to a sportive self-esteem, which, in spite of overall disappointment, continued to be at quite another level than what it had been for most of the twentieth century. Since 1992, Norwegian athletes had been performing on a broader and higher level than before, bringing home an increasing number of medals from both Summer and Winter Olympics. According to most observers, the modern elite sports system adopted by the Norwegian Sports Federation, 'Olympiatoppen', was highly influential in this relative success, creating a belief in continued achievements.[30] The support apparatus of Olympiatoppen was undoubtedly behind both the Norwegian gold medals of 2012.

The other gold medal came in men's kayaking, admittedly not a big sport in Norway, nor internationally. Perhaps therefore, it was a sport where the knowledge and the strategies of the elite sports system could excel and prove its value. All the same, Eirik Verås Larsen could add another Olympic medal to the ones he already had from 2004 and 2008.[31] More of a sensation, however, was the achievement of Bartosz Piasecki. Piasecki, son of a Polish immigrant who was also his coach, brought home a silver medal in the hitherto relatively unknown sport of fencing. Representing a national sports association with barely 1000 members, he created a totally new situation.[32] Never before had a Norwegian athlete progressed to an Olympic final in this sport. Nor had they been anywhere close, for that matter. The best Olympic performance so far was an 11th place from 1984. When Piasecki fenced for Olympic gold in the men's epée final on the evening of August 1, 2012, it led the biggest TV network in Norway to throw away its original schedule for this Olympic Wednesday, to show fencing primetime – a slightly surreal situation for Norwegian fencing enthusiasts. Piacecki's performances on the *piste* attracted so many viewers during the evening that this final match – where he lost to the Venezuelan Ruben Limardo – ranked among the top 10 of Olympic TV-events in Norway.[33] In fact, it made fencing the third most popular Olympic TV sport, beaten only by team handball and athletics.

These pleasant individual achievements could not deter, however, that the general impression was one of discontent. The amount of medals was far below expectations. What could be the reason? The elite sports system, 'Olympiatoppen', for the last twenty years had seemed to work after its intentions; to improve Norwegian top-level sports achievements. One of its acknowledged advantages has been its flexibility and will to bring the different sports together in order to make cross-sports learning possible. Particularly, the smaller sports seem to have benefitted from this.[34] Did the meagre harvest of medals in London 2012 mean an end to this success story? It is, of course too early to tell, but one thing it did lead to was renewed evaluation work. A so-called 'heavy' committee was established by the Norwegian Sports Federation to once more scrutinise the elite sports system. Their report will not be available, however, until spring 2013.[35]

That the English performed well in their own Olympics was easily observed from abroad. Many of these triumphs can be called usual success stories from sport with their individual twists. However, Bradley Wiggins' gold medal in cycling's time trial was especially noticed in Norway, as it was in England, where he from 2013 became 'Sir' Bradley Wiggins. His gold medal in the otherwise not particularly attractive event, from a spectator's view at least, individual time trial, generated the peak traffic moment of the whole Olympics on the BBC online services.[36] Also in Norway, his feats attracted interest. Why? Cycling is a relatively recent link in the Anglo-Norwegian sporting relations. In both nations, cycling has seen a significant increase in popularity over the last years. The interest for races like Tour de France, particularly, has accelerated, and both nations have seen talented riders rising to fame. While the English for the first time can boast an overall Tour de France winner, the Norwegians have gone to cycling heaven over (green) jersey wins and stage triumphs. Such feats are not to be despised in a young and fresh cycling nation, simmering with interest during the summer season. One of the young Norwegian prospects, Edvald Boasson Hagen, rides on the same professional team as English hero Bradley Wiggins. Hence, the link is clear: They are teammates. Norwegian media likes to remind people of this. Also, Norway had other promising riders from which the nation had hopes. One of them, Alexander Kristoff, actually seized a bronze medal in the road race.

The London 2012 Olympics was also called 'The Digital Games'. As was the case in England, the Games in Norway saw a new reality for wired and televised sports events. The Norwegian public was given more offers to watch and experience Olympic sports than ever before. However, 'offering everything is not enough in the age of multiple devices', as one BBC spokesperson stated[37]: The Norwegian state public broadcaster, NRK (the Norwegian equivalent to the BBC) who had the rights for TV- and web-broadcasting, distributed live images from the Games via two main TV channels and seven so-called event channels on the web. The new technological opportunities made possible ambitious statements from the NRK people: It was possible 'to geek out in all directions'.[38] The Olympics should be accessible wherever people were – 'on the beach, at the cabin, anywhere'[39] and whenever they wanted, on all sorts of platforms; TV, PC, tablet and mobile. NRK also provided extensive radio coverage. And the viewer interest lived up to expectations. Viewer figures were higher than from any recent Summer Olympic Games.

Saying something about Norwegians' sport preferences, an NRK representative informed that only the ratings from the Winter Olympics in Vancouver 2010 could beat the figures from London 2012.[40] Typically perhaps of Norwegian summer habits, large portions go to their family cabins at the seaside or in the mountains, and unavoidably some Norwegians complained about receiving conditions for streaming by mobile phones outdoors at the high mountains.

However, in the Norwegian summer of 2012, nobody could beat handball. Athletics, which is usually a main sport during summer Olympics, had to face the role of being the second most popular. The Norwegian handball women went into the Olympic tournament as favourites. They were also TV favourites, pulling the sport of handball along. Among the 10 most watched events at the Olympics, six were handball games where Norway was involved, the final against Montenegro, not surprisingly, topping the list. The men's 100-metre final, a secure international bet on most watched Olympic events, only ranked fourth among Norwegian viewers, beaten by three games of Norwegian women performing the, for the English, obscure game of handball. The no. 2 athletics event, seen from a Norwegian TV perspective, was the men's javelin final. Here, Norway could list one of the favourites, former multiple Olympic, world and European champion Andreas Thorkildsen. Even though he disappointed his followers, it seems fair to say that – English affections nonetheless – the Norwegian viewers let their national emotions be their guiding principles.[41]

The extended TV- and web-coverage made it possible to see all the 'minor' sports to an even greater sense than what is normal during the Olympics. It also made possible more reports and features from the local environment and the locals. It could be said, as well, that these reports were done journalistically, with the desired 'human touch'. The reporters would, in principle, have done the same thing if the Games were hosted by another country. At the same time, the digitalisation of the Games, and the massive BBC transmissions, also meant that much of the production and editing work could be done from the home base in Norway. NRK had relatively less people on the ground in London, compared to earlier Olympic Games. In that sense, London risked being just another facade or backdrop against which spectacular sports performances were staged.

One other question remains. Why did not Norwegian TV, or the BBC for that matter, follow up on an opportunity inspired by the 1996 European championship in football, when the all-conquering slogan was 'Football's coming home'? To state that 'sport is coming home' would perhaps not go well together with the role of a welcoming Olympic host embracing the entire world? It could be interpreted as not appropriate for polite English hosts, and as bragging better suited for the football culture. Perhaps popular knowledge is not that clear when it comes to the historical ownership of modern sport in general. Is it more challenging to state that England is the 'land of sport', as opposed to the commonly held view that England is the home of football? This was an opportunity missed, but not rued.

The English Sports' Impact

The three London Olympics have also taken place in the larger sports historical context of the impact of the English sport in general. This context has to be taken into consideration if one aims to understand the whole role of the London Olympics of 2012. The impact partly rested on structural connections that saw Norwegians travelling to Britain for work or studies and Britons coming to Norway for work (sailors and engineers) and for recreational purposes. The Norwegians would pick up a sport they had never experienced at home, while the Brits in effect introduced English sports to Norway.

One example of how personal knowledge of British culture could lead to local initiatives to promote British sports could be seen in the city of Bergen, on the Norwegian west coast, where shipping lines to Britain were frequent. Here, the English language teacher Johan Dahl in 1874 wrote several pieces in the local newspapers where he advocated the advantages of living the sports life that the British did. He was convinced that it was only a question of time before the English conditions would spread to Norway. With deep concern, he expressed: 'It would be strange if the neighbour (i.e. Norway) for all eternity would be content to sit passively, indifferent and satisfied with a weak resonance of the jubilation which regularly reaches us from near and distant neighbours'.[42]

Dahl was proven right. It did not take many years before the historical phenomenon that was called 'the English Sport' also reached Norway. From around 1880 through the turn of century, new sports clubs were founded. From England came the introduction of new and hitherto unknown sports, such as football, (lawn-) tennis and others. Also new ideas and ways were introduced to sports which were already known, as rowing and sailing. They were given new frames, new equipments and new ways of competing.

Transferred to a new culture, the English sport was given a distinct and different meaning. This led to an ideological schism in the development of the broad movement of Norwegian sports, based upon national political cleavages. Traditional 'idrett' with its values and virtues derived from the national culture and its claimed needs stood against the foreign 'Sport', a newcomer and a stranger in the cultural landscape.

Did the English sports influence bring about a 'colonisation of meaning' of what had previously been known by the Norwegian equivalent 'idrett'?[43] The historical discourse around the two words can be indicative here. The English sport was, by Norwegian nationalist conservatives, seen as the contrast of what Norwegian sporting life ought to be. In the word 'idrett', there was an implicit moral (value) and ideological element, which the Norwegian conservatives could not find in their understanding of the English sport. The main difference lay in the goal of the physical activities, or in other words, what was considered important in sporting exercise. The Norwegians chose to see the English sport as 'sport for sport's sake' and could not or would not see any deeper purpose in its performance. This antipathy to the 'foreign' sport was connected to an ideological contrast between versatile and specialised sport. The versatile sport, according to the Norwegians, was better suited for cultivating healthy young men with a sound constituency to make them good soldiers capable of defending the fatherland, all the things the nation needed from their youth.

The English sport would only lead to a 'sporting celebration of extraordinary and amazing abilities', with no other serious purposes attached to it.[44] It was portrayed as a dangerous physical practice coming from abroad; 'the sport madness [...] brings us nothing good', Laurentius Urdahl said. He was supported by the polar explorer and national hero Fridtjof Nansen who put it another way: 'Practice healthy idrett. Despise sport and modern competitive exaggerations'.[45] Skiing was a good example of a healthy activity. According to Nansen: *Nothing strengthens the muscles, renders the body so strong and elastic, teaches the qualities of dexterity and resource, calls for decision and resolution, and give the same vigour and exhilaration to mind and body alike...*[46] The English sports on the other side were the negation of all this. This, of course, was a caricature with small resemblance to how British sports ideologues portrayed their activities; as athleticism promoting character-building, morality and manliness.[47]

In spite of all this, there existed people, amongst others educators, with a more favourable view of the British sports.[48] And among young males from the middle classes, less bothered with ideological hang-ups, interest for English sports grew. Particularly football became popular as a class-transcending activity, while the other English sports, athletics, cycling, lawn-tennis, rowing and sailing had a tendency to fit into a class-based sports distribution; many of them evolving into typical middle or even upper class sports. English sports in that sense became tools for creating social and cultural distinctions.

However, the transfer of foreign expressions into a new culture was uncertain business. A sportsman risked being interpreted as a 'dandy' who had nothing better to do with his time and money than to show off with purposeless pastimes; in other words, the definition of an economic elite, with its 'conspicuous consumption' according to Thorstein Veblen.[49] Although the English sports were portrayed in disapproving ways, this is not to say that favourable characteristics of 'the Englishman' were downplayed. In the twentieth century, he was presented in rather admiring ways, as the fair and energetic gentleman.[50] Jørgen Juve offered a much-used stereotype in his (by Norwegian standards) ambitious work on football from 1934 when he reported that among English football's foremost characteristics were its 'stoic calmness, tactical sense and fairness'.[51]

Practice and Symbols: Cricket and Skiing

Hence, there was a deep Norwegian admiration for many things English. However, with the exception of football, there were not that many contact points or activities in common. The practice of British sports was in many ways markedly unlike the Norwegian. Team handball in 2012 and ice-skating in 1908 were examples of this. Cricket and skiing can provide further insight into how dissimilar the same sports can be experienced even among neighbours.

Until recently, cricket has been presented as the unchallenged provider of British culture in the sports field. Invented as a modern sport in England, with Marylebone Cricket Club (f.1787) for long being the sport's governing body, cricket, played the right way, presented attitudes and virtues that were characterised as typically English. Cricket vocabulary went into the national lingo. Cricket expressions came to mean more than their technical translations should indicate. 'A level playing field', 'Keep a straight bat' and 'Play the game' are some of many expressions that have become catch phrases in a wider vocabulary expected to be understood on a broad basis inside the English culture.

Cricket actually seems to have been the first of the new English sports to reach Norwegian shores in the nineteenth century, almost 20 years before football. Not much historical evidence is left to cast light on cricket's first phase. It is fair to say, however, that cricket struggled to catch a grip on the population. Some initial attempts occurred in 1866, when British engineers working in and around Oslo played matches probably against each other. Christiania Cricket Club played Britisk (sic) Cricket Club in a 'match' over 6 h, the newspaper Morgenbladet reported.[52] Apart from another match 2 weeks later, little or nothing is heard from the Norwegian cricket scene after that.

More than a hundred years passed, before this symbol of Englishness and the Empire was taken up once more in Norway, now by another group of immigrants. People from India and Pakistan mainly, as well as from Sri Lanka and Bangladesh, reintroduced cricket. Again as a typical immigrant sport, however, the difference from the first attempt is that cricket now is beginning to make a presence in the Norwegian sports landscape, with an aim to attract also native Norwegians.

Hence, the reintroduction of cricket in Norway more than a hundred years after its first landing was contingent upon post-colonial conditions. The first time representatives from Britain themselves tried to introduce the foreign game to Norwegians. The second time Britain's former colonial subjects, now Commonwealth associates, with more success have reintroduced their former colonial master's game – after having made it into a game of their own. That Norway's population today has a substantial element of immigrants not from Britain, but from the former British Indian Empire (the British Raj) is an obvious element in this story.[53] They have been eager to display a game that now symbolise Indian, Pakistani and other identities, thus demonstrating a post-colonial and globalised world.

The Norwegian equivalent to cricket when it comes to the symbolic role of the sport is skiing – also a sport that is very small with the (English) neighbour's, while it holds all sorts of symbolic and historic importance in Norway. Skiing was the distinction that made the people living in Norway into Norwegians. National heroes derived their status from their use of skis. Skiing was 'the most national of all sports'.[54]

In winter, sports literature Norwegians are given most of the credit for the spread of skiing as a leisure activity and as a sport, to Europe and North America, predominantly.[55] Skiing clubs were founded in Germany, France and other places on the European Continent. In Britain, however, the situation was different. That had to do with both natural conditions in Britain and a lacking Norwegian interest for Alpine skiing. This, so to say, opened up a field where a British interest for skiing could manifest itself in an independent way. Skiing the Norwegian, or 'Nordic' way, the latter is the present correct term to describe ski-jumping and cross-country skiing, never took off in a degree worth mentioning inside Britain.[56] Nevertheless, British skiers played a central role in the development of Alpine skiing outside of Britain, with The Public Schools Alpine Sports Club and Arnold Lunn as crucial agents, making it an Olympic event from 1936.[57]

Skiing has been named – by Norwegian historians – Norway's 'gift to the world'.[58] This 'gift' must have been to live with for the rest of the world, as it came in the form of a small winter sport, which claimed particular conditions; stable snow for a longer period of time, conditions that narrowed and limited the real field of influence.[59] However, as always with gifts, the Norwegians expected a return; that their values and skiing ideology should govern the sport of skiing. Hence, the Norwegians found it vital to dominate the International Ski Federation (FIS) from where they could dispute British, Continental and American ideas and competitive forms. In the long run, though, as skiing spread to more and more places, the Norwegians fought a lost case. As national symbols, though, skis still stand.

The London Olympics 2012 coincided with the centenary for the 'Race to the South Pole'. Although this concurrence mainly was passed over by the London organisers, the history of the conquest of the geographical poles as sports achievements provides one of very few Anglo-Norwegian contact fields on snow. When Norwegian Roald Amundsen beat the Englishman Robert F. Scott for the South Pole in 1911–1912, this was in Norway interpreted as a victory for a national skiing tradition with its emphasis on practicable and humble attitudes as well as preparing and training for the challenges. While Scott's 'defeat' in conquering one of the few remaining blank spots of the map was taken not only as a national, but also as an Imperial downfall. This may have contributed to an expanding Norwegian self-image when it comes to winter conditions and sports.[60] Nevertheless, winter culture, snow and skiing, was an exception from the regular sports scene where Britain was the undisputed master and example.

Football as a Specific Part of Norway–England Relations

In 2012, Norway is the country in Europe with relatively the largest amount of organised supporters of English football, outside of Britain.[61] The history of this love affair illustrates extraordinary Anglo-Norwegian sporting relations where influence runs one way and affection the other: In 1886, crews from the battle ships Agincourt and Iron Duke and four others introduced football to the two largest cities; Oslo and Bergen, during a visit from Her Majesty's Navy. They did so, however, in ways that on the surface at least, looked far from 'imperialistic'. Foremost the football games came about as an offer to restless cadets eager to entertain themselves physically during a long spell at quay. In Bergen, a local entrepreneur saw the possibility of making money by transforming this into a show with entrance fees for spectators. Posters advertising 'For the first time in Bergen ... Grand Football Match' played between crew members from the English naval ships were put up around the city. Curious spectators were also informed that 'English Musik' (sic) would be played during the game. However, through this display, early football was brought into close contact with representatives of law and order. The enthusiastic organiser had not bothered to acquire the necessary legal permissions, and it did not help him that during the game, there was also sale of 'beer and champagne'. Alas, for 'organising a public display of Englishmen playing football' and hence causing public disorder, he was brought to justice and sentenced to pay a relatively stiff fine in the police court.[62] The role of the locals was unclear. In Bergen, they were meant to be paying on-lookers. When a similar event took place in Oslo, there was also an element of possible learning among the spectators. Here, football had been tried out by representatives from the local youth who had organised themselves in Christiania Football Club – the name reveals the source of inspiration – shortly before. They met the British cadets for football.[63]

When the fleet departed, they left the part of the Norwegians who had actually watched the display, astounded. This was activity of a different kind compared to what in Norway passed under the heading of 'idrett'. The Norwegian activities were either individual (e.g. skiing) while the collective activities, e.g. group gymnastics, were characterised by discipline and strict movement patterns. Ball games were unknown outside of the children's sphere. Hence, the first impression of football was of a wild, anarchic and violent game. This was a game hard to understand and challenging to emulate. The British were the ones to explain and teach if this was to become more than 'hard and intensive fighting for the ball'.[64]

From the outset, it was clear that the game was British, they were the ones to be looked up to and admired – the surprising side of it is perhaps that this has continued to characterise Norwegian relations to English football until today. Anyone who could claim a past experience from the English game was given an almost automatic increase in authority on the field. A romantic picture of the English game was painted. This trans-national fascination and devotion for English football does not only affect the big and glamorous clubs, although they have the largest following. At the time being Norway has around 50 supporters' clubs for all sorts of clubs, from Manchester United to Macclesfield.[65]

Also players on the highest level seem to have been affected by a mentality of willing subordination, to a degree that some journalists found embarrassing. Particularly, one episode has stuck with the story of the national team of the pre-1990s. In 1980, Norway visited England to play a World Cup qualifier. The story goes that inexperienced Norwegian players full of respect for the historical ground they were about to step on to, the green grass of Wembley Stadium, for their first training session brought photo-cameras to eternalise this big moment of their lives. Nobody could deny that it obviously was a big moment. However, there was a backside; the media now could portray them as wide-eyed tourists, not as serious football players.

Since the first years of the twentieth century, Norwegian newspapers and sports periodicals had presented their readers with the weekend's English football results. It was a strong signal of the position of the English game, that when the Norwegian parliament voted to establish a state controlled betting company in action from 1948, the betting objects were without particular discussion decided to be English football matches. From 1948 then, Norwegians could place their money on Blackpool or Blackburn, Tottenham or Arsenal, with the blessing of Norwegian state authorities. The next step was to show English football on Norwegian TV. Late autumn 1969, Wolverhampton and Sunderland were brought directly into Norwegian living rooms. This match introduced a mighty tradition especially among Norwegian males; every Saturday afternoon in the winter season, there was an English game to follow on the TV, linked to the already existing football pools. The TV matches were run on the state public broadcasting system NRK until 1995 when commercial TV2 took over. The last years the tradition has more or less dissolved into pay-TV channels, making the still existing interest change from one particular, almost institutionalised time; 3 or 4 o'clock every Saturday and 2 h ahead, to commercial TV's needs for diversified and ever changing time slots.

The respect for England and English football is also there to be read from the football itself. Concerning achievements, these were the two nations who did not play 'in the same league'. Hence, when Great Britain lost to Norway during the Olympic football tournament in Antwerp in 1920, it came as a major surprise to both countries. Even *The Times of London* meant that this was a rather unexpected result and printed a drawn caricature with the title: 'The Downfall'. The Norwegian reactions could not disguise that the victory came as a shock. But the non-normality of the outcome had to be explained; this was the British (not English) Olympic amateur team. They were not representative for the strength of the real England, which were the professionals. The result caused no major stir in any of the countries. It seemed as if both nations agreed that this was not a representative result. The next decades proved that the footballing inequalities were perhaps stronger than ever.

It took until 1981 before a new sensational result occurred, and this time 'sensation' and similar expressions were definitely used. Norway beat England 2–1, real professional England, in a serious game, a World Cup qualifier in Oslo. From this game, radio reporter Bjørge Lillelien's comments reached international fame, when he reported on the match's dying seconds and really took off in a mix of Norwegian and English:

'There he (the referee) blows (his whistle), there he blows. Norway has beaten England 2-1 in football. We are the best in the world! We are the best in the world! We have beaten England 2-1 in football! It is absolutely incredible. We have beaten England – England, home of giants: *Lord Nelson, Lord Beaverbrook, Sir Winston Churchill, Sir Anthony Eden, Clement Atlee, Henry Cooper, Lady Diana*. We have beaten them all. We have beaten them all. *Maggie Thatcher, can you hear me? Maggie Thatcher*. I have a message to you, in your election campaign. I have a message to you. We have eliminated England from the World Cup in football. *Maggie Thatcher*. As they say in your language, around the boxing bars at Madison Square Garden in New York: *Your boys took a hell of a beating. Your boys took a hell of a beating. Maggie Thatcher*. Norway has beaten England in football. We are the best in the world'.[66]

What is worth noticing in this 'comment' is not the far-reaching interpretation of the meaning of the victory, 'the gloriously over the top response',[67] but the use of the inclusive '*we*'-form. *We* had beaten all the English heroes that Lillelien could come up with from the English history: *We have beaten them all!* Even if England's national team in 1981 was not what it once had been, Norway had clearly bought into the history, the reputation and the

'Football's coming home' tale. When little Norway could beat England in their own game, it was the height of sporting prowess. In the years to follow, the match has been remembered perhaps just as much because of the radio reporting, as for the result. Internationally – and perhaps especially in Britain[68] – Lillelien's outbursts have become an example of national 'patos' and ecstatic joy displayed during football matches.

2012 Aftermath: England Just Another Foreign Country?

At the 1908 Olympic Games, Norway was eager to be an independent nation, waving its flag among other independent nations. In 1948, Norway was an allied, Western nation among friends. While in 2012, Norway displayed itself as an economically strong nation with an advanced elite sports system, in competition with other modern nations in a situation where there were no dramatic external incidents that could give participation an extra symbolic edge.

In 2012, England still was a close friend and ally, even though, due to the EU issue, the two nations politically had drifted slightly apart. Culturally however, in spite of frequent travelling opportunities and increasing chances of becoming familiar with English society, England in many ways is as distant as it has been. Its class-based social hierarchy for once represents huge contrasts to the Norwegian society, in everything from the role and power of the aristocracy, to social manners. Norway has no aristocracy, and a Norwegian 'Sir' is also impossible. England is as close and as strange as it always has been. For the large amount of football lovers, however, London and England was well-known territory. Perhaps therefore, Norwegian media did not present England and London significantly different than it has presented other former Olympic organisers.[69]

In that way, it was the closing ceremony (produced by the English BBC) that again reinforced the cultural bridge across the North Sea. To end the Olympics with an overload of popular cultural symbols has become the norm in the TV age. However, to a Norwegian audience, these were symbols to which there was attached a popular resonance.[70] They brought together generations of Norwegians who were familiar with the sports stars, the pop music, the TV personalities, the movie stars and the other brands and icons of the modern English culture.

To host the Olympic Games always makes the most impression on the home ground. It could change the English impression of the English. On the other side, the 2012 Olympics did not drastically change the Norwegian impression of England. The English still are the fair, polite and humoristic people to which the Norwegians have friendly connections. And the Games did keep alive the memory of how close the two nations historically have been, although the longevity of such reminders is impossible to establish. For Norway then, does that mean that England has become just another foreign country? No, not yet. England holds a particular place in history and culture, including sports, and especially football.

Acknowledgements

I thank Prof. Dag Album, University of Oslo, Prof. Finn Olstad, Associate Prof. Lars Tore Ronglan and Research Fellow Gaute Heyerdahl at the Norwegian School of Sport Sciences for comments and suggestions.

Notes on Contributor

Matti Goksøyr is a professor in History at The Norwegian School of Sport Sciences, Oslo, Norway.

Notes

1. http://www.olympic.org/olympic-games, March 16, 2013.
2. Idrettsliv 1928, no. 37. cf. Furumo, *Norsk idrett og "utlendingen."*
3. M. Goksøyr, *Historien om norsk idrett*; Olstad and Tønnesson, *Norsk idrettshistorie*.
4. Guttmann, *Games and Empires*.
5. Gandhi, *Postcolonial Theory*, x. As Alan Bairner says, discussing Ireland, the value of post-colonial perspectives is certainly restricted. This can of course be said with increasing strength on Norway. Bairner "Irish Australians," 483, referring to Moore-Gilbert, *Postcolonial Theory*; Bale and Cronin, *Sport and Postcolonialism*, 4; Bairner, *Sport*, 159–74; Sugden and Tomlinson, Football and FIFA in the Postcolonial World, 175–196; Bairner, *Irish Australians*.
6. For example, Olstad, *Norsk idrettshistorie*, 75f; Goksøyr og F. Olstad, *Fotball!*.
7. http://www.oecdbetterlifeindex.org/, November 27, 2012; http://www.ssb.no/ur_okonomi/m, November 27, 2012.
8. Also if one does not include Spitsbergen. Norway $385,252 \text{ km}^2$ (or $148,746 \text{ sq mi}$) including Svalbard and Jan Mayen. Without these two areas, the area of Norway is $323,802 \text{ km}^2$. Britain (as England, Scotland and Wales) $229,848 \text{ km}^2$ (or $88,744.8 \text{ sq mi}$), including Shetland, the Orkney Isles, Hebrides and other smaller islands. England constitutes ca. 2/3 of the area of Great Britain.
9. After the Viking era which according to most historians ended in 1066 with the battle of Stamford Bridge (not the Chelsea football ground, but a small village outside of York, then two largest cities in England), where Norwegian Vikings were beaten by English king Harold Godwinsson, who just 14 days later was going to lose the Battle of Hastings to William the Conqueror.
10. http://www.ons.gov.uk/ons/rel/census/2011-census/population-and-household estimates for-england-and-wales/index.html, February 1, 2013.
11. For a general overview of the political and economical relationships, see Pharo and Patrick Salmon, *Britain and Norway*.
12. In 1986, British acid rain and nuclear waste became an issue casting shadows over Prime Minister M. Thatcher's visit to Norway. Pharo and Salmon, *Britain and Norway*, 17.
13. Norwegian Federation for sport and Paralympics. Board meetingNovember 6, 2012: http://www.idrett.no/omnif/idrettsstyret/Documents/IS-m%C3%B8te%2015%20(2011-2015)%20-%20protokoll.pdf, January 18, 2013.
14. For the Games in 1908, Norway sent 58 Olympic athletes. They returned home with two gold, three silver and three bronze medals. In 1948, the figures were 79 and 1-3-3.
15. Olstad, *Norsk idrettshistorie*, 159.
16. Krüger, "Forgotten Decision," 85–98.
17. M. Goksøyr, "Og så ein svensk-norsk landskamp!"
18. Lindroth, *Unionsupplösningen 1905 och Idrotten*.
19. Goksøyr, *Staten og idretten*.
20. The closest Norwegian equivalent to 'sport', though at that time not exactly the same.
21. Centralforeningen for Utbredelse av Idrett (The Central Association for the Spread of Sport ("Idrett")).
22. J. Martens in Olstad, *Norsk idrettshistorie*, 124.
23. In Dagbladet, April 6, 1913. Quoted in Olstad, *Norsk idrettshistorie*, 159–60.
24. Norges Riksforbund for Idræt (1910–1919).
25. Thor Thorvaldsen with crew won sailing's dragon class. He came back to do the same in Helsinki 1952. http://www.olympic.org/sailing-equipment-and-history, March 1, 2013.
26. Olympiaposten/Aftenposten, February 22, 1952.
27. "Britain indeed found quite a lot of female players in Scandinavia." http://www.britishhandball.com/2012-olympics/#, February 2, 2013.
28. For example, http://www.timeout.com/london/events/handball-guide-london-2012-olympic-games, February 2, 2013; http://www.telegraph.co.uk/sport/olympics/7904229/London-2012-Olympics-handball-guide.html, February 2, 2013.
29. http://www.dagsavisen.no/forside/hands-heter-det-pa-engelsk/, July 26, 2012.
30. Andersen and Ronglan, *Nordic Elite Sport*.
31. That is a gold and a bronze from Athens 2004 and a silver from Beijing 2008.
32. 1059 members in 2010. Norges Idrettsforbund, årsrapport 2010.

33. http://www.nrk.no/ol2012/nyheter/handball-finale-var-seervinner-1.8279580 (posted August 13, 2012, loaded March 18, 2013).
34. Andersen and Ronglan, *Nordic Elite Sport*.
35. Board meeting: Evaluation of the Olympic and Paralympic Games 2012. http://www.idrett.no/ nyheter/Sider/EvalueringavOLPL2012.aspx (February 16, 2013). On the new committee: http://sport.aftenposten.no/sport/idrettspolitikk/article256586.ece (November 5, 2012 and December 6, 2012). On mandate: http://www.nif.no/nyheter/Sider/evalueringutv_toppidrett. aspx (posted October 17, 2012, loaded March 16, 2013).
36. http://www.bbc.co.uk/blogs/internet/posts/digital_olympics_reach_stream_stats (first posted August 13, 2012. loaded March 18, 2013).
37. Cait ORiordan, head of product, BBC: The story of the digital Olympics: streams, browsers, most watched, four screens. http://www.bbc.co.uk/blogs/internet/posts/digital_olympics_ reach_stream_stats (first posted August 13, 2012, loaded March 18, 2013).
38. http://nrkbeta.no/2012/07/25/ol-strommene/ (posted July 25, 2012, loaded March 18, 2013).
39. http://www.nrk.no/ol2012/nyheter/stralende-fornoyd-med-apningshelgen-1.8262594 (posted July 30, 2012, loaded March 18, 2013).
40. http://www.nrk.no/ol2012/nyheter/handball-finale-var-seervinner-1.8279580 (posted August 13, 2012, loaded March 18, 2013).
41. http://www.nrk.no/ol2012/nyheter/handball-finale-var-seervinner-1.8279580 (posted August 13, 2012, loaded March 18, 2013).
42. Bergensposten 1874, no. 126. Dahl, as many Norwegians until today, quite openly mixed, or diffused the two terms English and British, seemingly without particular awareness.
43. Gandhi, *Postcolonial Theory*.
44. Norske Turnnotiser, no. 19–20, 1891. Quoted in Olstad, *Norsk idrettshistorie*, 85.
45. Laurentius Urdahl in Idrætsbladet no. 41, 1892. F. Nansen in: Centralforeningen for Udbredelse af Idræt. Aarsberetning 1902/03. Kristiania 1902/03.
46. Nansen, *Paa Ski over Grønland*.
47. Holt, *Sport and the British*; Mangan, *The Games Ethic and Imperialism*.
48. For example, Hans Hegna, I Centralforeningens Aarbok.
49. Veblen, *The Theory of the Leisure Class*.
50. Furumo, *Norsk idrett og "utlendingen."*
51. Jørgen Juve, *Alt om fotball*, 19.
52. Morgenbladet, 1866.
53. http://www.ssb.no/innvandring/, February 1, 2013. Britons are not by January 1, 2012 among the 15 largest immigrant groups in Norway, while Pakistanis constitute the third largest group.
54. Nansen, *Paa Ski over Grønland*; Olav Bø, *Skiing throughout history*.
55. Allen, *The Culture and Sport of Skiing from Antiquity to World War II*.
56. Except a limited, climate-dependant activity in the mountain areas in Scotland.
57. Allen, *The Culture and Sport of Skiing from Antiquity to World War II*, 102–106.
58. J. Vaage, *Norske ski erobrer verden*.
59. To say that the diffusion of the sport of skiing is to some extent dependent on climatic conditions and in the end to the amount of snow present is not to give into the influence of environmental determinism which John Bale discusses: Bale, "Lassitude and Latitude."
60. Today, it seems to be the ultimate humiliation to be beaten by a Brit on cross country skis. For example, http://www.dagbladet.no/2012/01/27/sport/nm/musgrave/langrenn/19974258/.
61. 105,590 organised supporters pr, May 31, 2012. http://www.supporterunionen.com/, (March 16, 2013).
62. Goksøyr and Olstad, *Fotball! Norges Fotballforbund 1902–2002*.
63. At this instance, rules were unclear; one played one half with a normal football and on half with a "ellipse-shaped" rugby ball. Much of the later newspaper comments dealt with what Norwegian observers found to be a violent and un-sophisticated game. Goksøyr and Olstad, *Fotball!*
64. Goksøyr and Olstad, *Fotball!*
65. Goksøyr and Hognestad, "No Longer Worlds Apart?"
66. NRK, radio. Here the whole part is translated. The italicised are the parts that also originally were in English.
67. http://www.guardian.co.uk/sport/2002/oct/06/sixnations2008.features.

68. For example, did the Observer Sport Monthly in 2002 rank it as no. 1 in their "ten greatest bits of commentary ever." http://www.guardian.co.uk/sport/2002/oct/06/sixnations2008.features.
69. Even though the main broadcaster; NRK, presented more hours of TV-production from an Olympic Games than ever before.
70. Hobsbawm and Ranger, *The Invention of Tradition*.

References

Allen, E. John B. *The Culture and Sport of Skiing from Antiquity to World War II*. Amherst: University of Massachusetts Press, 2007.

Andersen, Svein S., and Lars Tore Ronglan, eds. *Nordic Elite Sport: Same Ambitions – Different Tracks*. Oslo: Universitetsforlaget, 2012.

Bairner, Alan. *Sport, Nationality and Postcolonialism in Ireland*. 2003 In: Bale and Cronin 2003, Oxford, New York: Berg, p. 159–174.

Bairner, Alan. "Irish Australians, Postcolonialism and the English Game." *Sport in Society* 12, no. 4–5 (2009): 482–495.

Bale, John. "Lassitude and Latitude: Observations on Sport and Environmental Determinism." *International Review for the Sociology of Sport* 37 (2002): 147–158.

Bale, John, and Cronin, Mike, eds. *Sport and Postcolonialism*. Oxford, New York: Berg, 2003.

Bø, Olav. *Skiing Throughout History*. Oslo: Det Norske Samlaget, 1993.

Furumo, Asle. *Norsk idrett og "utlendingen"*. Norges idrettshøgskole: Hovedfagsoppgave, 2003.

Gandhi, Leela. *Postcolonial Theory: A Critical Introduction*. St. Leonards: Allen & Unwin, 1998.

Goksøyr, Matti. *Staten og idretten*. Oslo: Idrettsavdelingen, Det Kongelige Kulturdepartement, 1991.

Goksøyr, M. "'Og så ein svensk-norsk landskamp! Ein blir så patriotisk i slike stunder'. Norsk-svenske idrettsforbindelser etter 1905." In *Norsk-svenske relasjoner i 200 år*, edited by Ø. Sørensen, and T. Nilsson, Oslo: Aschehoug, 2005.

Goksøyr:, M. *Historien om norsk idrett*. Oslo: Abstrakt Forlag, 2008.

Goksøyr, Matti, and Hans Hognestad. "'No Longer Worlds Apart? British Impulses to the Creation of a Norwegian Football Tradition'." In *Football, Cultures and Identities*, edited by Gary Armstrong. Basingstoke: Macmillan, 1999.

Goksøyr, Matti, and Finn Olstad. *Fotball! Norges Fotballforbund 1902–2002*. Oslo: NFF, 2002.

Goksøyr, M., and F. Olstad. "Revolution and Resistance. The Rise and Fall of the Norwegian Playing Style." *Moving Bodies*, 1(1) (Football History and Culture), 133-140.

Guttmann, Allen. *Games and Empires. Modern Sports and Cultural Imperialism*. New York: Columbia University Press, 1994.

Hobsbawm, Eric, and Ranger, Terence, eds. *The Invention of Tradition*. Cambridge: Cambridge University Press, 1983.

Holt, Richard. *Sport and the British. A Modern History*. Oxford: Oxford University Press, 1989.

Juve, Jørgen. *Alt om fotball*. Oslo: Johan Grundt Tanum, 1934.

Krüger, Arnd. "'Forgotten Decision': The IOC on the Eve of World War I. The International Journal of the History of Sport." *OLYMPIKA: The International Journal of Olympic Studies* 6 (1997): 85–98.

Lindroth, Jan. *Unionsupplösningen 1905 och Idrotten. Den svenska idrottsrörelsen i en utrikespolitisk krissituation*. Sveriges Centralförenings för Idrottens Främjande årsbok 1977.

Mangan, James A. *The Games Ethic and Imperialism. Aspects of the Diffusion of an Ideal*. Harmondsworth: Viking Adult, 1986.

Moore-Gilbert, Bart. *Postcolonial Theory. Contexts, Practices, Politics*. London: Verso, 1997.

Nansen, F. *Paa Ski over Grønland*. Kristiania: Aschehoug, 1890.

Olstad, F., and Stein Tønnesson. *Norsk idrettshistorie*, Vol. 1–2. Oslo: Aschehoug, 1986, 1987.

Pharo, Helge Ø., and Patrick Salmon, eds. *Britain and Norway: Special Relationships*. Oslo: Akademika Forlag, 2012.

Sugden, John, and Alan Tomlinson. "Football and FIFA in the Postcolonial World." 2003 In: Bale and Cronin 2003, Oxford, New York: Berg, p. 175–196.

Vaage, J. *Norske ski erobrer verden*. Oslo: Gyldendal, 1952.

Veblen, Thorstein. *The Theory of the Leisure Class*. New York: Macmillan 1899, Dover Thrift Editions, 1994.

Newspapers/periodicals

Bergensposten 1874, no. 126.
Centralforeningen for Udbredelse af Idræt. Aarsberetning 1902/03. Kristiania 1902/03.
Dagbladet 2012.
Idrætsbladet no. 41, 1892.
Morgenbladet 1866.
Olympiaposten/Aftenposten 22.2.1952.
VG 2012.

Web sites

www.idrett.no
www.oecdbetterlifeindex.org
www.ssb.no
www.ons.gov.uk
www.britishhandball.com
www.fifa.com
www.nrk.no
www.guardian.co.uk
www.dagbladet.no
www.olympic.org
www.timeout.com
www.dagsavisen.no
http//:sport.aftenposten.no
www.telegraph.co.uk

Index

Note:
Page numbers followed by 'n' refer to notes
Figures and illustrations are in italics
Tables are in bold

www.routledge.com/9780415720601

Related titles from Routledge

From Beijing to London - Delivering Olympic and Elite Sport in a Cross Cultural Context
Edited by Fan Hong and Lu Zhouxiang

This book examines the impact of the 2008 Beijing Olympics and the 2012 London Olympic Games and highlights the latest findings in the areas of sport policy, elite sports system, sport media, sport facility management and sport social development in the two host countries - China and Britain. It identifies the role of national and local governments, universities and educational institutions in the delivery of elite sport in different cultural and social settings. Finally, the book considers the legacy of the Olympic Games in the areas of sport participation, public diplomacy, education and cultural communication in Europe and China.

This book was originally published as a special issue of *The International Journal of the History of Sport*.

Fan Hong is a Professor at the School of Asian Studies, University College Cork, Ireland.

Lu Zhouxiang is a Lecturer at the School of Modern Languages, Literatures and Cultures, National University of Ireland, Maynooth, Ireland.

Nov 2013: 246 x 174: 208pp
Hb: 978-0-415-72060-1
£85 / $145

For more information and to order a copy visit
www.routledge.com/9780415720601

Available from all good bookshops